THE UNHEARD TRUTH

THE UNHEARD TRUTH POVERTY AND HUMAN RIGHTS

Irene Khan

with

David Petrasek

Foreword by Kofi Annan
Secretary-General of the United Nations (1997–2006)
President, Kofi Annan Foundation

Viva Books

New Delhi | Mumbai | Chennai | Kolkata | Bangalore | Hyderabad | Kochi | Guwahati

First Indian Edition 2010

VIVA BOOKS PRIVATE LIMITED

- 4737/23 Ansari Road, Daryaganj, New Delhi 110 002
  E-mail: vivadelhi@vivagroupindia.net, Tel. 42242200
- 76, Service Industries, Shirvane, Sector 1, Nerul, Navi Mumbai 400 706
  E-mail: vivamumbai@vivagroupindia.net, Tel. 27721273, 27721274
- Jamals Fazal Chambers, 26 Greams Road, Chennai 600 006
  E-mail: vivachennai@vivagroupindia.net, Tel. 28290304, 28294241
- B-103, Jindal Towers, 21/1A/3 Darga Road, Kolkata 700 017
  E-mail: vivakolkata@vivagroupindia.net, Tel. 22836381, 22816713
- 7, Sovereign Park Apartments, 56-58, K. R. Road, Basavanagudi, Bangalore 560 004
  E-mail: vivabangalore@vivagroupindia.net, Tel. 26607409, 26607410
- 101-102 Mughal Marc Aptt., 3-4-637 to 641, Narayanguda, Hyderabad 500 029
  E-mail: vivahyderabad@vivagroupindia.net, Tel. 27564481, 27564482
- First Floor, Beevi Towers, SRM Road, Kaloor, Kochi 682 018, Kerala
  E-mail: vivakochi@vivagroupindia.net, Tel: 0484-2403055, 2403056
- 232, GNB Road, Beside UCO Bank, Silpukhuri, Guwahati 781 003
  E-mail: vivaguwahati@vivagroupindia.net, Tel: 0361-2666386

Published by arrangement with

W. W. Norton & Company, Inc.
500 Fifth Avenue, New York
N. Y. 10110

ISBN : 978-81-309-1316-2

Published by Vinod Vasishtha for Viva Books Private Limited, 4737/23, Ansari Road, Daryaganj, New Delhi - 110 002. Printed and bound by Sanat Printers, Kundli - 131 028, Sonepat, Haryana.

TO THE WOMEN OF BANGLADESH
WHOSE COURAGEOUS STRUGGLE FOR EQUALITY AND DIGNITY
INSPIRES, ENCOURAGES AND ENERGIZES ME

CONTENTS

FOREWORD
by KOFI ANNAN

Sixty years ago, the UN adopted the Universal Declaration of Human Rights, the first international proclamation of the inherent dignity and equal rights of all people. To this day, the Declaration remains the single most important reference point for discussion of ethical values across national, ideological and cultural divides. Yet, the Declaration's enlightened vision of individual freedom, social protection, economic opportunity and duty to community is still unfulfilled.

Today, leaders across the world are faced with multiple challenges, from the global economic crisis, to climate change and environmental degradation, from armed conflict and political instability, to hunger and pandemic disease. There is one challenge, however, that stands out – the plight of close to 3 billion human beings who live in poverty and are unable to meet their daily needs for adequate shelter, food, health care, clean water, or education for their children.

Poverty is perhaps our greatest shame. While gross inequalities between rich and poor persist, we cannot claim to be making adequate progress toward fulfilling the ambitions set down 60 years ago. It commands our attention not only for the scale of the suffering involved; but also because it is the poor who will fare worse if we fail to meet other global challenges.

The violence of war or that sparked by political crisis, the threats to livelihoods posed by climate change and economic collapse, the spread of disease – these and many other risks always hit the poor hardest. Moreover, they keep them poor. So too does pervasive discrimination, especially that experienced by women and girls, denying the poor the basic freedoms they need to organise to defend their interests, and excluding them from justice systems that might protect their assets, however meagre.

Many books and reports have been written that describe the problem of global poverty, and many propose solutions. Much of what is written focuses on ways to achieve and sustain economic growth, which enables developing countries to progress and meet the aspirations of their people. However, what this book does is to remind us that economic growth while necessary, is insufficient in itself. Poverty is not just about deprivation. It is equally about these other threats and challenges faced by those living in poverty.

People are beginning to understand that poverty is a human rights issue. The value of Irene's book is to make a clear and compelling case for the importance of human rights that goes far beyond the moral argument. Indeed, even as it appeals to universal values, hers is a deeply pragmatic proposal – that protecting the rights of the poor protects the livelihoods and freedoms they need to advance. Protecting rights provides protection against violence and discrimination, and securing basic freedoms gives the poor a voice so that they can play a meaningful role in determining their future. And it reminds us that basic needs like food and shelter are human rights that cannot be delivered by the market alone.

This is an argument that demands we throw aside what the book calls "Cold War categories" of economic and social versus civil and political rights. The Universal Declaration of Human Rights protects all rights. For the poor, securing freedom is essential as providing education, ending discrimination as fundamental as basic health care.

Drawing on a wealth of examples and her personal experience as a Bangladeshi and Secretary-General of Amnesty International, Irene makes a convincing case that putting human rights at the centre of the effort to end poverty will help us achieve this goal.

Some see the language of human rights as polarising. I disagree. Understood correctly, the appeal to respect human rights is an appeal to those universal values we share as human beings, across borders, cultures and ideologies. The programme Irene sets forth is grounded in obligations almost all governments have agreed to meet. If followed, it could provide a much needed and renewed sense of common purpose, so desperately needed in our divided world.

Kofi A. Annan
Secretary-General of the United Nations (1997-2006)
President, Kofi Annan Foundation

ACKNOWLEDGEMENTS

Many people contributed to the research, writing and publication of the book. I am enormously indebted, first and foremost, to David Petrasek for his advice, ideas, research and drafting of the text. Widney Brown, Claudio Cordone and Colm O'Cuanachain commented on an early draft. Audrey Gaughran contributed to one of the chapters. Steve Golub, Pamela Gomiez, Leila Kazami, Scott Leckie, Liam Mahoney and Matthew Winters contributed to the research. Helen Barron made important editorial changes to the first draft.

Philip Alston, Prof. Sakiko Fukuda-Parr, Usha Ramanathan, Salil Shetty and Alicia Ely Yamin acted as an informal review group of external experts, and provided insightful comments on the text.

This book would not have come about had it not been for Roby Harrington of W. W. Norton, who took the initiative to approach me two years ago and suggested that I write a book. Thanks go also to others at Norton for their support, including Wamiq Jawaid for his editorial help.

Many collegues at Amnesty International contributed to the production especially Lindsay Warmington who designed the text and Sara Wilbourne who coordinated the project. The book also benefitted from the scrupulous work of several skilled professionals namely Julia Bard, Debbie Millet, and Ian D Crane.

My warm appreciation goes to Kate Mardel-Ferreira and Patricia Melendez in my office and especially to Judit Arenas who brought great energy, ideas and commitment to every stage of the project in far too many ways to enumerate. Kate Gilmore, the Executive Deputy Secretary General, was a rock, backing me up as I juggled with competing commitments in the final stages of the book.

I could not have embarked on this project without the support of my husband, Josef and my daughter, Soraya who allowed me to take the time that I would have otherwise spent with them and put it in the Unheard Truth.

Finally, I want to acknowledge those brave individuals fighting for human rights and human dignity whom I have met in the course of my work and who inspired me to write this book. I recount some of their stories in the book, but have taken the liberty to change their names in order to preserve their privacy.

While the book draws heavily on my experience as Secretary General of Amnesty International and on material produced by the organization, the views expressed are my own and I take full responsibility for them.

Irene Khan

PHOTO ACKNOWLEDGEMENTS

I am grateful to the following photographers and agencies for permission to reproduce images on the cover and throughout the text: [listed in alphabetical order by photographer]:

Tanvir Ahmed for the cover image © Tanvir Ahmed/Majority World/Still Pictures;
G.M.B. Akash on pages 40-41 © G.M.B Akash/ Panos;
Amin on page 15, 201 © Amin/Amnesty International;
Amnesty International on pages 6-7, 100, 122, 164, 196, 201 © Amnesty International;
Cris Bouroncle on page 72, © AFP/Cris Bouroncle
Murtada H. Bulbul on page xiv, © Murtada H. Bulbul/Drik/Majority World;
Carlos Cazalis on pages 54-5 © Carlos Cazalis/Drik/Majority World;
Arturo Ramos Guerrero on page 22 © Arturo Ramos Guerrero/Majority World;
Robin Hammond on pages 132-3 © Robin Hammond/Panos;
Mark Henley on page 146 © Mark Henley/Panos;
Anna Kari on pages 65, 156-7 © Anna Kari/Documentography;
MaanImages/Magnus Johannson on page 80, © Amnesty International;
Sudharak Olwe on page 46 © Sudharak Olwe/Drik India/Majority World;
Moises Saman on pages 86-87 © Moises Saman/Panos;
Paul Smith on pages 212-3 © Paul Smith/Panos;
Boris Svartzman on page 32 © Boris Svartzman/Drik/Majority World;
Ash Sweeting on page 136 © Ash Sweeting/Panos;
Sven Torfinn on pages 182-3, 223 © Sven Torfinn/Panos;
Teun Voeten on page 170 © Teun Voeten/Panos;
Aubrey Wade on page 207 © Aubrey Wade/Panos;
Robert Wallis on page 141 © Robert Wallis/Panos;
WOZA on pages 230-1 © WOZA

ABBREVIATIONS

AGFE	Advisory Group on Forced Evictions
ALG	Alternative Law Groups
ANTHOC	Colombian Hospital Workers Union
ARB	Recyclers Association of Bogotá
BMA	Bangkok Metropolitan Administration
BRAC	Building Resources Across the Communities
CEDAW	Convention on the Elimination of Discrimination Against Women
CLEP	Commission on Legal Empowerment of the Poor
COHRE	Centre on Housing Rights and Evictions
DEG	German Investment and Development Company
DRC	Democratic Republic of the Congo
E.ON	German power and gas supplier
EITI	Extractive Industries Transparency Initiative
ERRC	European Roma Rights Centre
FGM	Female Genital Mutilation
FIAN	Food First Information and Action Network
GDP	Gross Domestic Product
HDI	Human Development Index
IANSA	International Action Network on Small Arms
ICCPR	International Covenant on Civil and Political Rights
ICESCR	International Covenant on Economic, Social and Cultural Rights
IDPs	Internally Displaced People
IFC	International Finance Corporation of the World Bank
IMF	International Monetary Fund
J4P	Justice for the Poor (World Bank programme)
KAIRP	Katchi Abadi Improvement and Regularisation Programme

LEAD	Legal Empowerment and Assistance for the Disadvantaged project
LTTE	Liberation Tigers of Tamil Eelam
MDGs	Millennium Development Goals
MKSS	Mazdoor Kisan Shakti Sangathan, Union for the Empowerment of Peasants and Labourers
NGO	Non-Governmental Organization
NK	Nijera Kori, Bangladeshi NGO
OECD	Organisation for Economic Co-operation and Development
OHCHR	UN Office of the High Commissioner for Human Rights
OMCT	World Organisation Against Torture
PRSP	World Bank's Poverty Reduction Strategy Papers
SEWA	Self-Employed Women's Association of India
SINTREMCALI	Union of Municipal Workers in Cali [Colombia]
SKAA	Sindh Katchi Abadis Authority
TFT	Task Force Tawhanong Pagpuyo
UDHR	Universal Declaration of Human Rights
UNDP	United Nations Development Programme
UNFPA	United Nations Population Fund
UN-HABITAT	United Nations Human Settlements Programme
UNHCR	United Nations High Commissioner for Refugees
UNICEF	United Nations Children's Fund
UPA	Urban Poor Associates
WACAM	Wassa Association of Communities Affected by Mining
WHO	World Health Organization

ONE
THE WORLD'S WORST HUMAN RIGHTS CRISIS

FIFTY YEARS AGO, TWO BABIES were born around the same time in my grandmother's house in Dhaka. One was a girl – myself. The other was a boy, Fajal, born to my grandmother's maid. Growing up as children in the same household, we often played together. I remember Fajal as a bright child, keen to draw pictures, make toys out of tin cans and pieces of string, and run around the yard, singing loudly.

As we grew older, our lives went their different ways. I went to school, then on to university abroad and a successful international career. Fajal was also sent to school but dropped out after a year because the teacher and his schoolmates teased and taunted him for being the child of a domestic servant. His mother put him to work in a state-run factory. Considered a man at the age of 18, he married a 14-year-old girl from a village, and soon became a father. When his factory was privatized a few years later, he agitated with other workers and was sacked. My family gave him money to buy a rickshaw and he did reasonably well until political violence and insecurity on the streets drove him out of business. He then drifted into petty crime and was badly beaten by the police. Unable to afford proper medical care, he never fully recovered from his injuries. Today, he is disabled and lives in a shack in one of Dhaka's sprawling slums with his children and grandchildren, surviving on handouts and his son's meagre income.

Children queuing for water. Mohammadpur, Dhaka, Bangladesh, May 2008. © Murtada H. Bulbul/Drik/Majority World

Fajal is one of 60 million Bangladeshis who live in extreme poverty. The different trajectories of his life and my own show that many factors, not all of them easy to analyze in economic terms, are crucial to understanding why people are poor.

Bangladesh won independence from Pakistan after a brutal and bloody liberation war in 1971. War was followed by famine and natural disaster. Overwhelmingly populated by small farmers and landless peasants, life expectancy in the country at that time was only 45 years, illiteracy was widespread and malnutrition rife. One out of every four children died before the age of five. The then US Secretary of State Henry Kissinger is said to have described Bangladesh as an "international basket case" for its dependence on foreign aid.

Today Bangladesh is still poor, but over the years the country has made remarkable progress. The poverty rate, as measured by the World Bank, has fallen from 74 per cent in 1973-74 to 40 per cent in 2000. Life expectancy has risen to almost 64 years, while infant mortality has halved. Trends in health, education, and income levels are moving in the right direction, even though the fight against poverty is still very far from being won.

Much has been written about Bangladesh's story of "poverty in retreat", as Jeffrey Sachs puts it in *The End of Poverty*.[1] Some of it reflects the achievements of civil society, social entrepreneurs and community-based organizations. But a lot of it is about Gross Domestic Product (GDP) and growth percentages, job creation, levels of foreign investment, savings and debt, access to international markets and the rapid integration of Bangladesh into the global economy, especially since 1991. I find it hard to locate Fajal's story in such accounts.

I find it equally hard to relate Fajal's experiences to the global effort to end poverty through economic growth. Most solutions to poverty concentrate on investment, trade, new technology and, where needed, foreign aid, which are seen as the primary paths to growth. Ending poverty has become the rallying cry of international organizations, political and business leaders, philanthropists and rock stars. Though this unprecedented attention is a good thing, I do not believe that more aid, fairer trade, or increased foreign investments can by themselves ensure that individuals like Fajal are able to improve their situation.

I was not born poor but I was born in a poor country. My experience as a citizen of Bangladesh and as a human rights activist tells me that discrimination, state repression, corruption, insecurity and violence are defining features of poverty. They are human rights abuses. To me, therefore, poverty is the denial of human rights and an affront to human dignity.

The premise of this book is that the poor are denied freedom and justice. These are not abstract notions. Their precise definitions can be found in international law and human rights treaties. Economic growth and increased income levels are important, but unless and until we address the rights of poor people we will fail to meet the challenge of ending poverty. Current global efforts to end poverty pay lip service to human rights, but include no serious attempt to make rights real.

In this book I will explain why I believe ending poverty is first and foremost about securing respect for human rights. I want to convince you, the reader, that not only are the poor denied their human rights, but also – and more importantly – that if we act in effective ways to protect those rights, our efforts to end poverty stand a far greater chance of success. In short, I speak of the human rights of people living in poverty not to point fingers and apportion blame (though there is plenty to go round) but because I believe that doing so points to solutions.

IT'S NOT *JUST* THE ECONOMY

Ciudad Juárez is a sprawling, ramshackle Mexican city on the United States border, just metres away from the gleaming towers of El Paso, Texas. It is host to the *maquiladoras* – assembly plants set up by international companies to take advantage of tax benefits and cheaper labour in Mexico to produce goods for export to North America. Young women migrate to Ciudad Juárez to find jobs in the *maquiladoras* and to escape rural poverty. Many come from the poorest regions of Mexico. In the last 10 years, hundreds of these poor, young women – many of them only girls – have been abducted, raped and brutally murdered in Ciudad Juárez and areas of Chihuahua state. They were killed while walking home from work or night school, their bodies dumped in the empty lots or scrubland around the shanty towns where they lived. Until 2005 there were no convictions, nor even serious police investigations or prosecutions. Amnesty International has been working with the families of the victims for the past five years. I have met many of them during my visits to Mexico. Norma Ledesma, whose 16-year-old daughter Paloma was raped and murdered on her way back from night school in 2003, said to me, "No one listens to us. We count for nothing – simply nothing to the government."

In economic terms, the women of Ciudad Juárez had improved their lot. But their security had worsened. They were thrust into sprawling shanty towns where poor and corrupt policing and the lack of community support networks exposed them to horrifying new threats. Through their labour they were contributing to the global economy but as poor women they were discriminated against and had no power, no political clout. Their voices were not heard.

Government officials and policy-makers are required to define and quantify poverty in the same way as crime, disease, or climate change. While recognizing the complexity of poverty, the most common official response is to define it in terms of income. According to the World Bank, those earning less than $1.25 a day are living in "extreme poverty", and those below $2 a day are "poor". According to this measure, over 1 billion people live in extreme poverty while another 2 billion are poor.

Defining poverty through income levels may have advantages, but it certainly has one major drawback. It leads to the conclusion that the only solution to poverty is to raise those income levels, and for this to happen on the massive scale needed, given the numbers involved, poor countries must experience substantial economic growth. Seen in this light, the solution is to foster growth – through increased productivity and investment, supplemented by foreign aid. Most books on global poverty highlight the need to boost economic growth; this is not surprising, as most are written by economists.

I do not wish to decry economic growth or belittle efforts made in good faith to boost the resources of developing countries or increase the income of poor people. To be sure, if those living in poverty had more material assets, it would benefit them, not least in their ability to obtain things they lack, such as food, shelter, education and health-care. But growth alone is not a panacea. Countries with impressive growth rates do not always see improved living standards. Bangladesh has seen a steady rise in national income, but some studies show that despite economic growth between 1990 and 2006, there was in the same period rising child malnourishment (worse among girls), and a decline in access to clean water in urban areas.[2] What's more, material benefits alone do not guarantee political power, end discrimination or improve security for poor people simply because they have increased their income above $2 a day. Investment may boost crop yields for impoverished farmers, but it does not automatically provide them security of tenure against unscrupulous landlords or corrupt officials. Nor does building new schools guarantee that girls will be able to access education on an equal footing with boys, nor that children of minority communities will be welcome. And greater income does not automatically make poor women more secure, as the mothers of Ciudad Juárez will testify.

In fact, where countries experience overall economic growth, it is common to see growing inequalities in access to those basic goods that are essential to a dignified life. Too often, those left behind are marginalized on grounds of gender, race, language, ethnicity or caste. If we do not explicitly address discrimination, marginalization and exclusion, some groups may advance but others will not.

The unfolding economic crisis that beset the world in 2008 demonstrates the fragility of an approach that focuses narrowly on economic growth as a response to poverty. Economies worldwide are in recession. Growth rates are slowing in China, India and Brazil, and falling in countries throughout Africa. Reduced demands for exports to the most developed countries and lower foreign investment will mean less growth for export-oriented economies. Countries like Bangladesh that are heavily dependent on remittances from migrant workers are likely to be badly affected. The consequences for those living in poverty, we are warned, will be catastrophic. The leaders of the G8, the chiefs of the development banks, corporate leaders have all pointed to declining growth rates as spelling the end of a global economic boom in which, they assert, "hundreds of millions were lifted out of poverty".

Overleaf: **Wreath laid by Irene Khan on behalf of Amnesty International at a memorial in Campo Algodonero, Ciudad Juárez, Mexico, where the bodies of eight women were found in 2001. Three cases of the murdered women were brought before the Inter-American Court of Human Rights in 2008.**

Brenda
2001
Lupita

2001
2001
Esmeralda

The extent to which this is true is hotly debated. But true or not, the conclusion seems to be that only through a new round of rapid global economic growth can we bring millions more people out of poverty. But by that logic, progress and improvements in the lives of poor people are hostage to boom and bust in the world economy. Economic growth is an important component of a strategy to tackle poverty, but it cannot be the only element. We must also give attention to other components: those that empower people living in poverty to claim their human rights so that they can be in control, rather than victims, of their destiny.

What I am saying is not new. The Nobel Prize-winning economist Amartya Sen (incidentally, a fellow Bengali) has argued powerfully that freedom is both a constituent component of development and a contributing factor to its achievement. He urges us to go beyond income levels when we measure the efforts to end poverty. The imperfect relationship between economic growth and the eradication of poverty led the United Nations, in 1990, to put forward a more comprehensive test for measuring progress – the Human Development Index (HDI). Countries are scored against a variety of benchmarks, such as per capita income, literacy levels, average lifespan, percentage of children in school, equality between the sexes and the incidence of death in childbirth. A country's HDI score will improve where progress is shown in relation to these and other indicators.

Few dispute the appropriateness of this more comprehensive measure of progress in development. Nevertheless, it is still the case that global policy looks overwhelmingly to economic solutions as the answer to poverty.

THE VICIOUS CIRCLE

Economic analysis does not capture the full picture of poverty, and economic solutions alone cannot fully address the problem of poverty. We need to look beyond economics – at deprivation, insecurity, exclusion and voicelessness – and to recognize these issues for what they are: human rights problems. We also need to understand that they are interlinked and form a vicious circle that impoverishes people and keeps them poor.

In September 2001, I was in South Africa and visited a counselling centre set up by the provincial government of Natal, just outside Durban. The purpose of the centre was to assist women in making complaints about family violence, and to improve the police take-up of complaints and the enforcement of protection orders from the local magistrate. There I heard the story of Rosie, a woman with five children, who was regularly brutalized by her husband until one day he beat her so badly that she died. I asked why she hadn't complained to the police or applied for a protection order from the magistrate, since South African law contains provisions to protect women from domestic violence that are among the most progressive in the world. The counsellor replied: "Rosie did not have the money for the bus fare to go from her village to the nearest magistrates' court."

Clearly, Rosie's inability to scrape together a bus fare is a sign of poverty. Those living in poverty lack the goods and services that are essential to a dignified life. They often do not have access to basic health-care. Their shelter is inadequate; they may not have access to clean water and sanitation; their children cannot attend school; they lack food and often go to bed hungry. People who live in poverty are deprived of the opportunity to better their position – through education, through secure employment, and through the protection of whatever meagre assets they can accumulate.

What is less well understood, though, is that deprivation dramatically affects the security of poor people. This was evident in Rosie's case; she was too poor to get to a magistrates court for protection. It goes further than this: the absence of security keeps people poor.

Poor people live in perpetual insecurity, and their insecurity reinforces their poverty. Poor neighbourhoods suffer from high rates of violent crime. Poor people often lack legal security in relation to their home, possessions and livelihood, and social security that would promise some minimal protection in the event of illness, crop failure, or unemployment. A recent UN-sponsored commission reported that tens of millions of people – including 70 per cent of children born in the least developed countries – lack a legal identity: their very existence is not officially acknowledged.[3] They have no rights in relation to those who exercise power over them – they are day labourers subject to the vagaries of the casual employment market, landless peasants at the mercy of landowners, slum dwellers evicted by developers, and women at risk from their employers, their communities and families. Without rights they are insecure, and insecurity means they are less able to fight their deprivation.

The state constantly fails poor people. They are disproportionately affected by police brutality and official corruption. Courts, administrative tribunals, welfare bodies, municipal councils, water and land-use authorities, boards of education – all ostensibly meant to treat all citizens equally – too often treat people living in poverty with contempt or indifference. This may be because less developed countries lack the resources or skills to provide the services, but more often the exclusion and neglect of poor people is the result of discrimination.

I spoke earlier of Fajal. His poverty was closely interlinked with the discrimination and violence he faced because of his low social status. Take the situation of women in Bangladesh. The country has one of the highest ratios of maternal mortality and violence against women in Asia. One of the most horrific forms of gender violence is acid attacks, often perpetrated by angry young men against teenage girls who refuse a proposal of marriage. Malnutrition is high among girls and pregnant women. On average women earn less than half the wages of men. Under Islamic personal law they are not able to inherit property, or to divorce or take custody of their children on the same terms as men, even though the national constitution guarantees equality and equal protection for all citizens. To me, the degree to which women have control over their own lives is an essential element in overcoming poverty, which in almost every country affects women disproportionately. Or take the situation of minorities. In Bangladesh, 500,000 Gypsies or travelling people (Bede), who are not recognized as a minority, are excluded from any state initiatives on health or education, and Bede women are almost all illiterate, in a country which is aspiring to gender equality in education.

Bangladesh is hardly unique. Significant proportions of people living in poverty worldwide belong to minority or marginalized communities, who are discriminated against on grounds that include gender, sexuality, ethnicity, creed, caste and disability. Poverty in rich countries comes into sharp focus through the lens of discrimination and exclusion. In the USA, tens of thousands of homeless people are not eligible to vote. Consider the Roma communities of Europe; in almost all the countries where they live their living standards fall far below those of the majority. In some of the worst cases, Amnesty International has found that the public authorities are complicit in or indifferent to policies that keep Roma children out of school or in inferior schools, or turn a blind eye to discrimination and racism by the police and courts.

As in the case of security, discrimination and exclusion mean that poor people do not have access to the entitlements available to the better off, and because of this, they are trapped in poverty. It is a vicious circle that is difficult to break because those living in poverty lack the power to change their situation.

Whether through deliberate repression or through indifference, those in power do not hear the voices of poor people. It is no coincidence that some of the poorest countries are also among the world's most repressive. But even in countries committed to democratic principles, those living in poverty consistently feel ignored, their voices often unheard by the authorities. For instance, in my many meetings with Indigenous Peoples in Oaxaca and Guerrero in Mexico, and Temuco and Calama in Chile, they constantly spoke of how their concerns were ignored or overridden by the authorities: their efforts to organize were met with repression; information relevant to their situation was withheld; processes for consultation were rigged or ineffective – all this despite laws recognizing their rights and status as Indigenous Peoples.

When poor people have no voice, when they are excluded and shut out, they cannot hold governments accountable for their failure to provide security or equality of access to public services. Under the agenda of "good governance", there is an effort to reform state structures to make them fair and efficient. But this would advance much more quickly if the voices of those who stood to benefit the most were not silenced or ignored. It is again no coincidence that some of the poorest countries of the world are also the most corrupt and poorly governed. Take the example of Bangladesh again. Greed, corruption and patronage thrive under the veneer of democracy among self-serving political and business elites. From petty bribery to grand larceny of government funds, corruption has deprived the poor, and driven resources into the hands of the rich in my country.

I raise the issue of "voice" because I have also seen its positive side in fighting poverty. Bangladesh is remarkable for its vibrant civil society, social entrepreneurs, community-based development organizations, and self-help schemes. Many of these grew exponentially in the wake of the independence war, when the new state was particularly weak. Bangladesh is the home of BRAC, the world's largest non-governmental organization (NGO), Grameen Bank, which pioneered the micro-credit revolution in providing small loans to the extreme poor, and Gonoshasthaya Kendra (People's Health Centre), known for its community health clinics for poor people. Investing in the empowerment of people living in poverty has been a fundamental part of the modest success that the country has had in the fight against poverty, despite its poor governance record.

MORE HUMAN RIGHTS EQUAL LESS POVERTY

Denied education, health-care, shelter or other necessities, and exposed to insecurity, poor people lack the essential elements to live a dignified life. Excluded and unheard, they are unable to improve their lot. Unable to get a fair hearing or influence events, they are left exposed to further threats and more deprivation, deepening the downward spiral of impoverishment. This experience of those living in poverty repeats itself over and over again, whether among villagers in Bangladesh, women in Ciudad Juárez, victims of violence in South Africa, the Roma minority in Europe or Indigenous Peoples in the Americas.

Taken together, they add up to a problem of power; more explicitly the *powerlessness* that those living in poverty feel in relation to the events and people that have an impact on their daily lives. They are powerless to obtain what they need to live a dignified life; to manage insecurity; to hold to account institutions that affect their lives, and to play an active role in society.

In the words of Professor Muhammad Yunus, my compatriot who won the Nobel Peace Prize for his pioneering work to eradicate poverty through micro-credit: "Because poverty denies people any semblance of control over their destiny, it is the ultimate denial of human rights."[4]

The pervasive powerlessness experienced by poor people is confirmed by the World Bank, which in 1999-2000 carried out the most comprehensive survey undertaken of poor communities, involving 60,000 participants in 20 countries. The resulting report, *Voices of the Poor*, concluded:

> *From poor people's perspectives, ill-being or bad quality of life is much more than just material poverty. It has multiple, interlocking dimensions. The dimensions combine to create and sustain powerlessness, a lack of freedom of choice and action.*[5]

The report identified several dimensions to the experience of living in poverty, including insecurity, being shut out by official institutions and being denied a voice and ignored. The report noted:

> *While each of the individual dimensions of poverty is important, it is even more important to understand that the dimensions form a powerful web. They interlock to create, perpetuate and deepen powerlessness and deprivation.*[6]

If this is a fair description of the actual, lived experience of poor people, then it should be obvious that the foremost challenge is not their enrichment but their empowerment.

This is why I insist on defining poverty as a human rights problem that can be addressed most effectively through respect for human rights. Framing poverty in human rights terms provides an empowering framework for rights holders (people living in poverty), and an accountability framework for duty holders (those who exercise power over poor people) to respect and protect rights. By asserting their rights, those living in poverty place themselves at the centre of the debate and gain the dignity to fight the conditions that keep them poor. By identifying obligations, we require the powerful to behave according to internationally recognized standards, rather than relying on market forces. It is currently fashionable to speak of government agencies as "service providers", but they should be seen as duty bearers, entrusted with obligations to deliver on specific rights. This strengthens the link of accountability between the government and the governed. Seen in this way, the relevance of the human rights approach to poverty eradication becomes apparent: if rights were protected and fulfilled, this would address the abuses which help to create and perpetuate poverty.

Human rights give a voice to the voiceless. Individuals have a right to express their views freely, to organize, to assemble peacefully and to make their views known. Human rights demand transparent and accountable government, so that people are informed and can participate actively and effectively in decision-making. Of course, full respect for human rights requires that governments are democratically elected and truly accountable to the electorate, and when they are, as I will argue later, we are more likely to win the struggle against poverty.

Equally, however, the deprivations experienced by the poor are a denial of rights. Access to clean water, basic shelter, health-care, education and food are basic needs that every human being must have to live in dignity. But they are more than that – they are internationally recognized economic, social and cultural rights. The Universal Declaration of Human Rights (UDHR) and other international instruments proclaim these rights, alongside the rights to freedom of speech and religion and to equality. The overwhelming majority of the world's governments have entered into binding treaties that commit them to fulfilling these rights, but there are still many who deny their validity. Acknowledging economic and social rights puts meeting basic human needs squarely within the framework of national and international accountability, and empowers people to expect and demand that their basic needs will be met.

Human rights shield people from insecurity because they provide protections and guarantees against the arbitrary exercise of power by the state. They also place an obligation on the state to protect individuals from the abuse of power by others – the employer in the workplace, the leader in the community and the partner at home. Further, rights establish equality before the law, so that the poor no less than the rich are assured of a fair hearing and their assets, however meagre, are protected against unjust seizure. There are rights to social security guaranteed in the Universal Declaration – they oblige the state to provide a social safety net to protect people's livelihoods in the event of illness and unemployment.

Irene Khan at the Microfinance Village organization meeting of BRAC at Tangail, Bangladesh, December 2007.
© Amin/Amnesty International

Finally, human rights address exclusion and inequality because they place duties on the powerful to act without bias or favour. International human rights are grounded in the premise of a common humanity – "All human beings are born free and equal in dignity and rights", declares the first article of the Universal Declaration. What more powerful appeal could be made to challenge the bigotry and prejudice at work in the world?

It is essential, however, that action to protect rights occurs concurrently in all four areas to tackle deprivation, insecurity, exclusion and lack of voice because, just as the problems are interlinked, so too are the different elements of the response mutually reinforcing. For instance, providing security against threats to life and livelihood, and ending discrimination, provides those living in poverty with the opportunity to meet their needs, just as it creates the space for them to demand action from governments where this is needed. Action in one direction alone, however, will be insufficient. Intervening simply to create democratic space may ignore the fact that the basic needs of some people can remain unfulfilled even in a truly representative democracy. Improving the education of girls without addressing discrimination against women will do little to address the feminization of poverty. If little is done to tackle violence in poor neighbourhoods, how can those who live there work or go to school?

In arguing my case for a human rights approach to ending poverty, I lay no claim to original thinking. Many people, including in governments and the UN, would agree with me that rights are relevant to tackling global poverty. The overwhelming majority of the world's governments have ratified international treaties, committing themselves to meeting their citizens' rights to an adequate standard of living, and to basic health-care, education and shelter. The Universal Declaration proclaimed these rights as far back as 1948, and the treaties commit states to work together to progressively bring people out of poverty. Former UN Secretary-General Kofi Annan pledged in 1996 that the UN would henceforth factor human rights into all its development work. UN agencies, many states, and others, including, to a limited extent the World Bank, have adopted human rights policies for addressing poverty and/or committed themselves to "rights-based approaches". All of this is good news – so where is the problem?

In reality, the acknowledgement that rights matter in the fight against poverty isn't complete, nor is there sufficient action resulting from that acknowledgement. There is a big gap in the international consensus on human rights as the basis for fighting poverty. Neither China nor the United States of America – the two powers that wield enormous influence in setting global policy – accept the full spectrum of human rights. China refuses to ratify the International Covenant on Civil and Political Rights (ICCPR), thereby challenging the importance both of these freedoms and of accountable government. The USA refuses to ratify the International Covenant on Economic, Social and Cultural Rights (ICESCR), thereby challenging the notion of a state's duty to meet basic needs. How can the vicious cycle of abuse that entrenches poverty be overcome if rights are not affirmed in their entirety by the leading nations of the world?

Even where the full gamut of rights is acknowledged, there is far too little concrete action to protect the rights of those living in poverty. When rights are invoked, it is most often done as a moral imperative to end poverty, but with no substantial obligation to act in a different way. When rights are incorporated in development strategies, it is usually without reference to the accountability of governments, business and international institutions.

The UN Millennium Declaration of 2000 invokes the language of rights to address global poverty. But the manner in which the Millennium Development Goals (MDGs) – the concrete targets drawn up to give effect to the pledges made in the Declaration – have been translated into concrete action, virtually exempts states from any requirement to address discrimination, protect the rights of the poor to organize or open up the development process to meaningful scrutiny by those whose rights need to be met.

Although policies are in place, very few development strategies actually incorporate rights in a meaningful way, even 10 years after the UN Secretary-General first called for this to happen. Overplaying the rhetoric and downplaying the application of human rights means little attention is given to the accountability of governments, donors and institutions, and even less to the real empowerment of the people living in poverty.

The persistence of poverty which inhibits the lives of billions of people is an indication of human rights abuse on a massive scale. This is not only because poor people are denied those basic necessities essential to a dignified life, but equally because so often this also indicates a denial of their rights to equality, to protection against harm, and to full participation in public life. Poor people do not have greater rights than anyone else; they have equal rights, and these deserve to be respected.

WHAT CAN BE DONE?

Sceptics will ask: "What difference does it make to acknowledge poverty as a human rights crisis? What concrete action will follow?" This book is written to answer the sceptics: to show why rights matter and what can and must be done to overcome poverty.

In the next three chapters I will look at the ways in which deprivation, insecurity, exclusion and voicelessness interact. Chapter 2 looks at the importance of "voice" and the right of those living in poverty to take part in decisions that affect them. I challenge the argument, led by a resurgent China, that authoritarian governments are better able to tackle poverty. Chapter 3 discusses the impact of discrimination on poverty and the growing inequality gap in the world today. Chapter 4 shows how insecurity is central to the experience of poverty. I look at armed conflict, criminal violence and violence against women to make my case for better protection of lives and livelihoods of poor people.

Identifying the human rights abuses that keep people poor is one goal of my book. It is equally important, however, to demonstrate the value of bringing the language and tools of human rights to bear on the debate. Therefore, in these opening chapters I aim through examples to show how asserting the rights to "voice" and inclusion, and to counter insecurity and deprivation makes a difference.

The human rights response to poverty cannot be partial, focusing only on people's rights to inclusion and security, while neglecting deprivation and voicelessness, or vice-versa. Unfortunately, government strategies and global anti-poverty efforts are doing precisely that. In Chapter 5, I look at the poisoned legacy of the Cold War, which pitted one set of rights against another – civil and political, versus economic, social and cultural. I develop a critique of the MDGs, but I also take a self-critical look at Amnesty International's own partial approach to human rights until some years ago, and describe the journey it has made to set that straight.

In Chapters 6, 7 and 8 I look at whether what appears to be convincing in theory, actually works in practice by applying the human rights frame of reference to specific harms and specific situations where the rights of poor people are at risk.

Chapter 6 examines maternal mortality, which is the leading killer of young women in the less developed world, despite being almost entirely preventable. Often portrayed as a health problem, I see it primarily in terms of the powerlessness of women.

The number of people living in slums is growing worldwide. Already home to over 1 billion people, the size of the world's slums will double by 2030. Chapter 7 shows the dramatic and daily experience of deprivation and insecurity of slum life, and argues that asserting the rights of people who live in slums is an essential component in tackling the challenges they face.

Economic growth may help the poor but it does not always do so. Chapter 8 looks at less developed countries enriched by oil and mineral extraction. Human rights abuses too often accompany extraction, and the revenues too rarely go to fulfilling basic rights. Governments in those countries must be made more accountable, but so, too, must the large foreign companies involved. Asserting rights helps in both respects.

If the problem is powerlessness, then laws that are supposed to put constraints on power ought to be essential. For the poor, however, the law is often another source of oppression. In Chapter 9, I describe what bottom-up strategies of legal empowerment can achieve, and how poor communities can claim their rights through using the law.

A NEW URGENCY

The world today is beset by a perfect storm of crises: a warming planet and environmental damage; global recession; threats to peace and security; and the plight of almost half the world's population, who live in poverty. These crises are interlinked, each impacting on the other. Climate change will, in most cases, be felt first and worst by those living in poverty. Many of the least developed countries are prone to conflict. Economic recession will set back progress in bringing people out of poverty and create more sources of instability. Solving any one of these crises is a challenge; put together they appear almost insurmountable.

I believe, perhaps perversely, that crises present opportunities. The economic crisis has forced us to rethink the old model that focused overwhelmingly on markets and diminished the role and responsibilities of governments. In recent years, we witnessed a progressive weakening of states, or at least of their ability, individually and collectively, to meet the challenges posed. Throughout the world, and from all sides of the political spectrum, there is now growing acceptance that the retreat of the state must halt. State action has regained its legitimacy, and not only as regards the economy. It is to states that we look to set the rules that will reduce carbon emissions and contain the spread of weapons that fuels conflict. This renewed focus on state action is good news for the agenda proposed here.

Human rights activists have always believed that effective and accountable states are best able to deliver the collective promise of human rights for all. Only such states can end poverty, the world's worst human rights crisis.[7] Rights have been seen traditionally as putting constraints on state power and being a shield for citizens against arbitrary state action. This remains a central purpose of enshrining human rights in law. Increasingly, however, rights are pointed as a sword to claim protection against other sources of power too – in the workplace, the community and the home. When this happens, it is a plea for protection to which only the state, through its laws, can respond. In other words, rights are also about demands for positive state action, not just calls to the state to refrain from illegal acts. A state must act to establish machinery for fair elections, to ensure that courts work fairly, that all children can go to school, and that the benefits of growth are shared equitably. States must protect individuals against the abuses of employers. Multinational corporations pose specific challenges in this regard, as many are bigger than states and make a virtue of being "nation-less". Crucially, states must act to protect the rights of women against the multiple threats they face in the home and the community.

The failures of states to act in this way are legion, of course, and it is not surprising that people look elsewhere for solutions. But asserting the rights of those living in poverty is a powerful means to make states work – because it clearly identifies duties and demands accountability in the face of inaction or the abuse of rights.

The international human rights system should complement local pressure with international oversight and support. It does not do this very effectively now, although the machinery is in place. But it could do this better if it were to position itself more centrally in global anti-poverty efforts. Just as development organizations must incorporate human rights more effectively in their strategies, plans and programmes, the UN's human rights institutions need to see the rights of poor people as a cross-cutting issue in all their endeavours, equally relevant to the eradication of torture as to the promotion of education.

Asserting rights is a call for state action, but those making the call are themselves empowered by their ability to claim rights on their own behalf when the duties owed to them are ignored and pledges are unfulfilled. When the women of Ciudad Juárez organized themselves and demanded their right to justice and protection for themselves and their daughters, the government could not ignore them any longer. With the support of Amnesty International and other national and international organizations, they forced the Mexican federal government, which had until then claimed it was a problem for state authorities, to intervene.

Poverty is not primarily about economics and income levels. It is about the powerlessness experienced in so many ways by those living in poverty. Human rights are claims that the weak advance to hold the powerful to account, and that is why poverty is first and foremost about rights. Though many acknowledge the rights dimension, too little effective action follows. Dominant global efforts to eradicate poverty are trapped in a frame of reference that focuses primarily on growth, in which rights are seen as obstacles, or mere slogans that can be invoked without consequence. In fact, unless and until the rights dimension to poverty is acknowledged and acted on, I believe these global efforts will make little sustained progress.

On a recent trip to Bangladesh, I went to see a legal literacy project run by BRAC. A group of women in brightly coloured saris sat on bamboo mats in a village enclosure. They were all recipients of micro-credit loans. They listened attentively as their teacher, using posters with graphic designs, explained the law prohibiting child marriage and requiring the informed consent of a woman to marriage. I asked one of the women why she was there. "I want to know more about my rights," she said. "I don't want my daughters to suffer the way I have, and so I need to learn how to protect my rights and theirs."

The struggle to end poverty is not only a struggle to increase material assets but is a struggle for freedom, justice and dignity. That is why invoking human rights gives us the best hope of winning.

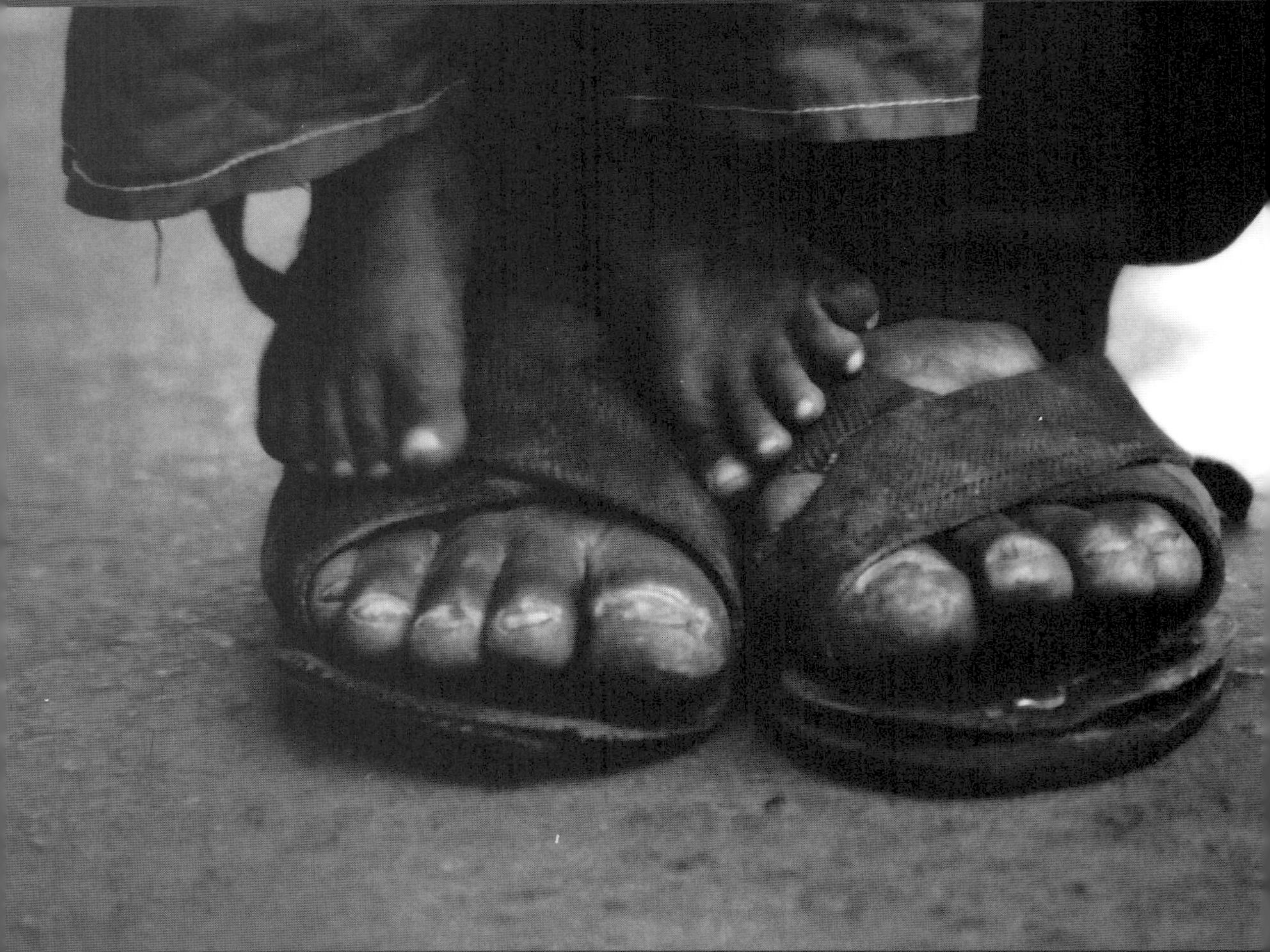

TWO
FREEDOM AND ITS CRITICS – WHY 'VOICE' MATTERS

IT TOOK THE AMNESTY INTERNATIONAL delegation less than 45 minutes to drive from Acapulco – known for its golden beaches, five-star hotels and luxury resorts – to the mountains where some of the poorest communities of peasants and Indigenous Peoples live in the Guerrero state of Mexico. The villagers led us to the banks of the Papagaya River where the authorities are planning to build La Parota Dam, the largest hydro-electric project in Mexico. The people pointed to their corn fields on the slopes and to the clusters of huts in the valleys in the distance and told us that all that – their homes, land and livelihoods – would be flooded if the dam were built. Further downstream, peasant farmers showed us vast stretches of orchards and fields they would have to abandon because there would be no water for irrigation when the river is diverted.

La Parota is part of a multi-billion dollar investment plan in infrastructure, communications and energy in Latin America. The project is expected to fuel economic growth by generating a very large part of eastern Mexico's electricity needs. But, if constructed, the dam will flood 17,000 hectares and displace over 100,000 people. Already poor, they will be made destitute by the development project. Yet, those likely to be most directly affected by the project were the least informed about what was about to happen. One farmer said to me, "The plan was made in 1976 but we were told

The bare feet of an Indigenous child resting on her father during a recess after a march from the mountains of Guerrero to Mexico City. Mexico City, Mexico, 2000.

nothing about it until the electricity company began digging last year." That was in August 2006.

The consultations initiated by the state-owned electricity company were deeply flawed. Many people had received only inadequate information or no information at all. Impact assessment studies did not cover all relevant aspects, and dramatically played down the numbers of people who would be affected. Many women were excluded from the consultation process because the company and the authorities based the exercise on a land registration system going back to the early part of the 20th century when women's land rights were not recognized. Most people did not know the extent to which they would be affected and even less what compensation, if any, they would receive. Differences within the communities between those who supported the project and those who opposed it had led to tensions, intimidation, harassment and threats, and at least three deaths.

Some of the communities organized themselves and brought legal action in the local courts, but the electricity corporation and the government appeared to be ignoring the judgments that were made in favour of the communities. Finally, as a result of a combination of local, national and international pressure, to which Amnesty International contributed, the authorities were forced to back down. They suspended the project and promised fresh consultations in 2007. The government had been thwarted in its economic development plans, the local people were left angry and embittered at having been ignored and excluded, and the future remained uncertain.

Participation of poor communities is essential to good development. Yet too often, and in too many countries, people's right to be informed and consulted about public policy is ignored; their right to express their views, protest or organize themselves is curtailed. The restrictions on liberty are justified in the name of advancing collective living standards. That argument is demonstrably false and clearly in breach of international human rights treaties to which governments have subscribed.

There is nothing new about the argument that freedom must be suppressed for the sake of economic growth and stability. During the Cold War, governments from both ends of the political spectrum – communist as well as authoritarian capitalist – used it to clamp down on civil liberties. Although most countries in the world are now wedded to the market economy, and many have adopted democratic models of governance, the idea that suppression of freedom is necessary for economic development still lingers on. Open economies need not be accompanied by open societies, the argument goes, because sometimes it is necessary to suppress liberty in order to raise living standards. Just look at China, they say. I fear that, as we enter a period of global recession, such arguments will gain a new lease of life. In 2008, when people took to the streets to protest against rising food prices and worsening economic conditions, even peaceful protests were met with force in many countries.

In this chapter, I will show that respecting freedom, and in particular giving people who live in poverty a chance to be heard, is a better strategy for development than repression. The value of freedom, both as a means to achieving development as well as an end in itself, cannot be overstated. Overcoming poverty is a struggle for freedom, waged primarily by those living in poverty. Freedom is denied when people live in conditions they cannot control and which deny them choices and opportunities that would improve their situation. Only when poor people have a "voice", when they are able to organize, speak out and take part in making decisions that affect their lives and livelihoods, can they tackle the deprivation, exclusion and insecurity they confront. In that process, they overcome their experience of being ignored and regain their dignity and sense of self-worth.

By the term "voice" I mean more than the right to protest. The right to information is the key that opens the door to effective participation, so giving poor people a voice means giving them information about the development choices that are available, including the expenditure of public funds. It also means responding to the claims and concerns of poor people because real participation can only truly work if the state is responsive and its officials are accountable to the population.

Consider this example, where participation, training and the empowerment of local leaders brought about change. In Cebu City in the Philippines, more than 70 per cent of the population lives in dismal conditions in shanty towns where they have no security of tenure. In the name of development, the government started to demolish their homes. The people who were affected were not consulted. In response a group of NGOs joined together to form the Task Force Tawhanong Pagpuyo (TFT), which organized the leaders of the urban poor. They suggested alternative proposals. Education and information campaigns were started for the communities as well as for judges who issued the demolition and eviction orders. Pressure on the authorities resulted in the creation of a local housing board, which included representatives from among the urban poor, as well as the NGOs that were helping them. The results were impressive. A comprehensive shelter plan for Cebu City was drawn up, including provision of basic services to the urban poor. The number of demolitions and evictions in publicly owned lots fell, and alternative housing was provided for those who did have to leave their homes. The judges' awareness of the issues meant that they consulted with the local housing board before issuing eviction orders.[1]

The importance of participation is not disputed on paper. Innumerable international declarations and national policy statements from governments and development agencies, state that "participation" is a good thing and that governments must consult with affected communities. In the UN Millennium Declaration in 2000, all the world's governments committed themselves "[t]o work collectively for more inclusive political processes, allowing genuine participation by all citizens in all our countries". The private sector, too, increasingly subscribes to the idea of involving "stakeholders" in consultations before proceeding with major projects.

On the ground, though, the reality is very different. Community leaders are harassed and intimidated. Governments refuse to allow independent organizations to register. People seeking to challenge legislation through the courts are denied access. Trade unions are restricted in their activities and their leaders arrested, attacked or killed. Peaceful protests are broken up by force. Those who criticize government policy are arrested or silenced in other ways. These are not isolated incidents. In 2008, Amnesty International documented at least 37 countries that currently hold Prisoners of Conscience – people who are locked up simply for what they say or believe – and at least 81 countries with severe restrictions on freedom of expression and the press. The International Center for Not-for-Profit Law says that in

2005-2006, 19 more countries introduced restrictive legislation, bringing to more than 50 the total number of countries whose laws, policies and practices stifle the work of civil society organizations, actively discouraging "participation".

To give an example, in Cambodia, community representatives and advocates working to halt forced evictions are harassed, and many arrested on trumped-up charges. In a recent land dispute which, on 24 January 2009, led to the forced eviction of 400 families at Dey Kraham in central Phnom Penh, 17 residents, including informal community representatives, were charged with criminal offences. Several of them have already been convicted, two to prison terms, while three others were given suspended sentences.

To give another example, in Colombia over 2,000 trade unionists have been killed in the last 20 years, and another 138 have disappeared. The situation for trade unionists in Colombia has been so consistently dire that the International Labour Organization (ILO) appointed a permanent representative to Colombia in 2006. Amnesty International has documented the fact that the majority of attacks on trade unions happen in the context of ongoing labour struggles. The hospital workers union ANTHOC received death threats after participating in a humanitarian camp for the right to health. ANTHOC had earlier been the victim of a bomb attack during a meeting called to discuss moves towards the privatization of health-care in Colombia. SINTREMCALI, the union of municipal workers in Cali, was targeted after campaigning against government plans to privatize Cali's electricity, water and sanitation companies.

There is a yawning gap between the rhetorical commitment to "participation" and the reality of repression and the experience of being ignored in communities and villages where people live in poverty. Why is this so? Are governments deliberately lying to us?

Some governments certainly are deceitful on this point. But more fundamentally there are, I think, three reasons to explain this gap. Firstly, "participation" is seen as a technical issue, something to strive for in development projects, but treated in isolation from the overall climate of freedom in the country and the willingness of the government to live up to its human rights obligations under international law. Secondly, there is a surprisingly widespread tolerance for an authoritarian approach to development, for the idea that we should put "bread before ballots". This is despite a lack of any evidence that restricting freedoms is a quicker route to raising living standards. Thirdly, the tools for effective participation – information, civilian engagement and accountability – are not always understood or available.

PARTICIPATION AS FREEDOM

Participation is too often viewed not as an empowering tool, a question of rights and dignity, but as an aspect of good project design. When participation is seen merely as a step to go through in implementing development projects, the ensuing consultation is only just sufficient to ensure that the condition is met. It is not treated with the seriousness it deserves. Like so many other items on the "to do" list of projects, it gets squeezed by time, budget and logistical constraints.

Take as an example the consultation processes that are part of the World Bank's Poverty Reduction Strategy Papers (PRSP). This process requires governments that receive World Bank funding to prepare papers outlining their plans to reduce poverty. Governments are expected to draft these through broad and inclusive consultation with civil society. In many countries the process has left civil society groups deeply frustrated because lack of access to information and to the process bars effective engagement.

Participation of people in the development process is regarded as a privilege rather than a right, with governments carefully limiting and controlling entry points. In the PRSP process, governments are often reluctant to allow citizens' groups in, or do so only under pressure from donors. Even then, discretion and discrimination are frequently exercised in deciding which groups should participate. Often those groups that are least likely to challenge the government significantly are invited. It's no surprise, then, that a forum organized by the World Bank in 2005 to look at the process noted that "...governments often treat civil society as the opposition rather than as the people."

Furthermore, many important issues – including human rights violations – are simply not up for discussion. The World Bank makes no mention of human rights in its monitoring and evaluation guidelines for the PRSP process, nor is there any conspicuous reference to human rights on the Bank's PRSP website or any of the major documents posted there. A 2005 document published jointly by the World Bank and the International Monetary Fund (IMF) frankly acknowledged that, "While interests in better financial management and results-oriented performance align, tensions can arise, particularly around political issues, human rights, and deep-rooted governance problems, most of which are not addressed in the [PRSP process]."[2]

How can there be real participation on poverty reduction strategies in countries where independent political parties are not tolerated, where the press is tightly controlled and where people are routinely locked up for expressing dissident views? Can participation be meaningful in a country where individuals who speak freely on the internet or who seek to form peaceful activist coalitions are routinely imprisoned? When intellectuals, who are members of the elite, are denounced and imprisoned for criticizing the authorities, people who are powerless and living in poverty understand that there are strict limits to what they can say.

People can only truly have a say in their own future in an environment where respect for basic rights is assured. That is what I call a voice-enabling environment. It is one where there is an active civil society. Individuals acting alone will always face formidable obstacles, hence the need for them to act through community groups, associations, NGOs and social movements. A voice-enabling environment encourages diverse groups to organize and make their views known. Such an environment protects the right to free expression, including a free press, and permits the free flow of information by electronic and other means. That is the surest way to create an engaged citizenry, and to nurture a culture where conversations about development, economic policies, and budget choices can flourish.

The voice-enabling environment that I speak of has an analogy in the "investment-friendly" climate referred to in the world of business. Foreign investors in less developed countries seek assurances that the legal and institutional environment will protect their investment. Rich countries and international financial institutions have set minimum standards for this purpose. They regularly put pressure on less developed countries to adhere to these standards, often, indeed, making aid and loans conditional on adherence. And from their perspective, this makes sense. What reasonable investor would proceed where contract and property rights were left to the whim of the regime?

Poor people must not be denied the same guarantees that are given to those who are rich. The right of those living in poverty to participate must be viewed as the basic minimum for a "development-friendly climate". International human rights law provides a ready and universal code that all governments should respect. Dozens of international treaties and declarations guarantee and describe in some detail the rights and freedoms relevant to participation – including what limits can lawfully be placed on these rights. If there is to be a serious effort to tackle poverty, then the legal and institutional environment must guarantee these freedoms. Which rational citizen would speak out against government plans, or indeed even treat a request for her or his views to be taken seriously, without such guarantees being in place?

BREAD BEFORE BALLOTS?

"Human rights are a luxury poor countries cannot afford." Those were the words of a Malaysian business magnate to me at the World Economic Forum in Davos during a discussion we had about the investments his company was contemplating in Sudan. He echoed the sentiments of many other political and business leaders from the developing world, who see human rights as a western export of little relevance and considerable hindrance to their national development. I have also heard similar views from western business leaders.

As Secretary General of Amnesty International, when I have complained about the arrest of trade union leaders, attacks on peaceful demonstrators or the suppression of popular protest or criticism, I have often been told that governments are acting in the interest of greater economic efficiency and progress, or to push through unpopular economic reforms that are required for longer-term economic development; that they must be able to impose painful but necessary discipline on the economy without fear of popular backlash. Such governments see freedom as destabilizing, and therefore an obstacle to economic growth. Suppression of dissent is often seen as the way to maintain stability, especially in countries that are split along ethnic, religious or linguistic lines, although in practice it ends up having the opposite effect, driving the opposition underground and sometimes into a violent response.

Unfortunately, the view that it is sometimes necessary to curtail liberty in order to promote prosperity is not confined to the developing world. Recently I had occasion to call on the foreign minister of a leading European Union member state, who is known to be a strong humanitarian and human rights advocate. I raised with him Amnesty International's concerns about the restriction of free speech and attacks on trade unionists in Tunisia. His response: Tunisia is making good economic progress, and some human rights restrictions are inevitable when a country is opening up its economy. How readily western governments turn a blind eye to the human rights abuses of market-friendly allies!

This argument, sometimes called "bread before ballots", is not new. It was advanced forcefully by many newly independent countries in Africa and Asia in the 1960s and 1970s, as they resisted pressure to democratize. Invoked by both socialist and free market ideologues, the case for postponing democracy and restricting freedoms was largely discredited in the 1980s as authoritarian regimes – most notably, but not only, in the Soviet bloc – proved unable to meet the aspirations of their citizens. Today, there is unprecedented support for democratic reform, and the overwhelming majority of countries have formally committed themselves to upholding basic political and civil rights. UN resolutions and diplomatic communiqués routinely cite the importance of democracy and human rights in development efforts. But, as my encounter with the western European foreign minister showed, much of this enthusiasm is just skin deep.

There persists a powerful current of opinion that is quite tolerant of repressive approaches. It takes strength from the incredible economic growth in China, and the belief that impressive reductions in poverty levels were achieved in that country despite – or possibly because of – the severe restrictions on civil and political rights. It is driven, too, by the experiences of South Korea, Taiwan, Thailand, Malaysia and Singapore – all countries which either postponed or curtailed freedom and managed to achieve impressive economic growth and improved

living standards. Vietnam is another such example, where it is reported that the proportion of those living in poverty has declined from 58 per cent to 16 per cent since 1993, even as repression and the imprisonment of pro-democracy and human rights activists continue. Then there is the experience of Russia, which, in the more open and democratic period immediately following the collapse of the Soviet Union, witnessed a decline in health, literacy and other indicators of well-being (as well as an upsurge in conflict). This decline, it is argued, was reversed under President Putin's increasingly authoritarian leadership.

I do not believe that authoritarian regimes are any better at tackling poverty than governments that commit themselves to respecting human rights. The case of China has been overblown. True, China's economic success over the last few decades has been impressive. True, tens of millions of Chinese have seen real improvements in their standard of living. And equally true that throughout this period the rights to free expression, assembly, information and organization have been severely restricted. Indeed, Chinese policy-makers often argue that China has made this progress *because* of its restrictions on basic freedoms. However, on closer inspection this argument looks very shaky.

First, the rise in economic growth, and the decrease in the number of those living in poverty in China has been accompanied by growing disparities that impact on hundreds of millions of people. Progress has been very uneven. The 2005 UN Human Development Report shows Shanghai province as having achieved a HDI score comparable to Portugal, but Guizhou province ranks only slightly above Namibia.[3] The income disparity between the top 10 per cent and bottom 10 per cent of Chinese society is 30:1.[4] Rural Chinese citizens benefit from only a fraction of the income and spending on health and education that their urban counterparts enjoy, and company ownership is heavily concentrated in the hands of a few. Growing gender inequalities have also accompanied China's development.[5] In April 2007, the state-run *China Daily* reported that the number of illiterate Chinese adults was increasing: between 2000 and 2005 the number grew by 30 million.[6] China does not provide free education to poor children and spends less than 1 per cent of its GDP on health-care, putting it in 156th place out of 196 UN

This man and his wife lost their home when their neighbourhood was demolished to make way for property development. Shanghai, China, 2005. © Boris Svartzman/Drik/Majority World

member states, according to the World Health Organization (WHO). A recent report by the UN Development Programme (UNDP) and the China Institute for Reform and Development has called on China to invest heavily in its social welfare system so that health, education, retirement and employment benefits are available to all its citizens.

Many Chinese would – if they were permitted to – hotly contest the idea that economic growth has improved their quality of life.[7] Take the case of Cha Guoqun, who left his village to do odd jobs in the city of Hangzhou in eastern China. When a cut on his leg became infected in November 2006, preventing him from working, he visited a state hospital. As Cha had no health insurance, the doctor gave him two options: either pay 1,000 yuan (US$146) a day for treatment, the equivalent of his entire monthly income, or have his leg amputated. Luckily for Cha, a Christian charity hospital stepped in and subsidized his treatment.[8]

The vast majority of the nearly 200 million urban migrants who have moved from rural areas to China's cities in search of work and better lives are not as lucky as Cha. Internal migrants are subject to discrimination, with little or no right to health-care, education or fair and non-exploitative employment. Migrant labour has helped to fuel China's economy and transformed the country's cities into modern, gleaming, metropolises. But the workers are refused permanent residency in urban areas. As the global economic downturn takes its hold in China, and the demand for Chinese exports falls, millions of migrant workers are losing their jobs and must return to the countryside.

Internal migrants in China have insecure legal status (due to the household registration system of *hukou*, which is set at birth and defines access to services). They suffer from social isolation and a sense of cultural inferiority. Their relative lack of knowledge of their rights leaves them particularly vulnerable. Their children are either left at home in the countryside, or find themselves facing exclusion in the cities.

In August 2006 local authorities initiated a sweep of schools for the children of internal migrants in Haidian district, Beijing, on the grounds that they were not licensed, operated dangerously, and violated health and safety regulations. Many schools were forcibly shut down, against the resistance of parents, students, teachers and school administrators. In Haidian district, only one school was allowed to remain open, serving around 2,000 children. This left almost 5,000 others without access to education. The local authorities said the children would eventually be reassigned to state schools. Many parents were unhappy with this option, partly because the fees were beyond their means, and partly because the atmosphere in state schools is hostile to migrant children. In the end some children were forced to return to their home towns.[9]

Secondly, whatever gains may be attributable to China's model of authoritarian development, autocratic rule in China has a long history of disastrous outcomes. Rulers in Maoist China precipitated widespread famine, which resulted in an estimated 20-40 million deaths. Policy mistakes combined with a lack of transparency also allowed HIV/AIDS to spread rapidly in China. In 2006, a joint report released by the Chinese Ministry of Health, UNAIDS and the WHO estimated that 70,000 new HIV infections occurred in 2005, and that 650,000 people were living with HIV. And mistakes have, without doubt, contributed to China's very poor environmental record: by some estimates air and water pollution lead to 750,000 deaths per year.[10]

Because the government punishes harshly those who criticize its policies and practices, official corruption and corporate malpractices are often not reported or not acted upon until considerable harm has been done and the scandal can no longer be suppressed. The government then responds with high-profile executions of officials found wanting – but such action has done little or nothing to stop or change corporate or official behaviour in China.

Thirdly, how might restricting freedoms promote economic growth in China? There is the abstract claim that China's authoritarian system has promoted stability and prevented a descent into chaos. This is hard to test. Perhaps a more plausible argument is that it allows the Chinese state to keep labour costs low and productivity high by preventing unionization and strikes. Today, however, China's labour costs are not the lowest in the world, and have not been for several years. Factors such as infrastructure, entrepreneurship and other variables that are independent of the type of government are more likely to explain China's economic success than any repression of rights. There is little evidence to suggest these could not have been pursued in a rights-respecting environment.

Finally, China's model of high growth alongside political repression is likely to be tested sorely by the global economic downturn if social discontent increases. Millions of workers have been laid off and sent back to their villages, with no social safety net. The government has announced spending on health and education as part of its economic bail-out package but there is a great deal of scepticism as to how seriously that will be prioritized or pursued by the provincial authorities. As three decades of the growth boom comes to an end, will the Chinese system – which allows little space for debate or dissent – be able to adjust itself in a way that is as responsive to the poor as to those with power? What effect the economic downturn will have on poverty reduction in China, and whether it will fare any better than countries with more open political systems, is a big question mark.

Furthermore, for every China, Vietnam, Taiwan or South Korea that appears to have demonstrated economic success without opening up political space, there are many contrary examples of authoritarian regimes past and present that have made terrible choices and impoverished their people – from Mobutu's Zaire, and Argentina and Brazil under military regimes in the 1970s, to North Korea and Myanmar today.

One high-profile example is Zimbabwe, where millions of people have been impoverished by years of political oppression and economic mismanagement. For almost a decade the government brutally silenced all critics of its policies. Thousands of people were arbitrarily arrested and unlawfully detained for peaceful protest, and tortured while in police custody, with total impunity. Many people are still missing following the wave of state-sponsored violence in the run-up to the elections in June 2008. By the end of 2008, years of retrogressive economic policies and practices, including the use of food as a political weapon, left 5 million people dependent on food aid and Zimbabwe's health system on the verge of total collapse. An outbreak of cholera in 2008 affected nine out of Zimbabwe's 10 provinces, causing hundreds of preventable deaths. Major hospitals failed to provide medical care to those in need. The system was paralyzed by shortages of drugs and medical supplies, a dilapidated infrastructure, equipment failures and a brain drain as health workers fled the country to seek refuge from political persecution and economic deprivation. In January 2009, most public schools could not open as teachers were on strike over poor salaries or could not afford transport to work. Hundreds of thousands of people who were forcibly evicted by the authorities in 2005 continue to live in destitution.

When dictators get things wrong, there are few channels for feedback, and so, often, there is very little that can be done to stop the situation from escalating into a full-blown economic and social crisis. In more open, democratic, rights-respecting systems, transparency and accountability are a powerful check on bad policies getting worse. Amartya Sen has famously examined the evidence on famines and other crises, concluding that the freedoms and transparency associated with democracies make them better placed to avert situations in which policy mishaps escalate into full-blown crises.[11] Popular backlash can be a good thing!

There are plenty of empirical reasons to doubt arguments based around the wisdom of the unaccountable. Experts agree that there is simply no large-scale data to support the view that authoritarian models result in better economic growth, let alone that they achieve more impressive poverty-reduction figures.[12]

Those who cite China, South Korea and Taiwan need to explain economic successes in democratic countries where, on balance, basic freedoms are respected, like Costa Rica and Botswana. Or, indeed, India. Its growth rates have rivalled those of China for the past few years. Though its human rights record is far from perfect, there is a free press and a vibrant and active civil society. And the same World Bank sources that point to declining poverty in China indicate that, since the early 1990s, India too has dramatically reduced the proportion of the population living in poverty, from 36 per cent to 26 per cent.

TRANSPARENCY AND ACCOUNTABILITY

If there are few grounds for believing that authoritarian governments are better able to tackle the problems of underdevelopment and poverty, what about the contrary? Can we prove that freedom helps to end poverty? That anchoring participation in a rights-enabling environment improves people's prospects?

Surprisingly, there have been few comprehensive studies that have looked at this question. Countries that belong to the Organisation for Economic Co-operation and Development (OECD), the club of the world's richest nations, have better socio-economic outcomes and most also tend to give greater protection to basic freedoms. It would be hard, however, based on their histories, to conclude which came first.

If we look only at poor countries, the evidence to date does show some correlation between respect for basic freedoms and higher scores on the UN's HDI. One study established a close link between respect for freedom of expression and civil liberties and better outcomes for measures of child mortality and per capita income.[13] We also know that corruption impairs socio-economic development, and that it seems to be more prevalent in places where respect for political and civil liberties is low. Studies on corruption and the delivery of basic services show that people with more information, more knowledge about "the system" and about their rights, are better able to represent their own interests effectively and obtain the services to which they are entitled.[14] If promoting civil and political rights checks corruption, which in turn improves development prospects (relative to those of a more corrupt system), then it is clear that human rights do in fact promote better human development.

Freedom of expression and the right to organize are essential ingredients in creating a society where the citizenry is actively engaged in debates on development. But to participate fully in government, to influence policy and to shape decision-making requires access to the information on which decisions and policies are based. People who are rich and powerful know how to play this game through their networks and resources. Those living in poverty are clearly at a disadvantage.

Democratizing access to information is essential if poor people are to play a part in the decisions that affect their lives. Take an experience from India. In the early 1990s, Indian workers saw corruption among public officials as a direct cause of their poverty. They demanded transparency as a means to improving their lives and changed the law in the process. It began in Rajasthan, when some state workers found that they were being underpaid. Their managers claimed that, according to the record books, they were not working as many hours as they believed they were. But could the workers see the record books where their hours were logged? No. They were officially a "state secret" under a pre-independence colonial law that was still in effect. Managers all over India were abusing this law to make a profit for themselves. They were receiving money from the state for the real hours worked, but were only paying the workers for the falsified, lower number of hours, and pocketing billions of their employees' rupees.

The Mazdoor Kisan Shakti Sangathan (Union for the Empowerment of Peasants and Labourers, MKSS), which had been advocating for the payment of minimum wages to labourers in Rajasthan, began a state-wide campaign to open up the record books to the public. According to one MKSS leader, "What has been significantly different about this campaign is that poor people made a connection between deprivation, endemic poverty, exploitation, denial of participation in institutions of governance, and secrecy, opaqueness, and unaccountable governance. Their slogan says it all: 'The right to know, the right to live'."[15]

The MKSS used public hearings, mass mobilization and creative street theatre to keep the issue alive, and eventually forced through new legislation in Rajasthan, which made all local authority records public and ensured stronger accountability for government officials. The Rajasthan campaign for transparency led the way for the subsequent National Campaign for the People's Right to Information. In May 2005, the Indian Parliament passed the Right to Information Act. Under this landmark legislation, government officials can be fined or have disciplinary action taken against them if they refuse or delay a request for information, provide false information or destroy information.

I was in India just six months after that law was passed. One MKSS leader gave me a practical example of how the law was empowering the poor to demand change. She said that in one village in Rajasthan, people had begun to demand information from the local officials about how much food aid was being provided by the state authorities to that village, and then took it upon themselves to check that figure against the actual distribution of food. When they discovered discrepancies, they complained to higher district level administrators and insisted on investigations. Eventually, the villagers found that there were fewer and fewer discrepancies between the allocation and the distribution of food. Pilferage and corruption had tapered off because of transparency and accountability brought about by stronger citizen engagement.

Information is a powerful vector for change. A 1996 study in Uganda revealed that up to 80 per cent of grant funds intended for schools were not reaching their final destination. In order to improve

the situation, the Ugandan central government began to publish data in national newspapers and their local language editions regarding the size of the monthly grants that communities were supposed to be receiving. When a second public expenditure tracking survey was conducted in 2002, it found that the proportion of funds that were intercepted had been reduced to 20 per cent. Information had enabled parents to monitor local officials. There was a significant relationship between the distance to the nearest newspaper outlet and the reduction in the diversion of funds.[16]

The voices of people living in poverty are made more effective by information but they will remain no more than "protest" unless and until people with power engage and respond. "Voice" is not simply about the right and opportunity to speak out. For poor people's participation to work, not only must information be available, but the state must be accountable to the voices that are raised.

Just as "voice" is more than protest, "accountability" means more than democratic elections. In many fledgling democracies, the elected leaders are not representative of the people, or may have grabbed votes by playing upon ethnic divisions and nationalistic fears. Without the checks and balances of a more thorough system of accountability, based on transparency, citizen engagement and the rule of law, democratic rule can rapidly degenerate into misrule based on corruption and abuse of power. My own country, Bangladesh, has been a classic case of successive, democratically elected governments promoting "kleptocracy" – a system that runs on greed and corruption.

How power is exercised is at least as important as how it is won. Democratic elections alone are insufficient to protect against this outcome. Indeed, those studying the issue report that electoral democracy on its own may even make things worse.[17]

The dangers of ignoring this side of the problem have been well-documented in relation to poor countries enriched by oil booms. For many years now, economists have spoken of the "resource curse" – where countries with an abundance of natural resources, such as minerals or oil, exhibit less economic growth and development and suffer from more corruption, violence and conflict, than those with fewer natural resources. They have noted how many oil-rich countries

Previous pages: Rai women, one of the many ethnic minority groups in Nepal, celebrate their new year. Kathmandu, Nepal, May 2008. © G.M.B. Akash/Panos

were poorly governed and tended to squander their wealth – many even became poorer. Similarly, a major lesson drawn from the collapse of authoritarian communist states was that secret and unresponsive bureaucracies were ill-equipped to meet the challenges of late 20th-century development. A consensus emerged in the early 1990s, based among other things on World Bank assessments of failed development efforts in Africa, that good governance mattered. Corruption, weak institutions, sclerotic courts, arbitrary rule and the politics of patronage were all undermining development – which is hardly surprising.

Demands for accountable and transparent government have been around for some time. Some would argue that international efforts to promote "good governance" and the rule of law, and which challenge corruption, take up this agenda. The truth is that, despite many years of attention to the problem of corruption in government and its negative consequences for development, we do not appear to be making much headway in reducing it. A major evaluation of the World Bank's funding for public sector reform, including anti-corruption efforts, carried out by the Bank's own auditors, concluded that there had been little progress to show for Bank lending in this area.

The voice of people living in poverty – their participation, access to information and the obligation of the state to engage and respond to them – needs to be recognized more explicitly as a key issue of good governance. In other words, accountability for human rights needs to be put in the mainstream of the development agenda.

Neither the eight UN MDGs – the main international strategy for eradicating poverty – nor their associated 20 targets, make any demand on governments to respect and protect those basic freedoms that are essential if participation is to be meaningful. The resources and high-level attention given to the MDG process include no serious examination of restrictions on freedom and participation in so many less developed countries. The monitoring of those issues is left to the under-funded, over-stretched and politically weak UN human rights systems, unconnected to the MDG process. This glaring gap in the MDGs needs urgent repair.

The billions of dollars that are being poured into the MDGs and foreign aid may produce better results if more attention is paid to protection of the participation rights of the poor. In a 1997 study that looked at more than 600 World Bank-financed projects, the authors consistently found a positive association between the protection of civil liberties and the economic rate of return in World Bank projects.[18] The authors also found a positive correlation between citizen protests (demonstrations) and the economic rate of return for projects. This last finding is particularly significant in suggesting that increased voice leads to improved outcomes. As the authors write: "The results support a chain of causation that runs from greater civil liberties to higher levels of citizen involvement and political participation – including as one dimension civil manifestations – to better projects."

Turning from poor to rich countries, the experience of Indigenous Peoples in Canada, Australia, New Zealand and the United States points to how effective participation can help in tackling poverty. All these groups score worse than the general population for levels of health, education and well-being. Indigenous Peoples in the USA, for example, are four times more likely to live in poverty than members of the average population, while their college enrolment is at half the national level. In these wealthy countries, with highly developed health systems, Indigenous Peoples suffer from a higher prevalence of nearly every major disease.

Indigenous Peoples have been engaged for decades – in some cases centuries – in struggles and collaborative processes with their respective states to achieve greater control over the implementation of social services for their communities. In recent decades, the degree of self-governance by the Indigenous Peoples of Canada and the USA has increased with respect to a number of services, and evidence suggests that this correlates with a measurable improvement in a range of social indicators. A recent landmark study by the Harvard Project on American Indian Economic Development concluded that, when Indigenous Peoples make their own decisions, they consistently outperform external decision-makers in areas such as natural resource management, economic development, health-care and social service provision.[19]

Canadian policy has been moving steadily over decades to transfer responsibility for health-care management to Indigenous Peoples. According to a government evaluation of the long-term impacts of this transfer policy, "First Nations and Inuit organizations have thrived as a result; service responsiveness has improved; mandatory programs are being delivered; and the accountability of Chief and Council in health matters has improved from pre-transfer times."[20]

Self-government and transferring control over social services to local communities will not always be appropriate; Indigenous Peoples, especially those living on traditional lands, have special claims in this respect. Nevertheless, the essential point remains that giving the people who are affected a real say and genuine control over development options and outcomes is essential. In my view, respect for rights and basic freedoms is the surest means to do so.

Empower those who need reform most, and let them claim it from those who rule in their name, rather than leaving it to the whims of those in power, pushed and prodded from time to time by donors. "Voice" of the citizenry combined with effective and fair "response" from those in power is one of the key links in the chain of deprivation, exclusion and insecurity that defines poverty. When information flows freely and state structures work to consult and involve affected communities, freedom becomes the means for releasing people from the yoke of poverty.

Voice is more than a licence to protest, but states also have to allow for protest and dissent if the reform is to reap true rewards. In other words, the supply of good government is intricately linked to the demand for it, freely expressed by the people. The market mechanism that links the two is the people's right to information and free expression.

Freedom is a value in and of itself, but it is also a means to eroding deprivation when poor people have the space to define and implement solutions to poverty. And it goes in the other direction too. When deprived of education or basic health-care, weakened by chronic hunger, denied legal identity, or lacking a fixed address, people are trapped in poverty and meaningful engagement will be difficult. Knowing that means putting the human rights of poor people at the centre of the effort to end poverty. It means recognizing poverty as a human rights problem.

THREE
FREEDOM FROM DISCRIMINATION – ENDING EXCLUSION

I come from a community of scavengers. Until I was eight years old I had never met anyone outside my own community. Everyone I knew was poor. We lived in a slum on the edge of the city. None of us kids went to school. No one from outside our neighbourhood ever visited us. When I was about eight years old, one day my father took me to the local fair. It was my first visit outside my neighbourhood. I was very excited. I wanted to go into the café, sit on the plastic chairs and eat like other people but my father bought me some food from a stall and said, "No, we have to sit out on the pavement and eat." We ate our food on a piece of newspaper. I remember crying because I could see other children eat from plates and I wanted to do the same. My father told me that the stall owner could not give us food on a plate because no one would ever touch the plate from which we ate. That is when I first realized what it means to be a Dalit, an untouchable. I was determined to change my life. I worked hard to get an education. I went to a free school run by a Catholic priest. I am the first person from my community to have a high-school diploma but still I cannot get a good job. When employers hear I am a Dalit, they say no one will want to sit next to a Dalit. The only job I could find was as a garbage collector for the municipality.

Bissanya, a Dalit woman, survived the horror of rape by an upper caste man just months after her child was born. Bandha, Uttar Pradesh, India 2007.
© Sudharak Olwe/Drik India/Majority World

I HEARD THIS STORY FROM Ranjit, a union leader of Dhaka's garbage collectors. Amnesty International together with a Bangladeshi NGO, Manusher Jonno, had invited activists to a seminar on Human Rights and Human Dignity. Ranjit was one of many who took the floor to speak. Bangladesh is a predominantly Muslim country with about 8 per cent Hindus and smaller numbers of Christians and Buddhists. It is composed mainly of ethnic Bengalis with a small minority of tribal peoples. Although not without problems, the country is making progress on fighting poverty. It was all the more striking, therefore, that each speaker told a similar story – of how their caste, gender, social status, religion or ethnicity kept them excluded from the mainstream.

When asked to diagnose the causes of poverty, the economist is likely to look first at the obstacles to growth. Is the banking system sound? Are the tools to implement trade policy in place? Is taxation fair and are public revenues properly directed and administered? These and others are the vital signs that economists take as an indication of overall economic health.

When asked the same question, the human rights advocate is likely to look first at the presence and treatment of diverse groups. Such groups might be defined on ethnic, religious, linguistic or other grounds, including caste, or mental or physical ability. The situation of women and girls will always be relevant. The human rights advocate wants to know how such groups perform according to such indicators as literacy, life expectancy, maternal mortality, and access to education, employment and justice. The other vital signs are the degree to which all groups in the society can participate in government, and whether they are free to practise their faith, use their language or organize themselves. Put another way, the first question the human rights advocate will ask in relation to poverty is: "Who is being left behind?" Experiences such as the seminar in Dhaka are not uncommon; those left behind are often members of marginalized groups.

It is logical to assess human rights by measuring discrimination because those rights are based on the idea that our common humanity transcends borders, class, belief, and ideology. International human rights standards promote tolerance for and protection of diversity, but decree that distinctions along these lines must not affect the enjoyment of core human rights. Indeed, all the major international human rights treaties prominently prohibit discrimination. When allowance is made for suspending rights in times of emergency, or for the gradual implementation of rights, it is always conditional on guaranteeing non-discrimination. Measuring equality is no easy task, but the presence and persistence of discrimination, in law or practice, is a sign that commitments to equality remain unfulfilled. When migrants, women, or members of certain ethnic, racial or religious groups are over-represented among the poor, and when they have disproportionately low scores on basic measures of human wellbeing, it is almost certain they are being denied equality of access to rights and opportunities.

The sad reality is that such groups are too often over-represented among poor people, including in the most developed countries. The persistence of poverty has many causes. No doubt failures of economic policy rank high on the list, but so does discrimination. Diagnosing poverty by looking at human rights shows this in sharp relief, and is as valid as measuring it by using economic factors. Moreover, when discrimination works to exclude certain groups from the benefits of development and economic progress, it must be tackled head on. Economic growth alone is unlikely to help.

This chapter looks at the links between discrimination and poverty, to show how the former is both a cause and consequence of the latter. Recognizing this fact is important because, until the problem of discrimination is acknowledged, little can be done to remedy poverty. Global anti-poverty policy – as reflected in the MDGs – has largely failed to take this fundamental first step. In addition, the problem of discrimination *within* countries is compounded by inequality *between* countries, where wealth too often determines people's access to even the most basic rights. What looks increasingly like a two-track world is not only morally wrong but also politically unwise. It creates fertile ground for global insecurity and conflict, as the next chapter will show. Overcoming discrimination is not easy but I am convinced that a human rights approach can help policy-makers better understand the challenge and so enable them to develop more effective responses.

DISCRIMINATION AND DENIAL

In the last chapter I described the exclusion experienced by poor communities, their sense of not being heard, of being shut out by institutions that enact and administer state policy – by courts, land and birth registration offices, systems of protection such as the police, schools and health centres, and certainly by distant legislatures. Exclusion is often underpinned by discrimination or unequal treatment. In the overwhelming majority of cases, women and religious or ethnic minorities are worse off than men and majority communities.

Take an emerging economy like India, which has seen impressive growth in recent years. As of 2005, 42 per cent of females over the age of six, compared with 22 per cent of males, had never attended school. There are huge differences in illiteracy rates across regions, ranging from 5 per cent for men in Kerala to 60 per cent for women in Bihar.

The traditional caste system in India attributes status, power, and therefore economic security, according to an accident of birth, from which there is no escape until death. This dictates the lived experience of a huge slice of the population and traps them in poverty from which they cannot easily escape. People who belong to groups known, according to the Indian Constitution, as Scheduled Castes (some of whom are Dalits) and Scheduled Tribes (some of whom are Adivasis), who together make up almost a quarter of the country's population, display much higher levels of deprivation than other members of the population. For example, even though infant mortality rates are declining among these groups, in 2005 they were still 30 per cent higher than the national average. Members of Scheduled Castes and Scheduled Tribes also have markedly higher levels of malnutrition than the general population; this, according to some indicators, has actually got worse in recent years.

I began this chapter with Ranjit, a Dalit from Bangladesh. Discrimination against Dalits is severe throughout South Asia. For thousands of years they have been so marginalized that they are excluded even from the region's discriminatory caste system. Treated as untouchables, Dalits lie outside the segregated hierarchy of the four main caste categories of Brahmins, Kshatriyas, Vaishyas and Shudras. In India, the practice of untouchability was formally outlawed by the Constitution in 1950, and numerous affirmative action laws and policies have been introduced by the government to ensure that Dalits can, for example, attend university or get jobs in the public service. Yet these policies have done little to challenge entrenched social attitudes of members of the dominant castes, and so have made few inroads into ending inequality and injustice.

Despite making up 16 per cent of the total population of India, – over 160 million people – Dalit communities are still subjected to extreme forms of social and economic exclusion and discrimination. Their lack of access to education is reflected in the statistic that literacy rates for Dalits hover below 40 per cent.[1]

Like India, Brazil is also an emerging economy. And here too, poverty, whether measured in terms of income or levels of access to basic necessities such as health-care, education, food or shelter, has disproportionately affected racial minorities and women. Afro-Brazilians are highly over-represented among the ranks of the poor in Brazil, and experience far worse outcomes than their white counterparts across a variety of social and economic indicators. As of 1999, they made up only 45 per cent of the total population but comprised 69 per cent of people living in extreme poverty. They have considerably less access to adequate housing and they have higher numbers of children in the labour force. White Brazilians consistently earn higher wages than Afro-Brazilians, and are more likely to advance to managerial/directorial positions. When race intersects with gender, the disparities are even more pronounced. Female income and education levels lag behind males by a significant margin. Women of African descent have some of the lowest paying jobs with the poorest working conditions of any members of society.[2]

The very fact of being poor – even where those affected belong to majority communities – may also lead to discrimination and therefore reinforce exclusion, further entrenching poverty. People living in poverty are often denied equal access to services – sometimes because of lack of money or social status, sometimes because of lack of information, but more often because those with power lack the political will to address their exclusion. This can operate so perniciously as to keep families poor over many generations.

That is why it is important not only to understand the progress of particular groups, but also to measure the progress of the poorest sectors of the population. One way to do this is to divide a country's population into fifths or "quintiles", based on their share of national income. Tracking the progress of the bottom quintile is a means of assessing whether improvements and wealth are being enjoyed equally. Where such data is available, the results often show that the poorest among poor people progress little.

In Nepal, for example, despite moderate economic growth, the data show the poorest quintile in the country actually had a smaller share of national income at its disposal in 2006 than in 1996. In Uganda significant progress has been made in reducing the number of new cases of HIV/AIDS overall. But this trend has not been mirrored among the poorest parts of the population. In Bangladesh and Peru in the 1990s, children living in poverty saw less improvement in access to education than the general population (in the case of Peru, there was an actual decline). Aggregate national figures in these cases belie variations within countries. In Zimbabwe, between 1988 and 1999, "a decline in average under-5 mortality masked a rise in the number of deaths of children in the poorest fifth of the population".[3]

The statistics tell a powerful story. But statistics do not tell us why discrimination is wrong, nor what can be done about it. The human rights perspective brings added value here. It insists on equality in access to basic rights; every human life ought to be lived in the dignity provided by basic education, health-care, shelter and adequate food. The persistence of discrimination is not simply a regrettable feature of economic life; it is morally repugnant, and a violation of rights and international treaties. At a practical level, it undermines the efforts to eradicate poverty.

As noted earlier, traditional measures of poverty make reference to income levels. Progress is often reported as an increase in a country's average income level. But even where economic growth does raise aggregate levels of income, so that per capita income levels rise, the evidence is mixed regarding the degree to which the income levels of the poorest also rise. Income inequality within many, if not most, countries is rising. And even where economic growth does result in increased income for poor people and improved spending to fulfil basic rights, too often groups which are already marginalized are overlooked and left behind. In many countries, rising GDP and income levels exist alongside stagnant or worsening indicators of health, education, and wellbeing for such groups, which may include ethnic, racial, religious or linguistic minorities, migrants or women.

This is not an argument against the value of economic growth as part of a solution to poverty. In many countries impressive growth rates have raised the incomes of millions of people and, as a result, many are able to gain greater access to what they need to live in dignity. But if the current economic crisis teaches us anything, it is the fragility of a policy based on growth alone. For when growth falters, those millions who have advanced may fall back very quickly, and the most vulnerable are hit hardest. The World Bank estimates that upwards of 50 million people have fallen back into poverty in 2009 as a result of the global recession; this is on top of the 100 million who did so in the previous year due to rising food prices. Relying on growth alone generally means the poorest are the last to benefit in the boom and the first to suffer in the bust. The human rights perspective alerts us to the reality that deprivation may arise from discrimination, whether in law or practice, or disadvantage due to past discrimination and exclusion. And where this is so, general increases in income levels, when and where they do occur, are unlikely to be a complete solution. Discrimination itself must be confronted.

But how? The human rights diagnosis brings into sharp focus the problem of discrimination and exclusion. But what does it offer in terms of remedial action? Much depends on the context. At the risk of over-simplifying, there are three scenarios in which discrimination drives and deepens poverty.

In the first scenario, discrimination is open and finds formal expression in law, policy and practice. Such overt, systematic, deliberate and discriminatory impoverishment can be seen in a number of countries today when it comes to the status of women. There are still laws in many countries that restrict women's right to

own property or land. Despite producing 60-80 per cent of the food in developing countries, women own only 1 per cent of the land.[4] In many countries laws also restrict women from enjoying equal status with men in terms of work and family or personal life. Examples can also be found in several countries where particular ethnic or religious groups are deliberately disenfranchised, denied equal protection of the law and face restrictions on their movement and work. The Rohingya, a Muslim minority in Myanmar, are a prime example: they are treated as "foreigners", even though they have lived there for generations. In many countries, immigrants, refugees and asylum-seekers are explicitly denied rights to work, to go to school or to access health-care.

Though most shocking in terms of intent, this discrimination may, paradoxically, be easier to confront for the very reason that it is plain to see. An immediate remedial action is also apparent: changes in law and policy to bring the government into line with its international human rights commitments. Indeed, international treaties like the Convention on the Elimination of Discrimination against Women (CEDAW) seek precisely to ensure formal equality of women. Other human rights treaties guarantee equal rights for minorities, or set limits on when it is permissible to deny rights to non-citizens. Similarly, treaties dealing with refugees set out the circumstances under which they are entitled to basic services and access to health and education. Experience shows, however, that laws, while important, are only a first step in eradicating discrimination that is rooted in politics and culture.

A second scenario, perhaps more common, is where there is official denial that discrimination or racism persist. In this situation, formal, constitutional guarantees of equality are often in place, and overt discrimination in law may be hard to find. But the government's failure to implement these laws effectively or to counter social and other forms of discrimination means that systematic discrimination continues in practice. Statistics show disproportionately low HDI scores among Indigenous Peoples in Latin American countries or Roma in Europe, as compared with members of the dominant (and richer) communities, though in both cases there is formal legal equality.

Previous pages: **Children from the slum of Paraisópolis eat oranges from the garbage of the upper-class neighbourhood surrounding the slum. São Paulo, Brazil.**
© Carlos Cazalis/Drik/Majority World

In a third scenario, there may be an acknowledgement of the discrimination or disadvantage suffered by marginalized people. Often this is expressed in terms of a historical injustice that needs to be corrected. Formal constitutional guarantees might be complemented by government bodies tasked to advance equality. There may also be in place special economic or social programmes to assist disadvantaged groups. These may include affirmative action or "positive discrimination" measures or may even take the form of quotas for representation in elected bodies, the civil service, institutions of higher learning or company boards.

But in this third scenario problems arise when, despite special measures, marginalized groups continue to progress slowly if at all. The mainstream community may resent the special measures and blame the marginalized groups for their own condition of poverty or exclusion. In practice, we end up with the same denial of the problem encountered in scenario two. It just takes longer to emerge and may even be harder to counter. I discussed above the situation of the Dalits: laws guarantee their equality and affirmative action policies are in place, yet it is all too common for their higher caste fellow citizens to blame them for their continuing poverty.

Such denial is hard to address because, by its very nature, it does not acknowledge the problem.[5] In the second scenario, the government denies the problem, pointing to formal guarantees of equality; in the third, though, even where there is government acknowledgement and remedial action, denial is pervasive among those who are not themselves experiencing discrimination. The value of the human rights framework is first and foremost to force an acknowledgement of the problem by the state and society – formally through change of law but also socially through acceptance of universal values. Without this, there can be no solution. Acknowledging that some groups are being left behind highlights the *current* impact of *historical* experiences of racism. Experience repeatedly shows that past systemic and institutional discrimination is not easily or rapidly overcome, even where the law is invoked to end it.

The multiple levels at which exclusion operates – systematic and deliberate discrimination, formal equality coupled with continued discrimination in practice, or continued exclusion even where efforts are made to redress past discrimination – means there is no uniform or simple response. Combinations of these various forms of exclusion may co-exist in the same country, such that different marginalized groups may experience different forms of discrimination. As noted above, the most straightforward action is to ensure that laws guaranteeing equality and non-discrimination are in place and implemented. This is, in any case, what governments have agreed to do through their adherence to international human rights standards. But often, additional and specific measures are required, which are targeted to improve the political representation of marginalized groups, their ability to access and benefit from public services that contribute to meeting basic needs, or to dedicate specific funds to their advancement. Again, many such policies are elaborated in various human rights standards or in the views expressed by UN and regional bodies that oversee their implementation. The human rights framework also requires that we stress the "voice", or empowerment, of those living in poverty (of which I spoke in the previous chapter). This is a critical ingredient in fighting exclusion.

Political will is also key to countering entrenched attitudes and prejudice. As long as discrimination is denied, no government programme is likely to succeed. Exposure and acknowledgement are vital to generating the will to change. Defining the problem as a breach of international legal commitments adds to the pressure to generate this political leadership.

Finally, and beyond law and government policy, lies the moral issue: how to convince a general public that denies racism of the need to address it? The appeal of human rights is not only to governments to act differently but to everyone. In the words of the UDHR, we must all "act towards one another in a spirit of brotherhood". A cliché? Some will say so. But my many years of work in the United Nations and Amnesty International have convinced me that the universal value of human rights is a powerful motivation – one that can inspire and unite people across divides.

Discrimination in law or practice drives and deepens poverty. Whichever example we look at, whether it be the Roma, Dalits, Indigenous Peoples or any other marginalized group, the significant correlation between discrimination and poverty is evident. And yet global anti-poverty policy fails to encourage governments to acknowledge the problem of discrimination, except to some limited extent in the case of women and girls.

THE MILLENNIUM DEVELOPMENT GOALS

We are wallowing in a state of collective denial. The MDGs, the world's pre-eminent anti-poverty plan, fail to throw light on the problems of discrimination and exclusion. The official UN guide to applying the various MDG indicators repeatedly notes that there are likely to be differences in progress towards the goals among different groups in a particular country. It then goes on to note, in relation to many of the MDG indicators, that "showing and analysing data on specific ethnic groups may be a sensitive issue in the country"; the guide does not recommend UN agencies do so.[6] Putting blinkers on or brushing the issue under the carpet is no answer.

The MDGs are the major global response to the scourge of poverty. Although only developing countries have to report on their progress towards them, they were agreed to by all governments at the 2000 UN Millennium Summit. The MDGs comprise eight distinct goals to be achieved by 2015: to eradicate extreme poverty and hunger; achieve universal primary education; promote gender equality and empower women; reduce child mortality; improve maternal health; combat HIV/AIDS, malaria and other diseases; ensure environmental sustainability; and develop a global partnership for development. Each goal has specific targets that set out in more detail the precise objectives. The goal to end extreme poverty translates into target commitments to halve the number of those living on less than $1 a day, to achieve full and productive employment for all and to halve the number of those who suffer from hunger. The goal to empower women translates into a target commitment to eliminate gender disparity at all levels of education. And the goal to improve maternal health entails target commitments to reduce by three-quarters the maternal mortality ratio and achieve universal access to reproductive health.

I will leave aside for now the debate on the overall extent to which the MDGs take full account of human rights, and return to this in later chapters. What I want to point out here is that the MDGs fail to fully acknowledge and account for the role of discrimination in perpetuating poverty. Countries report on their progress to meet the targets using aggregate data – general numbers for the country as a whole. But, as we've seen, in countries where the overall trends in poverty reduction appear positive, these do not always translate into improvements for minority and marginalized groups. The experience of national progress can be highly unequal and uneven in practice, often due to discrimination against particular groups. Statistics on those whose incomes are above $1.25 a day, or enrolments in primary school, or on maternal mortality are not broken down by race, religion, region, caste or other social group. It is entirely possible, therefore, that the position of already marginalized groups may stagnate or worsen, even as the country reports a general decline in the numbers of people living in poverty or progress on education or health.

Only with regard to ensuring that girls are attending school do specific MDG targets demand disaggregated data, in this case on the basis of gender. There is additionally a specific indicator regarding the proportion of seats held by women in national parliaments, as a means of measuring progress towards women's empowerment.

It is not enough to know what proportion of the population suffers from hunger, has access to clean water or dies of malaria. We need to know whether they are male or female, white or black, rural or urban, more prevalent in the north, south, east or west of the country. As the population rises, the use of proportionality masks underlying absolute increases in malnutrition and chronic hunger. For example, the absolute numbers of people suffering from hunger globally have increased steadily since 2000. Crucially, we also need to know who makes up these proportions and numbers. We need to translate figures into people. Only then is exclusion identified, and only then can it be seriously tackled. In the words of the UN Office of the High Commissioner for Human Rights (OHCHR), we need to "include the excluded".[7]

There is no dispute that, across a range of development indicators, women and girls generally fare less well than their male counterparts. Women are over-represented among those living in poverty and under-represented among the literate, healthy and politically active. Young women, for example, experience markedly higher rates of HIV/AIDS infection than young men, but this is in no way apparent from the formulation of the sixth MDG.[8] In Asia, mortality rates for girls under five are markedly higher than for boys, again, information that is not being taken into account in assessing progress on the first MDG's target of reducing infant mortality.

Or consider the situation of Indigenous Peoples. They comprise 5 per cent of the world's population, but 15 per cent of the world's poor; they make up a third of the world's 900 million people living in extreme poverty in rural areas. Malnutrition among women and children of Indigenous Peoples tends to be higher than among the rest of the population, as do rates of infant mortality and vulnerability to disease.[9] According to the UN, "Indigenous peoples face huge disparities in terms of access to and quality of education and health. In Guatemala, for example, 53.5 per cent of Indigenous young people aged 15-19 have not completed primary education, as compared with 32.2 per cent of non-Indigenous youth. In Bolivia, the infant mortality rate among the Indigenous population is close to 75/1000, as compared with 50/1000 for the non-Indigenous population."[10] Yet there is no specific target or indicator to measure the progress of Indigenous Peoples, and no obligation on countries to report on it.[11]

Who is being counted, and who is not, is more than an issue of numbers and data. It is deeply political, and fundamental to the struggle to end poverty. Power in almost all societies is divided along faultlines of gender, race, religion, language or wealth. For ruling elites, to collect and publish data on who is being excluded is an act of acknowledgement that is the first step towards confronting the problem. When disaggregated data is published it can also be a spur to action, as civil society and the groups themselves are able to mobilize on the basis of the information.

There may be practical difficulties in disaggregating data in some developing countries, but these can be overcome through capacity-building and technical assistance. Many countries, including Brazil, South Africa and India, do measure progress across different groups. In doing so they recognize that some groups are disproportionately affected by poverty. More importantly, such information equips them to tackle the underlying problems, as it brings to light continuing exclusion. We can no longer avoid this challenge. Everyone counts, and everyone must be counted individually, their own story told and their own voice heard.

Compounding the problem of who is not being counted, is the problem of which countries "count". The inattention to exclusion means global anti-poverty efforts largely ignore poverty and discrimination in rich countries. Indeed, many argue outright that we should focus our efforts only on the poorest countries.

In his book, *The Bottom Billion*, Paul Collier argues that efforts to alleviate poverty should be focused on the poorest countries, which are not growing and not meeting the basic needs of the vast majority of their citizens. In his view, there are "a total of five billion people who are already prosperous, or at least are on track to be so, and one billion who are stuck at the bottom". At one level, he is right – priority must be given to the poorest people. But this appears to overlook the fact that even in middle-income countries there are significant numbers of people living in similar poverty to those in the "bottom billion".

There are good reasons for ensuring that global efforts to tackle poverty do not ignore those living in middle-income countries. Though smaller as a proportion of the overall population, there are significant numbers of people living in extreme poverty in countries such as Brazil, Peru, Russia, Indonesia, Mexico and China. Using the income measure alone (which, as we've seen, is only part of the story), it is estimated that there are 140 million people living on less than $1 a day and 600 million living on less than $2 a day in middle-income countries alone.[12] In fact, middle-income countries account for almost one third of all those in the world who live on less than $1 a day.[13]

Where data is available, HDI indicators for poor people in middle-income countries are similar to the low scores registered for the "bottom billion". The fact that, in many cases, they are members of otherwise disadvantaged and marginalized groups is, or ought to be, further grounds for paying greater attention and applying remedial measures. Indeed, their lack of progress in relation to the mainstream itself points to the problem.

Middle-income countries are required to report on their progress on the MDGs but the most developed countries have no such obligations. Of course the number of poor people in these countries is much lower than in Africa or south Asia, for example. But although deaths from hunger and malnutrition are rare in rich countries, the poorer and more marginalized communities within them have noticeably higher maternal mortality ratios, and higher rates of illiteracy and disease, and shorter life expectancy. They are at greater risk of violence and their political voice is not heard as loudly. Over the past two decades there has been little improvement in their condition. The levels of inequality, mired in discrimination and deprivation, are shocking, even by the standards of less developed countries.

A distinguished group of researchers recently published the American Human Development Index, modelled on the global UN HDI, but looking at the specific performance of the USA and providing data disaggregated by gender, race/ethnicity and geography (state and congressional district).[14] The report found significant differences in human development in relation to race and ethnicity, with Latinos, Indigenous Peoples and African Americans scoring much worse than Asians or Caucasians. African Americans have a shorter life expectancy today than the US average in the 1970s. There are huge disparities between the estimates of net worth (the value of a person's assets) for Caucasians and others: in 2004 the median net worth for Caucasians was $140,800 compared with $24,900 for other racial/ethnic groups. African Americans and Latinos in full-time work earn 80 per cent and 70 per cent, respectively, of what Caucasians earn. The authors attribute this to "differing educational levels and work experiences, discrimination, residential segregation, and higher rates of incarceration".

The report noted significant geographic differences, even among congressional districts within the same state. They give an example in New York, where districts are just over two miles apart but have vastly unequal outcomes in terms of earnings, unemployment rates and education. The district that consistently ranked lower was almost entirely populated by marginalized groups (65 per cent Latino and 28 per cent African American) while the one that ranked higher (and was the highest-ranking congressional district in the country) was predominantly Caucasian (66.4 per cent).

The United States of America is not unique among developed countries in harbouring such disparity. Between 10 and 12 million Roma people live in Europe, and are the most chronically marginalized population on the continent, who are largely excluded from public life in many countries. Roma communities suffer the highest levels of poverty and unemployment, and the worst health status of any group within Europe. Many live in isolated ghettos with poor infrastructure and services.

The European Roma Rights Centre (ERRC) has documented systematic discrimination against Roma in the health systems in many European countries,[15] ranging from refusal of services, abusive and humiliating treatment by doctors and hospital staff, segregation into inadequate facilities, and much more. The WHO has warned that the discriminatory health-care poses a threat beyond that facing the Roma people themselves: "The inability of Roma to access health services is recognized as a serious impediment for 53 countries in the region if they are to maintain polio-free status and achieve the measles and rubella targets."[16] Social prejudice against Roma people is deeply ingrained. In one survey, 79 per cent of Czechs said they would not want Roma as neighbours. In another, 68 per cent of Germans had an unfavourable opinion of Roma. This underlying current of prejudice is often fed by politicians and state authorities. Amnesty International research has shown discrimination in education of Roma children.

I recall a chilling experience I had when I worked for the UN. I was in Macedonia in 1998. Thousands of people were streaming across the border from Kosovo. I was head of the UN's emergency operation for refugees. One night we had a major security incident in one of the camps. Several Roma families were surrounded by angry mobs of refugees of Albanian origin from Kosovo who claimed that one of the Roma men had colluded with the Serbian forces in Kosovo to kill Albanians. They beat up some of the Roma people. We managed to intervene and prevent further bloodshed, but only by removing the Roma families from the camp. We then spent several futile hours trying to find alternative accommodation for them. Among the Roma refugees were a heavily pregnant woman, several young children, and a man with a broken arm, but not a single hotel or pension in Skopje was willing to admit the Roma families, even with the assurance

Internally displaced Roma refugees in Mitrovica, Kosovo, 2006.
© Anna Kari/Documentography

that the UN would foot the bill. In the end we put them up in a tent on the UN premises for the night and moved them the next day to a Macedonian Roma community outside Skopje. Having worked in many refugee crises, I am familiar with the wariness of host populations. But what shocked me was the total marginalization these families faced. Demonized by the Macedonians as well as by their Albanian compatriots from Kosovo, they were the ultimate outsiders.

Refugees, asylum-seekers and migrants also face discrimination and exclusion around the world. To take examples from some of the richest countries, in Switzerland the denial of welfare payments has led asylum-seekers who have been refused refugee status into destitution; and in Germany migrants face restrictions on access to health-care and the possibility of redress where their labour rights are violated. Their children's access to education is also limited.

There is a difference between the threat of hunger and death faced by the rural poor in Africa, and the deprivation experienced by the urban poor in the cities of the rich world. But the thread that links them is exclusion. Viewing their poverty through the prism of human rights highlights this. Yes, global efforts should prioritize the people living in the most extreme poverty in Africa and other parts of the less developed world. But it makes no sense to ignore the poverty that persists in more developed countries.

In sum, using human rights to diagnose poverty brings discrimination into sharp focus, and forces an acknowledgement of the problem – an essential first step to addressing it. The next step will include legislation to guarantee equality and non-discrimination, remedial action such as affirmative action programmes to overcome the legacy of past discrimination, and public education to counter prejudice and bigotry. Political leadership is crucial for success. Studies have noted that the political participation of disadvantaged groups, and their access to higher education and a fairer share of economic resources, all contribute substantially to any effort to overcome discrimination.[17] This points, again, to the way in which action across all four dimensions of poverty is mutually reinforcing. If the benefits of economic reforms and growth are to be shared equally, then those leading such efforts need to integrate action in these areas into their plans.

GLOBAL APARTHEID, GLOBAL INEQUALITY

Imagine a country with 1,000 inhabitants, 200 of them of European descent and 800 of non-European descent. The 20 per cent of European descent are also the richest; they collect 70 per cent of the country's income. The bottom 40 per cent of the population – all non-Europeans – share a mere 5 per cent of national income. One half of the country (500 people) live in poverty, of whom 495 are of non-European descent, making non-Europeans 25 times more likely to be living in poverty than their counterparts of European descent. The life expectancy of the most privileged segment of society, those of European descent, is 14 years greater than the group making up the vast majority of the population. Infant mortality rates for families of European descent are 5-6 times lower than for the majority of the population. Adult literacy among the non-European majority group is just 66 per cent, compared with 97 per cent among those of European descent. The country I am describing is South Africa under apartheid.

Shockingly, the gross disparities it reflected are less than those we find in the world as a whole today. The richest 10 per cent of the world's current population collects 50 per cent of its income, while the poorest 10 per cent struggle to survive on mere 0.7 per cent of world income. Roughly 40 per cent of people live on less than $2 a day and almost half live below the $2.50 a day mark. Life expectancy among the OECD countries (some 25 industrialized democracies) is a full 19 years higher than the average life expectancy for low-income countries and 13 years higher than the combined averages for low- and middle-income countries. Infant mortality amongst rich countries is over 15 times lower than the rate for low-income countries, and 10 times lower than the averages for low- and middle-income countries combined. Adult literacy for low-income countries is 61 per cent, 79 per cent for the middle- and low-income countries combined and 99 per cent for OECD countries.

The parallel with apartheid of course is not exact. The rich world of today includes some Asian and Latin American countries, and in many poor countries there are very rich individuals. But the reality is that inequalities within countries, and across the world, are growing.

I raise this comparison to make the point that the discrimination and exclusion that deeply divide those with wealth from those living in poverty within societies are being replicated in global inequalities among countries. We live in a world of obscene disparity, where a privileged few reap disproportionate benefits while many more suffer very real deprivations that fundamentally affect both the length and quality of their lives.

There are several ways to measure inequality, within countries and internationally. At the international level, if we take the average per capita income for each country, compare them, and look at trends over the past few decades, we see a quite startling divergence. Rich countries have increased their lead over poor countries at an exponential rate. This measure, however, treats all countries the same, regardless of population. China and India together comprise one third of the world's population, and large numbers of the world's poor people. If we take this into account and weight a country's population, then measure inequalities between countries, we do see a decline in the gap between the richest and poorest countries. But if China and India are excluded (and they are major economic powerhouses), even a weighted index shows worsening inequality between countries.

The fairest means of measuring inequality, however, is to ignore borders and attempt to count inequality between human beings as if we were members of a single community. On this measure too, the "global inequality" gap is growing wider.

Some will say this is nothing but a numbers game. Admittedly, the data on which all such comparisons are made are not terribly reliable. Nor is there agreement about what points of comparison we should be focusing on. Those who say the overall number of poor people has not declined are challenged by those who point to a growing middle class in newly emerging economies – and both are right. It depends on what you are looking at and how you look at it.

Diagnosing poverty by looking at human rights takes the debate beyond disparities in income to disparities in access to basic rights – health-care, education, shelter and social assistance. The pragmatist in this case may be tempted to argue that, as long as the situation of most people is improving and the overall proportion of poor people is falling, the fact that by some measures the rich are growing richer much more quickly than people who are poor makes little difference. If improvement can be seen in rising life expectancy, falling illiteracy rates, more children in school and fewer deaths from preventable disease, then why worry about the growing gap in global income inequality?

Global inequality does matter. It risks entrenching a two-track world: not east/west, nor even north/south but rather rich people and poor people, insiders and outsiders. Even if those on the bottom rung in terms of life expectancy or susceptibility to disease are better off than their ancestors, that is of little consolation to them when they are still denied full access to health-care and education, and they can see that their rich compatriots have more than they could ever possibly need.

Even though some poor countries and communities are progressing, the gap between them and rich countries is not narrowing. Most accounts of the impact of growth on poverty only look at the progress of poor people. They note improvements in relation to specific indicators and highlight a broad trend towards better quality of life. But while such progress is taking place, rich countries, and rich people, are not standing still. Even though the average income of developed countries is growing at a slower rate than that in less developed countries – many of which like India and China have much higher growth rates – the developed countries started off so far ahead that the gap between them will continue to grow for the foreseeable future. Indeed, by some estimates, it will be 2100 before the average income in less developed countries reaches the level of the developed countries today, but by that time the gap between them will be eight times larger than it is today![18]

From a human rights perspective, the inequalities are shocking and indefensible. Not, as some would have it, because it is wrong to be rich. And not because everyone should go to the best schools or live in the best neighbourhoods. Rather, it is shocking that income too often determines whose rights are recognized and whose rights are ignored. It is shocking that we pay little attention to the fact that growth in many countries is not improving the situation of marginalized groups. And it is dangerous that the income gap between rich and poor people will continue to widen to levels that can only breed resentment and risk exploding into violence.

For me, the question is not so much who is moving ahead, but who is being left behind in each country across the world. Unabashed globalists trumpet a "flat earth" based on the success of software firms in Bangalore or entrepreneurs in Guangzhou. But in their excitement to celebrate the success of those who are prospering, they overlook the plight of those whom the global economy continues to fail. Countries with some of the highest inequalities in income are also countries where significant segments of society do not enjoy human rights.

When rich people get richer but are surrounded by poor people, they have shown in numerous countries an inclination to opt out of publicly funded services. Instead, they invest in private security, private schools and private health-care, and secure their own safe supply of water. When those at the top withdraw their support from the public provision of public goods, the result is a further weakening of the state, at precisely the time when its capacity to deliver ought to be strengthened. As a consequence, those who cannot afford to pay for the private provision of public goods find themselves falling further and further behind, as the social and economic resources at their disposal continue to contract. The prospect of a shrinking public sector is deeply troubling for those who are already woefully under-served.

At the national level, action to fulfil the rights of those being left behind will cost money. Growing income inequalities suggest that a fairer distribution (or redistribution) of resources is needed. The alternative could be costly. Beyond the moral argument, not investing in the health, education, and wellbeing of all members of society, regardless of their caste, gender, ethnicity, religion or social status, is bad economic policy: it holds back progress on many fronts and can also be a source of instability and insecurity.

A fairer approach may also be needed at the international level, where wealth gaps are as morally repugnant and economically unsustainable today as they were under apartheid in South Africa. The fact that these gaps are widening and will continue to do so should be a wake-up call to all of us. Do we want humanity to replicate an apartheid state on a global level? A global redistribution of resources is, of course, much more complicated than the pursuit of equality within countries. Foreign aid is undoubtedly part of the answer, but the richer and more powerful countries could do much more – in their trade and investment policies, in tackling the companies, banks and arms dealers over whom they have control, and who facilitate or benefit from corruption and an abuse of power that is pervasive in less developed countries, and, most importantly, in convincing their own electorates that their prosperity cannot be maintained if it is at the expense of the rights of others. There is a special burden on rich countries to invest more in securing rights and freedoms on a global basis.

Human rights derive from and are inherent in our common humanity. Everyone has these rights on an equal basis, not by virtue of citizenship of any particular state, but simply because we are human beings. This transcends borders and divisions of all kinds. Action to respect these rights, therefore, falls to each of us within the spheres of our competence and power. Much more could be done to promote equality, tolerance and diversity through the universal appeal of human rights. And much progress would be made on poverty as a result.

FOUR
LIVING IN FEAR – SECURING RIGHTS

ON MY WAY TO ELEMENTARY school every morning in Dhaka, I would see crowds of men lining up outside big construction sites, squatting on the pavement, waiting for the foreman to call out their number. The chosen ones would rush forward with big smiles on their faces, while the others would drift away forlornly. I could not understand why anyone would be happy to get backbreaking work. I was too young then to appreciate the joy of a daily wage to buy food for hungry mouths, as opposed to the fear of having to send children to bed with empty bellies.

To live in poverty is to live in uncertainty and insecurity. For poor people life is a daily struggle to secure survival: food, work, a roof over their heads. At every turn there is fear, not only of disease and hunger, but also of gangs and guns, police brutality, family violence or armed conflict. In this chapter I will look at some of these sources of insecurity, how they reinforce poverty, and what must be done to protect poor people from these threats. Most importantly, I want to show how the assertion of rights is crucial to this task.

For many people living in poverty, insecurity begins with not knowing where their next meal will come from. In a world where over one billion people are overweight, 300 million of them clinically obese,[1] a billion people go to bed hungry every night. The recent spike in food prices has increased the numbers of those hungry people. The crisis was brought on by several factors: a growing demand for grain, increased costs of

Irene Khan talking to internally displaced people at a camp outside al-Jeneina. Darfur, Sudan, 2004.
© AFP PHOTO/Cris Bouroncle

fertilizer and transport due to rising energy prices, the conversion of land producing food to land producing crops for biofuels, lack of investment in the agricultural sector, and speculation in commodity markets. The relative impact of each factor is debated. But there is no debate on the outcome – tens of millions of people who can no longer afford to buy enough to eat. There is perhaps no clearer example of what an insecure livelihood means. Sufficient food one day, and none or too little the next, on account of price rises beyond the individual's control and, indeed, beyond the control of many individual governments.

Insecurity of livelihood is experienced in many other ways. From city bankers to migrant workers, the economic downturn has thrown into sharp relief the fragility of job security. While the former have a cushion on which to lean, the latter have little to fall back on. According to some reports, over 20 million migrant workers in China have lost their jobs and been forced to return to the countryside. In Bangladesh, hundreds of young men are being sent back daily from the Middle East and South East Asia, their source of income having disappeared without warning, leaving them in penury, since many had sold everything they owned to gain the opportunity to work abroad.

The economic downturn is shining a spotlight on a situation that has been a reality for poor people for a long time. Day labourers, like those construction workers I watched on my way to school, have no guarantee of secure employment. Landless peasants rely on the goodwill of landlords or creditors. Poor farmers are dependent on marginal land and at the mercy of the weather, in so many regions increasingly adverse due to climate change. People living in slums face the fear of forced eviction. In most poor countries, poor people have no safety net when, despite their best efforts, their basic needs cannot be met. If they or family members fall sick, if crops fail, if the factory shuts down or their home is demolished, they are left with nothing.

I come from a country prone to natural disasters, but although floods and cyclones play havoc with the lives and livelihoods of poor people, their insecurity of livelihood is not simply a consequence of nature. To a greater extent it is a result of bad laws and policies, unscrupulous employers and corrupt officials. In the campaign in India for the right to information that I described in Chapter 2, the resources directed at very poor people were being stolen by those who were meant to be administering the scheme.

The UDHR proclaims the right of everyone to social security, specifically "to security in the event of unemployment, sickness, disability ... or other lack of livelihood in circumstances beyond his control". It also asserts the obligation on the state to ensure everyone "an existence worthy of human dignity" and, where necessary, supplementing income "by other means of social protection". Further treaties have elaborated these obligations in more detail. But few developing countries have reached those standards.

The point is not that each country must have in place cradle-to-grave welfare systems, which would be difficult, if not impossible. But every country has an obligation, within its means, to establish social protection measures for those most at risk. The contribution of the rights framework is to make clear that such forms of protection are not optional. Muhammad Yunus once said to me that, had he been a delegate at the United Nations in 1948 when the Universal Declaration was being drafted, he surely would have insisted on a right to micro-credit as an alternative form of social security.

Ensuring greater livelihood security for those living in poverty is a major thrust of development efforts but it remains a big challenge. There are many programmes – for decent work, to protect rural livelihoods, for the provision of micro-credit, or preparedness for disaster. There are some good examples of what can be achieved with political will. In Brazil, the Bolsa Familia scheme guarantees families a set amount of cash – on average $35 a month – from the federal government, if they ensure that their children stay in school and have them vaccinated. Eleven million families have benefited from the scheme so far – that is 44 million people or 20 per cent of the population. Half of those who receive the "family grant" live in the north-east, Brazil's most impoverished region.

Security of livelihood is of fundamental importance to poor people, but in this chapter I will focus in greater depth on the physical insecurity which drives people into poverty and traps them there. I will look at the risks posed by armed conflict and violent crime, and particularly women's experience of violence. I focus on these areas because, as a UN refugee official for 21 years, and then as Secretary

General of Amnesty International, I have seen at first hand the disproportionate and debilitating impact of such violence on the lives of poor people. My aim is twofold: to show how such threats and risks perpetuate poverty, and, more importantly, to highlight how the human rights perspective can assist in efforts to diminish these risks.

WAR, CONFLICT AND POVERTY

Driving across western Darfur in September 2004, I could see clear signs of villages that had been destroyed. Patches of grass were growing in circles where huts had once stood. Camels were grazing where once there had been homes. In one half-destroyed hut I saw broken clay pots and a child's shoe lying on the ground as testimony to the hasty flight of the occupants. Some farmers were sneaking back under cover of darkness to harvest their millet but most were too frightened to return. Hundreds of thousands people had sought refuge in camps for internally displaced people (IDPs). The camp we visited outside El Geneina was a desolate place, with people herded like cattle, living in tents and dependent on handouts. The Janjaweed militia roamed around the perimeter fence like animals circling their prey. The men rarely stepped outside the camp for fear of being killed. Women and girls who ventured out to fetch water or firewood were often raped and attacked by the militia.

Darfur was poor before armed conflict broke out, but five years of fighting has left the region devastated. Over 2 million displaced people or refugees are living on handouts, their land and livestock destroyed, with war preventing the resumption of farming and grazing on which the region's people depend.

It is no surprise that countries suffering from prolonged armed conflict dominate the lowest ranks of the HDI. Such countries also make up the bulk of the 10 poorest performers in terms of infant mortality and average income.[2] According to one analysis, in 2002 all of the 38 sub-Saharan countries included in the UN's list of low-income countries had recent experiences of armed conflict.[3]

Various studies have shown that countries with lower per capita incomes are more likely to experience civil war and simmering violence than their relatively better-off counterparts. This raises an interesting question. Is it the relative poverty of these countries that makes them more prone to conflict? Or is it the continuing conflict that keeps them poor? As one might expect, the relationship operates in both directions. In the case of Darfur, the war was as much a result of environmental degradation and pressure on land as political grievances, oppressive policies and an abundant supply of arms. Poverty creates the conditions for conflict, and conflict, in turn, further impoverishes people, creating the risk of more conflict.[4] A recent study concluded: "[A]rmed conflict is arguably now the single most important determinant of poverty in Africa; and certainly of the concentrated forms of poverty that develop when populations are displaced, livelihoods vanish and safety networks breakdown."[5]

When a conflict persists or is transformed into low-level violence that continues for a prolonged period, the effect on the population is devastating.[6] In December 2006 I was in Jayyus, a village on the West Bank of the Palestinian Occupied Territories. The village is now divided by the Wall – or more accurately an iron fence. Ostensibly to make Israel more secure, its main effect in Jayyus has been to cut off the Palestinian population of the village from their citrus groves and olive orchards. A once prosperous farming community is now impoverished. "The gate in the wall is opened only for two hours in the morning and two hours in the evening but the security checks take so long, that many of us can't go through to the other side before the gate closes. If I can't get to my orchards, if I cannot cultivate my olives, how will I survive?" cried one angry Palestinian farmer. The 700-km wall – 80 per cent of which runs inside the West Bank – restricts the access of thousands of Palestinians to their workplaces, health facilities and other services. Over 500 military checkpoints and restrictions on using roads have the same effect. In Gaza, the Israeli blockade that was strengthened in 2008 led to the closure of the few remaining factories and shortages of essential supplies including food and medicine. Over 80 per cent of the population is dependent on humanitarian assistance, and extreme poverty, malnutrition and other health problems have increased.

In many present-day conflicts, attacks on civilians and civilian infrastructure are not "collateral damage" but a deliberate strategy to terrorize and uproot populations and occupy land. Depriving people of their means of survival so that they are forced to flee becomes part of the military objective. In the former Yugoslavia "ethnic cleansing" was used to drive minority groups from their land and homes so that others could occupy them. On a trip to Croatia in April 2008 I met members of the minority Serb community, still living in desperate conditions almost 15 years after the war had ended, still threatened by the perpetrators, and still struggling to find jobs in the factories from which they had been fired because of their identity.

Much has been written about the correlation between ethnic conflict, genocide and poverty in the Great Lakes region of Africa. I will not repeat that, but instead will share a personal experience which illustrates more clearly than any statistic the cost of war for poor people. In September 2003 I led an Amnesty International delegation to Burundi, a country that had been torn by ethnic violence for many years. A week before we arrived, the military had carried out a "search operation" for rebels in the north of the country in which some 174 people had been killed. We were told that there were only four survivors and that they had been taken to the local district hospital, where we went to visit them. We were shown into a room and asked to wait, then the first survivor walked in. She was a little girl, naked with her arm in a sling and a dirty blanket wrapped around her. She told us her name but could not tell us her age – I guessed she was about five as she still had her milk teeth. She could not remember her family name but she recalled vividly the attack on her family. She described how the soldiers had burst into their hut, sprayed it with gunfire, killing her parents, grandfather and sisters, before bayoneting her baby brother. She was wounded but, because she was small, she had somehow managed to crawl between the legs of the soldiers and escape in the commotion without being noticed. A neighbour found her naked and unconscious in the forest the next day and brought her to the hospital, but neither the neighbour nor the hospital had the means to buy her any clothes. That is why the five-year-old survivor of a massacre was still naked, wrapped only in a blanket when we saw her.

Civil war impoverishes people by destroying lives and livelihoods in innumerable ways. I saw it after 1971 in my own country, Bangladesh, where war was followed by famine. I have seen it in many other countries where I have visited or worked. In Cambodia and Afghanistan, people could not gain access to fields that had been strewn with mines. In Nepal and northern Sri Lanka farmers could not take their products to the markets because the roads and bridges had been destroyed by decades of conflict between government forces and armed groups. When the infrastructure is destroyed, when those who provide vital services to the population – doctors, nurses, teachers, engineers – are killed or forced to flee, when government resources are diverted to military and security spending and away from social services such as health and education, people living in poverty suffer the most.[7]

War affects people's health in myriad ways, both directly and indirectly.[8] They are more vulnerable to communicable disease and sexual violence, they experience higher infant mortality and are more likely to suffer from illnesses associated with malnutrition and compromised water sources, and to have mental health problems resulting from the trauma of violence. The increase of disease during conflict is well documented, and is associated with displacement, overcrowding in refugee camps,[9] and the difficulties in carrying out (and sometimes the complete suspension of) government-sponsored immunization and health-care services. Increased risk of HIV infection often accompanies conflict, and is thought to be largely attributable to a combination of increased sexual violence (particularly targeting displaced populations) and the mobility of troops throughout the country.[10] Significant rises in the incidence of malaria, tuberculosis and respiratory infections are also linked to conflict.[11] Women and children are most vulnerable to the negative health effects of conflict, and these effects often continue long after the conflict itself is over.

War also has a catastrophic impact on education. As well as reducing available government funding, it destroys schools. Children may be taken out of education to help their families earn money to survive. In northern Sri Lanka some parents kept their children away from school because that was where the Liberation Tigers of Tamil Eelam (LTTE) armed group was recruiting child soldiers.

And of course, notwithstanding the argument that growth in the military sector during a war can create jobs and boost the economy, there

Irene Khan visits the gate of Ras Atja in Israel's separation fence in the West Bank near Quiplia, Occupied Territories, Israel, December 2006.
© MaanImages/Magnus Johansson/ Amnesty International

is considerable evidence to show that prolonged internal conflict in many less developed countries leads to poorer economic performance and therefore a decline in economic opportunity. Comparing 18 case studies, the World Bank found that: 15 of the cases experienced a drop in per capita income; 12 saw a drop in food production; 13 experienced declines in export growth; and all the cases resulted in increased external debt as a percentage of GDP.[12] Another study found that, as a result of the Rwandan genocide, 20 per cent of the population moved into poverty, of which one quarter of the sample moved into extreme poverty.[13]

It may seem obvious, but it bears repeating: to end poverty we must do all we can to prevent wars in the first place. If we cannot, then, at a minimum, we must lessen the deadly impact on civilians.

It is here that the rights perspective brings much to the debate. Invoking human rights compels one to look at war first and foremost from the perspective of those individuals caught up in it. This, in turn, creates a powerful force for change. Indeed, in the last two decades, there has been a profound shift in the global response to civil war – revolving around an awareness of human rights and the impact on civilians.

Putting the spotlight on individual suffering has resulted, in the last 20 years, in the creation of international tribunals and eventually the International Criminal Court to punish war crimes and crimes against humanity. New treaties have prohibited the use of child soldiers and land mines. We are on the way to achieving a ban on cluster bombs: 94 countries signed the UN Convention on Cluster Munitions at a conference in December 2008, and more are joining them. With the divisions of the Cold War over, the UN Security Council is more active in addressing internal conflicts and mass human rights abuses where they threaten regional security. Among other initiatives, it now monitors countries and armed groups that recruit children, denounces violence against women in conflict, deploys peacekeepers with a mandate to protect civilians, and imposes travel and financial sanctions on warlords. Civil society has joined with governments and business to set and monitor standards to end the trade in conflict diamonds. Peace settlements now routinely include provisions obliging the parties to protect human rights, and sometimes allow international monitors to oversee the fulfilment of this obligation. More than 100,000 UN troops are currently deployed to guarantee security in countries emerging from war – this is an all-time high.

Despite these efforts, however, much more needs to be done. Chronic conflicts persist in which hundreds of thousands of people continue to suffer – in Palestine, Sri Lanka, Colombia, the Caucasus, Darfur, the Democratic Republic of the Congo (DRC), Somalia and elsewhere. New wars loom on the horizon. The growing threat of terrorism including violence from armed groups in Iraq, Afghanistan and Pakistan has led to expanded military operations to counter them. In countries where political settlements have been negotiated, peace is often fragile and prone to degenerate into low-level violence or sudden flare-ups. UN peacekeeping operations are under-funded and over-stretched, and international criminal indictments are ignored – witness Darfur. In the testimonies of rape, massacre and torture that Amnesty

International researchers bring back from war zones, I see the proof of the collective failure of the international community to go far enough and deep enough in the protection of the rights of those caught up in violent conflict.

WHAT MORE CAN BE DONE?

We can do more. First, we must work harder to stop conflicts before they start. A lot of effort has gone into developing early-warning mechanisms and improved conflict analysis to assist in the prevention of deadly conflict. There is a growing capacity in the international NGO community as well as in multilateral organizations to analyze crucial information about what is happening in countries that are below the radar of media attention. The challenge remains to persuade powerful nations to pay attention to these warnings and muster the necessary political will to take preventive action. In early 2003, six months before a major humanitarian crisis emerged in Darfur, Amnesty International drew attention to the upsurge in conflict in the region, the government-sponsored attacks on civilians, and the need for international action to avert precisely such a crisis. No one would listen.

Second, once war has broken out, and in the post-conflict stage when low-level violence continues, it is essential to ensure the protection of civilians. One way to do this is through deploying UN or other foreign troops. In a major breakthrough in 2005, UN member states unanimously agreed that they had a "responsibility to protect" civilians when genocide and crimes against humanity were evident and the state where atrocities are being committed fails to act, either because it is unwilling or unable to do so. As we learned from the failure to respond to genocide in Rwanda, the UN must be prepared to use force as a last resort to protect people. But it is not easy to generate the political will and find the military means to make this happen. The US intervention in Iraq, justified in the name of human rights when the weapons of mass destruction argument proved hollow, has not helped.

Less controversial is the deployment of peacekeepers with the consent of the host country. There are already over 100,000 UN peacekeepers in the field. Some argue that we need to place tens of thousands more peacekeepers in countries at risk of new or renewed civil war in order to maintain the security that is essential to tackle poverty.[14] It is, of course, a costly option, but so too are the costs of a return to war. UN troops have contributed to stability, including for example in Sierra Leone, Liberia and southern Sudan. But in addition to preventing a return to war, they must do more to offer protection against continuing human rights abuses. The widespread violence against women in the eastern DRC took place despite thousands of UN troops being deployed in the area.

The focus on the human dimension means that security must be judged at this level. Are women safe? Can small farmers plant their crops? Are the roads free of banditry? Whether independently deployed or as a complement to peacekeepers, international human rights monitoring teams can help boost security for populations at risk. The UN has used them effectively in earlier conflicts in El Salvador and Guatemala, and more recently in Nepal. They achieved real successes, not only in reducing the human rights violations associated with conflict, but also as a confidence-building measure. Human rights monitors can be very useful in the tense post-war period, as belligerents turn from bullets to the ballot. Well-trained field officers in these monitoring operations not only gather information and produce reports for analysis, they carry out constant daily advocacy on behalf of people who are under attack. They use their presence and diplomacy to dissuade attackers, and they use their impartiality, and where they've won it, local credibility, to bring together polarized groups and reduce tensions. The potential of this approach is well-documented,[15] but it has not been matched by resources.

Third, we must improve our ability to help countries rebuild after war so that they remain peaceful. Far too often, the end of warfare signifies not peace but continuing violence that leaves civilians, and women in particular, at risk. In the eastern DRC, rape and sexual violence against women and girls reached epidemic proportions after the conclusion of an earlier peace treaty. Soldiers and members of various armed groups raped women and girls with complete impunity, bringing abject terror to a broad swathe of the countryside.[16]

We must rebuild in ways that do not retrench old inequalities, or create new ones. The human rights approach keeps the focus on more than stability: it demands constant attention to ensuring that the peace is truly just, and brings benefits to all, including the poorest people. As countries rebuild themselves, new laws and new institutions must be put in place that do not replicate past injustices. This, in turn, creates conditions that will prevent a return to war. Both in Iraq and Afghanistan, Amnesty International made extensive recommendations to governments on building systems for the rule of law based on human rights, but neither country proved receptive to those ideas.

Finally, using a human rights perspective also means ensuring that those who are responsible for abuse do not get away with it. We must use the courts, tribunals, truth commissions and other institutions for confronting the impunity of political leaders, armed forces and warlords. International humanitarian law, the rules of war, the Geneva and other Conventions, are not just academic exercises. They are instruments for bringing war criminals to account – just like any other accused murderer, rapist or arsonist.

One major obstacle to security at the end of a war is the easy availability of weapons. For many years Amnesty International has campaigned for governments not to supply weapons and equipment to countries or groups where they would be used to perpetuate human rights abuses. Some countries have passed legislation restricting exports unless human rights criteria are met. This has had little impact, however, as those seeking weapons could always find another supplier. In 2003 Amnesty International, together with Oxfam and the International Action Network on Small Arms (IANSA) launched the Control Arms campaign, in which we mobilized a million people from around the world to demand an Arms Trade Treaty which would oblige all states to end arms transfers that undermine development or contribute to human rights abuse. When we began, only a handful of governments indicated their support. Five years later, as of October 2008, almost 150 states had given their formal approval and a drafting process was underway in the UN. With continued pressure and campaigning, a treaty could be in place in the next few years.

Most crucially, whatever approach we take to limiting the impact of civil war and reducing the human rights abuses associated with it, we must not forget that the affected people themselves must be given the space and resources to lead the strategies to confront poverty and conflict.

Consider, for instance, the inspiring struggle of the Afro-Colombian people in Choco, Colombia. These communities had struggled for decades to achieve collective ownership over their territory. They didn't do it to confront paramilitary attacks but, when the attacks came, their legally protected titles and community development mechanisms helped them withstand the pressure. Their community strength, resistance to pressure to join either the paramilitaries or the guerillas, establishment of "humanitarian areas" where people could flee temporarily and safely return when fighting had passed, and systems for collectively protecting their villages' trade and livelihoods were groundbreaking. They invested in networking and organization, and this enabled them to react under pressure with creative collective strategies. Their experience in national and international organizing to protect their cultural identity and territorial autonomy also served them well when they needed to make effective denunciations of human rights abuses.

The example from Choco exemplifies the creativity, courage, and political astuteness of people in the worst of situations, who are struggling for answers, working with their families, their villages, or neighbourhoods, their religious communities and other networks to devise strategies to confront poverty and conflict. Choco is an example of the ways in which people around the world struggle for sustainable livelihoods, dignity and economic control over their destiny.

People under attack are the primary protagonists and should be the creators of solutions to their plight. It is incumbent on all of us to find ways to support these valiant efforts. International action must aim to complement the strategies of the people themselves. Again, we see the practical meaning of taking action to address all four dimensions of poverty. If we help people gain control over their lives, with "voice" and participation in the decisions that affect them, this empowers them not only to face their economic and social problems more effectively, but also enables them to confront violence and conflict.

CRIME – TOUGH ON POOR PEOPLE

Wealthy people build gated communities to protect themselves from what they see as the criminality of poor people. But in truth, it is those living in poverty who suffer the worst and most pervasive forms of crime. Being poor dramatically increases one's likelihood of being exposed to violent crime and decreases the possibility that the police will provide protection. In urban areas, poor neighbourhoods fall into the hands of criminal gangs. In rural areas poor people are left at the mercy of tyrannical landlords.

Amnesty International's research on slums shows that whole communities are living under the control of criminal gangs or "'slum lords". In the *favelas* of São Paolo I found people facing multiple threats: poverty and lack of public services as well as violence from drug gangs and the police. The residents of the *favelas* spoke of the gun violence of the drug gangs and of how the state has failed for decades to provide them with either public security or public services. In some places, they said, the drug gangs have been driven out by *milícias*, or paramilitary gangs made up of off-duty security officials, who then have taken control of the communities and charged the residents for protection and for access to basic services such as water or gas.

People living in the *favelas* are trapped in poverty. Their everyday life is dominated by violence and fear. The gangs use gun power and physical threats to impose curfews that keep people in their homes. If schools or health services are far from where the communities live, it is unsafe for people to travel from their own neighbourhood to access the services they need in areas controlled by rival gangs. Health-care workers are intimidated and told not to treat victims of gang violence. Residents may be at risk if they try to come together to improve services. The gangs can prohibit people from organizing themselves, and breaking the "rules" may result in violent punishment. A brave young woman human rights activist, whom I met in one of the *favelas* in São Paolo received death threats and had to be evacuated with the help of Amnesty International to the United States. Those in the *favelas* are disproportionately likely to be victims of violent crime. In 2001, 309 homicides were recorded in Jardim Ângela, a socially

Previous pages: **A labourer from the Afro-Colombian community in the village of Pie de Pato, Chocó region, Colombia, 2009.**
© Moises Saman/Panos

deprived district, in comparison with two homicides in Moema, a more affluent area located only a few kilometres away.[17]

It is a vicious cycle: poverty and isolation create a vacuum into which gangs move, bringing drugs, guns, violence and fear, further breaking down legitimate community structures. Everyone living in the community is tarred with the same brush and considered to be a criminal, or regarded as an "enemy of the state". The police response is often militarized assault, for instance in Brazil using the infamous *Caveirão* assault vehicles, and targeting whole communities. The violent police reaction further stigmatizes, terrorizes and alienates the community. Isolation increases and poverty deepens.

Police violence against poor communities is notoriously widespread. Amnesty International has documented police brutality in slums in Jamaica and Kenya,[18] including killings and executions. Women suffer verbal, physical and sexual abuse at the hands of the police. As in the case of Brazil, so too in Jamaica, where people in slums reported being treated with disrespect, prejudice, contempt and discrimination by the police because of the perception of the entire community as "criminals" or "accomplices to crime".

People living in poverty are victimized by criminals, and then often further victimized by the police who should be protecting them. The framework of human rights law calls for the state to be clearly accountable. Human rights groups, therefore, are usually among the first to highlight and criticize cases of police brutality and abuses of power against poor communities. But in difficult situations, where fear of criminal violence dominates the public consciousness, human rights organizations themselves may be labelled as "protecting the criminals."[19]

In the face of police failure to control crime, poor communities have at times taken law into their own hands, forming vigilante organizations that execute their own form of justice outside the rule of law, and often with considerable popular support. This was seen in Nigeria with the emergence of the Bakassi Boys, a gang that developed in the commercial centres of Aba and Onitsha. Local crimes rates were perceived to be skyrocketing, and merchants were fed up with paying protection money in the absence or with the collusion of the police. The Bakassi Boys took on the alleged criminals, and their use of violence in doing so was seen by local people as a major factor in reducing criminal violence. The problem wasn't solved, of course, as the gang came to be seen as armed militias for political factions, but initially they, and other vigilantes who followed, did enjoy widespread public support.[20]

Violence and lack of police protection are not just features of city life. The tyranny of rural poverty is perhaps most starkly illustrated by the prevalence of bonded labour – slavery by another name – in areas such as agricultural plantations or domestic work. The powerlessness of those living under this feudal control is an invitation to abuse, and violence against bonded labourers is widespread. As is violence against those deemed to be at the bottom of the social hierarchy in rural areas – such as Dalits in South Asia, or Indigenous Peoples in Latin America.

The World Bank's research confirms that people living in poverty do not see the police as a source of protection but too often as yet another source of insecurity. In *Voices of the Poor*, the authors noted:

> *Perhaps one of the most striking revelations of the study is the extent to which the police and official justice systems side with the rich, persecute poor people and make poor people more insecure, fearful and poorer. Particularly in urban areas, poor people perceive the police not as upholding justice, peace and fairness, but as threats and sources of insecurity. Women report feeling vulnerable to sexual assault by the police, and young men say they have been beaten up by the police without cause.*[21]

Corruption thrives in such situations of organized crime and poverty. In the example of the Bakassi Boys, the police were widely seen to be complicit in the criminal rackets, and hence the support for an extra-legal response. Amnesty International has been reporting for many years on police brutality, and has found that corruption in police forces is a major obstacle to overcoming the impunity that allows their abuses to continue.

The complex nature of the problem points to the need for a comprehensive approach. Crime hurts poor people, and it constrains their options for improving their livelihoods, health, education or other aspects of their welfare. Security is therefore essential for the poor, but to be effective it must be provided in a way that does not lead to more human rights abuse. Effective policing both provides security and protects rights – and is best done with transparency and accountability on the part of the state.

Human rights organizations within countries have been working on both sides of this problem for some time. Even while they are actively monitoring the justice system and standing up for the rights of the accused, they are also offering support and training for police, praising examples of good practice, engaging in debates and developing policy and legislation to strengthen the state's ability to deliver on its obligation to protect people while still respecting their rights.

This emphasis on security works best when it goes hand in hand with a continuing commitment to the active participation and "voice" of poor people in developing security policies. The justice system and the police need mechanisms to involve and listen to the concerns of poor people both about crime and about police approaches to crime. The communities that are most affected have a right to be involved in designing the policies and practices that are supposed to protect them. As the earlier example from Chocó illustrated, the involvement of the community makes a successful outcome much more likely.

Policing models that involve collaboration between the police and the local communities are increasingly common in the most developed countries. Although the statistical impact of community participation on crime is difficult to prove, there is broad acceptance that greater community participation improves the relationship between the police and the community and has many other advantages. The translation of these strategies to poorer nations has been more difficult.

In Kenya, civil society groups have begun to collaborate with the national police, with mixed results. One collaboration involved a downtown business association, which allowed local merchants to have an input into the prioritization of crime prevention concerns in the area, as well as establishing mechanisms to support police capacity-building. While some people point to a resulting reduction in crime, the collaboration has been criticized for excluding marginalized people from the process, including street vendors and poor people, and reinforcing police attitudes that criminalize poverty. In a parallel project, the Kenya Human Rights Commission established a collaboration with police in specific poor neighbourhoods, which tried to take into account the complexity of the police relationship with poor people – in particular that the police are perceived as oppressors and sources of corruption. This project recognizes that police action needs not simply to expand, but to change its attitude – a long-term process which, in practice, has been hampered by the distrust the police have of human rights organizations who tend to criticize them.[22]

In the slums of Mumbai, the former Police Commissioner described a similarly difficult relationship between the police and the people, rooted in decades of corruption, connivance between police and organized crime, and alienation of the public: "Police felt the slum dwellers were all squatters, criminals. Slum dwellers felt police were the oppressors, who only listened to the rich and would not hear legitimate complaints."[23] But in this case, a collaborative project seems to be rapidly changing that relationship. The police and local community members have set up local neighbourhood councils which have led to a rapid decrease in crime and an improvement in public perceptions of the police. These police *panchayats* build on an indigenous model of local decision-making. Each is made up of 10 local women and men: they resolve local disputes, decide compensation and restorative claims, and negotiate steps with those accused of criminal behaviour, before their alleged crime is formally brought to the police. This local structure allows the overstretched police to work more efficiently on tougher criminal matters. It gives the local community a say in dispute resolution and crime prevention. The whole process is done in close collaboration with the police, ensuring that this local justice structure is consistent with the formal legal system in its outcomes. There are 230 *panchayats* serving approximately 4 million people who live in slums. According to the Mumbai police, the process has reduced the caseload of the police by 90 per cent in many neighbourhoods, as well as significantly reducing crime and improving relationships.

Crime prevention and public security are extremely complex challenges but they are inextricably linked to human rights protection and are of crucial importance to people living in poverty. Victims need protection from crime, and the accused need the protection of due process and the rule of law. Police need capacity and training, but they also need credibility and legitimacy within the community if they are to succeed. Sadly, too often they lack both, and are undermined by widespread corruption and the temptation to be tough on crime by stigmatizing entire communities. Only strategies that are coherent, and nurture a long-term culture of respect for the law and human rights are likely to succeed. The rights framework tells us that there is no contradiction between supporting the police in confronting violent crime, and – as the examples above show – demanding that the police and justice systems remain accountable at all times to the rule of law.

VIOLENCE AGAINST WOMEN

The young woman sat with her back to me as she recounted in a low voice her ordeal of being attacked and raped by Janjaweed militia while collecting firewood on the outskirts of her village in western Darfur. She broke down in tears as she whispered that she was pregnant and did not know what she would do when her husband's family found out. The older woman sitting next to her said, "We send young women and girls to fetch the firewood because being young they can run fast when the Janjaweed militia come, but not all of them run fast enough." We met several rape survivors in that village, most of them teenagers. The normal course of action, if the girl was unmarried, was for the family to move elsewhere with the girl, to a place where no one would know what had happened. If she was married, then the likelihood was that she would be abandoned by her husband. As a rape survivor she had no future, only the risk of pregnancy, HIV infection and ostracization.

In the women's prison in Kabul, I listened to another rape survivor, this time a 16-year-old girl. She had been abducted from her home in Kunduz and forced into marriage. She was abused and raped until she could bear it no longer and ran away. She had no means of survival and was soon caught by the police and put into prison. She felt this was the safest place for her because, if her family found her, they would kill her for having destroyed their honour. There were 170 women and girls in the prison, almost all of them with similar stories of abuse, violence and a willingness to stay in prison rather than return to their own homes for fear of being killed.

For women living in poverty, whether in times of war or peace, at home or at work, insecurity manifests itself most commonly as sexual violence. Violence against women is universal, but it has a disproportionate impact on poor women.[24] Research shows that poor women are at increased risk of violence from their partners and of sexual violence including rape.[25] This is not because poor people are inherently more violent, but because poverty and insecurity provide fewer forms of escape or redress, and fewer opportunities for women to claim power over their own lives and assert themselves.

Gender violence is essentially an abuse of power. For families living in poverty, some people feel that the easiest way to establish power is physically. Compound that with a poor woman's lack of access to health services or resources to find alternative accommodation, and the consequences of violence are much more dangerous for her than for her wealthier sisters. Then position the scenario of sexual violence in the midst of insecurity where other power dynamics come into play, such as criminal gangs or corrupt officials or armed conflict, and you can understand why there are painfully few options for poor women to escape or protect themselves.

Poverty, for women, is both a cause and a consequence of violence. Think of the story of Rosie in Chapter 1, who died at the hands of a brutal husband because she could not afford the bus fare from her home to the magistrates' court to obtain a restraining order. Women may live in slums where gender violence is high.[26] They may be trapped in a war where rape is used as a military weapon. Or hunger and destitution may force women into situations of sexual exploitation.

By adversely affecting their health, education or work opportunities, the violence they face deepens the poverty trap in which they find themselves. Consider the situation of the women and girls of Ciudad Juárez I mentioned in Chapter 1. According to the WHO, many women suffering from poverty become migrant workers in order to survive economically. As such, they are "at high risk of experiencing abuse by employers including confinement, slave-like conditions, and physical and sexual assault."[27]

Or think of the violence to which refugee and displaced women and girls are exposed. As a UN refugee official working with the Vietnamese boat people in South East Asia in the 1980s, I witnessed the double trauma of young Vietnamese girls who had been raped by pirates on the South China Sea, and then by corrupt camp officials in the countries where they were seeking asylum. A decade later, the humanitarian community was rocked by scandals which exposed the rackets that some NGOs were running in camps in West Africa, sexually exploiting hundreds of refugee women and girls.

Poverty traps women into dangerous and violent domestic situations. Paradoxically, those who try to earn an income and gain a degree of autonomy face more violence from the men in their lives and the communities in which they live. Where a woman is working but her partner is not, or in patriarchal societies in which men traditionally hold most of the power, women can find that their efforts to improve their situation increase the likelihood of violence, as men resent their efforts to assert their freedom.[28] Going back to my experience as a UN refugee worker, I often felt that the high levels of domestic violence I saw in refugee camps resulted from men being so committed to traditional attitudes on gender that they found it difficult to adjust to a situation where the women were no longer economically dependent on them and resorted to physical force to impose their authority.

Education is a path out of poverty but gender violence impedes girls' access to education. Violence on the way to or within schools prevents girls from taking advantage of educational opportunities and so reduces their prospect of lifting themselves out of poverty.[29] Girls from poor families are sometimes pressurized into engaging in sex in exchange for fees, uniforms, books and even lunches.[30] The number of girls reporting incidents of sexual violence or unwanted sexual contact in or on the way to school is very high. A report prepared for the World Bank notes that recent studies in Africa have revealed a startling number of girls reporting sexual violence at the hands of their teachers and male classmates. For instance, in South Africa 37.7 per cent of high-school rape victims identified a teacher or principal as the rapist. A six-site African study revealed 16-47 per cent of girls in primary and secondary education reporting sexual abuse or harassment by a teacher or classmate.[31] Such violence not only undermines girls' ability to participate effectively at school but also drives some of them simply to give up on education.[32]

Good health is fundamental to overcoming poverty; this fact is central to the MDGs. Gender violence harms women's health in a number of significant ways which, in turn, induce or perpetuate their experience of poverty. A multi-site WHO study of violence against women by intimate partners found that, in the 15 sites under study, 19-55 per cent of women reported having been physically abused by their partners. And violence against women can have disastrous consequences for maternal and infant health. The health consequences are many and often long-lasting.[33] There is also a link between health and education: a study by the International Food Policy Research Institute identified improvements in women's education as the single most powerful contribution to reducing malnutrition over a 35-year period.[34]

Women are also more likely to be infected with HIV if they have been raped or sexually abused, as they are in no position to negotiate protection.[35] Evidence from Uganda shows a high level of correlation between domestic violence and the spread of HIV/AIDS. In some instances, the tragedy of HIV/AIDS has become just another tool for those who want to dominate, and inflict pain and suffering.[36] In addition, a Zambian study revealed that violence against women was a significant barrier to women accessing HIV treatment, thus exacerbating the impact on victims' health.[37]

Directly related to the negative impacts on health and education, violence against women also impedes their ability to work. One study in India revealed that women lose an average of seven workdays as a result of one incident of violence.[38] A study conducted in Chile and Nicaragua examining the impacts on work of domestic violence against women found that women who had suffered from domestic violence over the preceding 12 months were less likely to work outside the home and earn income than their non-abused counterparts. In addition, among women in that study who were working, victims of abuse earned considerably less than non-abused women – 46 per cent less in the Nicaraguan case for victims of sexual violence and 57 per cent less for victims of severe physical violence.[39]

The point should be clear by now. The violence women face keeps them poor, and it is poor women who are most exposed to violence. No MDG target, however, requires governments to work towards ending violence against women. This despite the fact that violence against women directly and indirectly obstructs progress on almost all of the MDGs. But governments are not obliged to report on their efforts in this area. Given the links between violence and poverty, would it not make sense for them to do so?

Women's groups around the world have been campaigning against gender violence for many years. In 2004 I launched Amnesty International's campaign to Stop Violence Against Women to join this effort. There have been real successes in reducing violence against women. Laws have been established to criminalize and punish violence against women; police forces have set up dedicated units to investigate violence against women; shelters for women at risk have been created. At the international level, rape in war has been explicitly outlawed, and international tribunals have prosecuted and punished some perpetrators. Most importantly, there is now greater awareness about violence against women. This is not to say that the problem has been resolved but that we know what can be done with political will and resources.

There are three distinct advantages to using the human rights framework to challenge violence against women. Firstly, it places clear duties on the state to take action, regardless of whether the violence is committed in the home, in the community or by state agents. It rejects the idea of a "private" sphere, where abuse can be tolerated. Secondly, human rights can challenge appeals to tradition, local culture or religion, that might be invoked in an effort to justify violence against women or prevent action to end it. Human rights are universal, and are spelt out in declarations and treaties that in one way or another all states have agreed to. And thirdly, if we focus on rights, we necessarily look to the rights of women themselves to challenge violence and demand the equal protection of the law. This puts the emphasis on women's empowerment as an essential part of the solution. It is only when women themselves become agents for change – as in the case of the women of Ciudad Juárez – that their situation will change.

THE CHALLENGE AHEAD

Lives lived in poverty are lives lived in fear. Asserting human rights in this context is the means to find security. By respecting rights, we could lessen the impact of war on people living in poverty, ensure fair and effective policing in poor communities, and curb violence against women.

Of course, there is a global dimension to the insecurity faced by those who live in poverty. War, criminality and violence do not always originate at home or persist only due to the failures of national governments. Arms flows can prolong wars. Regional interference can instigate or prolong internal conflicts. Organized crime in slums can be fed by illicit trade in drugs internationally. Trafficking of women can expand the scope of gender violence. International apathy to women's human rights can encourage some governments to neglect gender violence in their countries.

Similarly, threats to people's livelihoods have an international dimension. Increased speculation in world commodity markets dramatically raised the price of basic foodstuffs, pushing millions more people into hunger between 2006 and 2008. International trade rules and practices make poor farmers' crops uncompetitive. The global economic crisis has thrown millions of people back into poverty. Export-led jobs are disappearing as demand from abroad dries up, and reductions in remittances or international aid could lead to cuts in health and education programmes in some poor countries.

Perhaps the most pressing and dramatic insecurity overshadowing the lives and livelihoods of poor people is climate change. Poor farmers will see reduced yields on already marginal land. The numbers of landless people will grow when low-lying ground is flooded by rising sea levels. Clean water will become harder to obtain, and tens of million of people will be displaced. Disease will spread. Poor countries are ill-equipped to adapt to these conditions. The effects of climate change are likely to be immensely destabilizing, and may fuel political crisis and conflict. Global insecurity of this dimension will require global solutions based on global values and principles.

The human rights framework is borderless. Women in Kabul or Darfur have the same right to protection from violence as women in

Manhattan or Mayfair. The global nature of insecurity has its parallel in the global responsibility to uphold human rights as an antidote to it. The international community as a whole has a responsibility to fight the insecurity that pushes people into poverty and traps them there.

I have seen the power of human rights claims to release prisoners of conscience. I am convinced that – by abolishing fear and insecurity – the same power can release prisoners of poverty.

FIVE
POVERTY TRAPPED

IN MAY AND JUNE 2006 1,500 families living in Sambok Chab, Cambodia, were forced into trucks and dumped in a deserted flood plain 20 kms outside the city. During the course of multiple incursions, hundreds of security officials destroyed the families' homes. Those who tried to resist were arrested. "On the day of the eviction, I lost my belongings, including clothes, plates and mats. The police and military police ... came in and shouted: 'Dismantle, dismantle, and leave!' I pleaded [with] them not to beat me," Srey Mom, a mother of three, told Amnesty International researchers, a year later. "I agreed to pull down my house. Then they dumped us right here." Living under a tarpaulin on the flood plain with no income and no prospects, the day she was forcibly evicted from her home remained vivid in her memory. When she spoke to us, her son was still not permitted to attend school as his identity papers had been destroyed in the eviction.

Such evictions are all too common in Cambodia. They usually take place without court orders, without any prior consultation, and in violation of countless national regulations, as well as international human rights law. When residents resist, they are repressed. In March 2005, five people were killed when more than 200 homes were demolished in Kbal Spean – no one has ever been held accountable. Between 2005 and 2007, hundreds of

AI Belgium made the AI logo from 26,105 candles in a candle-lit vigil in support of Chinese human rights activists. In doing so they set a world record for the largest outdoor candle display. Sint-Truiden Grote Markt Belgium, June 2008.
© Amnesty International

people were arrested in Cambodia in land-related disputes. Many are still sitting in jail; some have been convicted, others are awaiting trial. Those who face such arbitrary action, in Cambodia and elsewhere, are usually from the poorest and most marginalized communities.

Srey Mom's plight evokes both outrage and compassion; outrage that she should be treated in this way, and compassion that motivates us to help her. But how can we help her? She needs food and proper shelter. At the same time, she deserves redress for her illegal eviction, including compensation for the losses she has suffered. Her son needs schooling. It would help too if the police and security forces were held to account and reformed, so that such acts will not occur in the future.

Clearly, it is woefully insufficient to address any one of these issues in isolation. Srey Mom's deprivation is not the whole story. She needs legal protection and a political voice if what has happened to her is not to be repeated. At the same time, such protections will not, on their own, meet all the needs of those in poverty.

When I met with Mapuche Indigenous leaders in Chile, they complained about insecurity and violence as well as the loss of their lands. In Darfur in Sudan, and in Goma in the DRC, women who have survived rape at the hands of armed militias and soldiers told me that they needed access to health services and also to justice. In Nepal, those displaced by the violence of the civil war spoke to me of threats to their lives and livelihoods.

Deprivation. Insecurity. Voicelessness. Exclusion. These are the conditions that define poverty. They are interlinked: the persistence of any one of them will have an impact on efforts to overcome the others. Action to end poverty, therefore, must tackle all four simultaneously. The human rights framework helps to identify the action needed across all four dimensions of poverty, and its basis in international law gives such action legitimacy.

The UDHR, proclaimed in 1948, sets out a comprehensive set of rights – to free speech, to freedom of religious worship and to a fair trial, and also to basic health and education and a minimal standard of living commensurate to a life lived in dignity. Article 25 of the UDHR specifically guarantees a right to adequate housing, so cruelly ignored in Srey Mom's case. In 1948, the emerging bloc of socialist countries pushed for the inclusion of these economic and social rights, but there was also widespread support from capitalist countries. The memory of the Great Depression was fresh, and so too was US President Franklin D. Roosevelt's championing of the Four Freedoms – freedom of speech and religion, and freedom from fear *and want*. Roosevelt explicitly linked rights in the political and economic realms when he said: "If the average citizen is guaranteed equal opportunity in the polling place, he must have equal opportunity in the market place."

The holistic approach implicit in the Four Freedoms, and explicitly set out in the UDHR, unravelled as Cold War rivalries intensified after 1948. The rhetoric of human rights became a weapon, used by both sides to delegitimize the other's ideology. It was convenient for the USA and its allies to champion civil and political rights, and convenient for the Soviet Union and its allies in the communist bloc to champion economic and social rights. That both sides evinced significant failures to respect the rights they championed – the USA, for example, in supporting military dictatorships in Latin America and the Soviet Union in backing poverty-stricken, failing socialist states in Africa – only served to underline the deeply political, ideological and hypocritical nature of the dispute. When the United Nations came to develop the aspirations of the UDHR into binding treaty commitments, the Cold War split meant states could not agree on the relative priority to be accorded to either set of rights. In the end it was decided to divide them into two distinct treaties.

In 1966 the UN adopted two separate human rights treaties – the Covenant on Economic, Social and Cultural Rights (ICESCR) and the Covenant on Civil and Political Rights (ICCPR). Under each distinct umbrella, separate systems of reporting and monitoring on compliance have emerged. This dual-track approach is evident throughout the UN's human rights machinery. There are separate agenda items for the two sets of rights in most UN meetings, and distinct experts and working groups are appointed for each category of rights. The Berlin Wall has fallen but the ideological barriers in human rights are yet to be fully dismantled. Even today, economic and social rights are identified with socialism, or at least with a philosophy that promotes active state intervention in the market. Civil and political rights are sometimes still seen as being dependent on – or strongly linked to – free market approaches.

This separation of human rights into two sets has real consequences. States may ratify one treaty without ratifying the other. For instance, the USA has bound itself to the ICCPR but not to the ICESCR. For China, it is the reverse. States that were once aligned East or West now often align along a North-South axis in relation to the two categories of rights. "Southern" states push for UN bodies to give greater attention to economic and social rights, and "Northern" states push for a focus on civil and political rights. Though any number of UN resolutions and declarations assert the "indivisibility" and "interdependence" of all human rights, the operational agenda of the UN, and even more so, the human rights politics in the UN, have entrenched a dual-track approach.

This split has greatly damaged approaches to the alleviation of poverty. The categorization of rights has lent credence to the view that some rights can be prioritized over others; or indeed to the view that only one or other category of rights is deserving of international attention. Many governments and business and opinion leaders are trapped in such political and ideological debates. Today, all sides are placing high levels of trust in the market to deliver rights – despite the global economic crisis exposing the fallacy of such an approach.

In this chapter I will argue that these debates and disputes trap and distort thinking on poverty. They prevent action to protect and fulfil rights across all four dimensions of the problem: deprivation, exclusion, insecurity and voicelessness. These can only be effectively tackled by assuring the full spectrum of rights.

I will also discuss the journey that Amnesty International has made to bridge the divide in human rights. For many years, the organization worked to protect a limited range of civil and political rights. My first undertaking as Secretary General of Amnesty International was to attend the organization's biennial international conference in August 2001, which took place in Dakar, Senegal. Hundreds of delegates from more than 70 countries debated and agreed a proposal to expand the organization's mission to include the defence of economic, social and cultural rights as well as civil and political rights.

THE POLITICS TRAP

Dom Hélder Câmara, then Archbishop of Olinda and Recife in Brazil, said of the military dictatorship governing his country: "When I feed the poor they call me a saint; when I ask why the poor have no food they call me a communist."

Much of the resistance to taking a holistic approach is grounded in the idea that rights are too "political". Many global discussions on poverty are led by economists or by organizations with a development mandate. It is natural that they should focus on material assets and conditions that impact on economic opportunities and aim to take practical steps to improve insufficient sanitation, lack of education, poor health or weak job prospects. While many of those working in the field of development are aware of the politics of poverty, they may find it controversial or difficult to address the underlying factors. Frankly, it is easier to engage in debate about how to provide the poor with the things they lack than to ask why such deprivation persists. Such an interrogation may inevitably lead to clashes with those in power, with whom one must co-operate in order to pursue development work.

The political obstacles to confronting the issues of powerlessness are very real. Until the late 1990s, for example, the World Bank insisted that human rights issues lay outside its mandate, as the Bank's articles of incorporation restricted it to "economic considerations". It took this constraint to mean that it could not interfere in internal politics. Throughout the period of structural adjustment policies, the Bank maintained the fiction that the conditionality it imposed on its loans was apolitical. In some cases it set conditions requiring governments that access bank finance to adopt specific macro-economic reforms. Is this not political? And is demanding an end to discrimination against women political? The Bank's work has expanded today to include significant efforts to fight corruption and make governments more transparent and attentive to inequalities. However, the legacy of its structural adjustment policies are still being felt in many countries – even more acutely in the current economic downturn. Furthermore, the Bank remains ambivalent on rights. It raises such issues in its research and publications but still fails to insist that human rights be included in the poverty reduction strategies at country level.

The question of what is political is largely one of perception. Just as the World Bank saw rights to free expression or minority protections as "political", some human rights advocates also felt that defending economic and social rights would lead them into "political" disputes, which would compromise their impartiality. Many of Amnesty International's own members argued in the past, for example, that defending economic and social rights would "politicize" its work by requiring the organization to delve into domestic debates on the allocation of public funds and the political orientation of economic policy. I recall meeting a group of Amnesty International activists in 2001, shortly before the organization decided to change its mandate. The activists were very positively disposed to overseas development assistance but concerned about the organization working on economic, social and cultural rights. "Amnesty International will appear political if it campaigns for the right to health-care and housing," they told me. Yet, for decades the organization had demanded the release of political dissidents, which is of course perceived as a political act by some but that did not deter Amnesty International!

The UK-based international affairs magazine *The Economist* took a similar line when it published a cover page editorial on the eve of Amnesty International's conference in August 2001, saying that the organization should reject the proposal to expand its mandate, as that would move it from the realm of law to the realm of politics. Amnesty International, it said, should stick to defending rights to free expression and fair trials, and documenting torture and political killings.

Of course, the advocacy of human rights – all human rights – is to some extent "political". As someone who worked in the field of refugee protection for 21 years, I know how politically sensitive it is to demand the release of asylum seekers from detention, even though it is a purely humanitarian act. Rights are claims on power, and challenging the exercise of power is seen by those in power as having a political dimension. Politics concerns making choices about the direction of government policy – choices that must be made to give effect to rights. But there is nothing inherent in the character of certain rights which makes them more or less political than others.

All rights have a firm basis in international law, and governments have committed themselves in one way or another to respect these rights. To demand that governments live up to their self-assumed obligations to respect all human rights – economic, social and cultural as well as political and civil – can be credibly defended as action driven by law, not politics. To argue otherwise is to be trapped in the ideological perceptions that hark back to the Cold War.

THE PHILOSOPHICAL TRAP

The attack on economic, social and cultural rights is deeply rooted in ideology that goes back to the Cold War and denies the validity of including health, education or shelter as "rights". This was also the position *The Economist* took in urging Amnesty International to reject expanding its work to include the defence of economic, social and cultural rights. More than 50 years after the UDHR had endorsed these rights, *The Economist* argued in 2001 and again in another article in 2007 that, unlike freedom from torture, rights to shelter and food are contested, and have not "attained the status of moral absolutes..."

> *Governments may intentionally torture their citizens; they do not usually intentionally inflict on them poverty and ill health. The moral imperative to stop poverty or disease is therefore not as convincing as the moral imperative to stop torture.*[1]

In other words, only civil and political rights count as true rights. Various reasons are given for this argument. It is said that economic, social and cultural rights do not place clear duties on identifiable authorities. The connection between the state as the perpetrator and the harm that occurs – ill-health, unemployment, homelessness or illiteracy – is not close enough to create as clear an obligation as is the case, for instance, with arbitrary detention, torture or unfair trial.

Then there is the resource argument. When a state cannot afford to build the medical services that might reduce maternal mortality, how can it be held responsible for not fulfilling a woman's "right" to health? Education and health cost money, and therefore, the argument goes, it is not feasible to expect developing countries to deliver such rights. Again, to quote *The Economist*: "To guarantee civil and political rights is relatively cheap, whereas to guarantee economic and social rights is potentially enormously costly."

The Economist is not alone in its scepticism. There are others – governments as well as legal scholars – who argue that economic, social and cultural rights cannot be regarded as creating the same obligations on governments as civil and political rights.[2] They claim that economic and social rights cannot be enforced through the courts because they lack sufficient specificity, and/or doing so would interfere with judgements best left to the political process. Health, education and housing require choices to be made – about the collection and allocation of public funds, about how far to encourage and allow for private provision, about which policies will be most effective and about which groups to prioritize. Making such choices is the proper job of governments, not the courts.

Therefore, according to these critics, rights to vote, to free speech and to assemble, to privacy and property, to due process and equality before the law should be protected. But when it comes to food, housing, health-care and education, these should be seen more as aspirations.

None of these arguments stands up to serious scrutiny. Just as government policy – and choices – can perpetuate torture, they can also perpetuate poverty. In the former case, a failure to investigate and punish torture prolongs the practice; in the latter case, a failure to end forced evictions condemns individuals like Srey Mom to destitution. Is one morally more repugnant than the other? *The Economist*'s argument would require us to accept the logic that the failure to act is not a choice made by governments. Not addressing the need for adequate shelter or primary education – even within the limited budget of a less developed country – is just as much a choice as ordering the detention of political opponents. Both action and inaction result from an exercise of state power.

Identifying clear and enforceable duties that would give effect to economic and social rights may indeed pose specific challenges. But in countries like India and South Africa, where such rights have been adjudicated and enforced, courts and public authorities seem quite capable of overcoming such challenges.

On the point about governments having to make political choices, most rights require trade-offs against other, often legitimate, goals of public policy. Rights to due process may place constraints on the timeliness of criminal justice. Tolerating dissident views and public protests may slow up a government's response to an economic or political crisis. The fact that the state may have to make hard choices in order to deliver economic, social and cultural rights – for instance by spending funds on health rather than on national defence – does not make the obligations any less valid.

As regards cost, most human rights require resources. Maintaining a fair and effective judicial system requires significant public investment. Without it many civil and political rights would be impossible to fulfil. Cost should not be a determinant of human rights.

It is often asserted that economic, social and cultural rights place positive obligations on states to fulfil them, to build schools, immunize children, ensure public housing for the poorest people, whereas civil and political rights place negative obligations on states – to refrain from interfering with free speech, not to violate the right to life by executing people, and so on. In fact, this is not true. Both sets of rights create negative and positive obligations. Building an effective court system to ensure fair trials is as positive an obligation as building schools to fulfil the right to universal primary education.

Some of the scepticism about economic, social and cultural rights arises from the recognition in international law that, in some circumstances and for some economic and social rights, the state can meet its obligations through "progressive realization", in other words, gradually, over a period of time.[3] To some, this is seen as a denial of the rights, but, in reality, it is merely an acknowledgement that the capacity of the state to deliver on these rights is an element to be taken into account when judging whether it has complied with its obligations. The obligation remains, at all times, to make progress, and there is no support whatsoever for the notion of postponement pending the realization of any other rights. In fact, international law also specifically acknowledges the need for international co-operation and assistance to deliver economic, social and cultural rights. In my view, this reinforces, rather than weakens, the international recognition of these rights.

THE MARKET TRAP

Increasingly the debate about the lesser nature of economic, social and cultural rights is being overshadowed by what I call the "market trap". This is the growing trend to set aside a state's obligation to fulfil all human rights – of whichever category – in the expectation that the market will lift people out of poverty. Health, education and housing are not seen as rights but as needs that will be met through economic growth alone and not through public policy. As for civil liberties, either they are not recognized as being relevant or it is assumed that a free economy will eventually and automatically lead to an open society. In Chapter 2, I spoke about the "bread before ballots" approach of some countries; here I note the increasing tendency to expect both "bread" and "ballot" to be delivered by market forces.

Following the end of the Cold War and the collapse of communism, all governments, no matter of what ideological stripe, have been united in their commitment to the free market. Market economies today are pursued not only by liberal democracies like the United States, the European Union and India, but also by authoritarian states like Saudi Arabia and nominally "communist" states like China. Bowing to the free market's potential to deliver economic growth, the state – whether democratic, autocratic, socialist or communist – has retreated, weakening or even destroying social safety nets, and abrogating on its human rights obligations.

The issue is not whether growth has led to improved living standards. Undeniably, living standards have improved in many countries for many people. Undeniably, too, they are stagnant in others, and desperate poverty remains all too common in many countries. The causality between growth and the eradication of poverty is not clear-cut. But that is only part of the problem. The other difficulty with the "market trap" is that it misses the point that eradicating poverty is not only about raising living standards through higher levels of income. It is, as I argue throughout this book, equally concerned with overcoming exclusion, ending insecurity and giving a voice to the powerless – in other words, with respecting human rights. To see housing, health, employment and education as rights, rather than simply the fulfilment of basic needs, is to recognize an empowering process that restores dignity to people living in poverty and to acknowledge the inherent indivisibility of rights.

The "market trap" also leads many analysts either to ignore civil and political rights as irrelevant, or to assume that these rights will follow once a country has progressed in economic development via a burgeoning market. In the past, the strong correlation between literacy, per capita income and democracy led some scholars to argue that wealth and income enable democracy, and therefore must be pursued prior to attempting to put democratic institutions in place.[4] However, there is no evidence to suggest that authoritarian governments which free up markets and perform well economically are then more likely to democratize and uphold civil and political rights. A recent and authoritative assessment of the data suggests that transitions to democracy are undertaken randomly, and that to the extent that there is a correlation between democracy and levels of wealth, this is not due to the need for particular thresholds to be met, but rather relates to the higher survival rate of democracies above a certain income.[5]

Nor do open markets automatically lead to open societies. Indeed, if income thresholds were sufficient for democratization to occur, we would have seen a wave of open societies emerging across energy-exporting countries in recent years, where average income has risen dramatically. Unfortunately, if anything, countries like Russia, Kazakstan, Azerbaijan, Turkmenistan, Equatorial Guinea and Saudi Arabia are proving to be as autocratic as ever. Furthermore, they are not always, or even usually, investing that wealth wisely to end income poverty – a point which I will address in Chapter 8. Their average incomes conceal extreme lows as well as extreme highs.

At the other end of the spectrum, countries which concentrate primarily on consolidating democracy and entrenching civil and political rights do not necessarily improve the living standards of their poorest citizens. As we saw in Chapter 3, examples abound of impoverished minorities in rich western countries. Detailed analysis of the situation of specific groups, as well as an explicit commitment to eradicating poverty, are necessary to ensure respect for the rights of all to health, education and housing.

As this book goes to press, global economic recession is dominating the news. While the depth and impact of the recession are as yet unknown, one response is already clear: there is a swing in favour of stronger state intervention and regulation. For the past two decades the state has been retreating or reneging on its responsibilities in favour of the market. But now governments are radically changing their position and are talking about new global financial architecture and an international governance system in which the state must play a stronger role. Such talk must not be limited only to the economic and financial architecture. There is also an opportunity now to halt the retreat of the state from the social sphere and redesign a more human-rights-friendly model of government than that which has characterized international policy-making for the past 20 years. The economic situation also creates the possibility of radically rethinking the role of international financial institutions in terms of respecting, protecting and fulfilling human rights, including economic and social rights. The exclusion and marginalization of people living in poverty, the threats of violence they face, their lack of political voice, cannot be left to the vagaries of the market to resolve.

THE SEQUENCING TRAP

Neither the political, moral or economic arguments for privileging one or other set of rights are valid. Why, then, does it continue to be so difficult to act on all rights in order to end poverty?

Some governments and commentators resist a holistic approach on practical grounds; they say that we need to deal first with certain rights in order to achieve concrete results. This is the sequencing trap – and it suffers from the fallacy that we can approach complex human rights problems in a piecemeal fashion. Unfortunately, the UN's policies and strategies lend implicit support to those who would pick and choose which rights to prioritize.

One camp of sequencers argues that once a country has reached a certain stage of economic development, democracy – or respect for civil and political freedoms – will follow. According to this view, the state should concentrate on economic growth and invest first in health, education and housing. From the other side, it is argued that primacy must be given to civil and political rights. The state should first ensure the rule of law, protection for basic freedoms and respect for democratic principles. Once that is achieved, an active and engaged citizenry can debate on equal terms the development options and inevitable trade-offs that the state will need to make as it determines the best allocation of economic resources.

The very existence of such diametrically opposed positions, both able to cite the experience of various countries in support of their case, should lead us to doubt the validity of either position. In any event, the empirical case for either side is weak. As pointed out in Chapter 2, for every China and South Korea that has succeeded in reducing poverty, there are many more autocratic regimes that have not. The idea that democracy and respect for human rights inevitably follow once a country has reached a certain stage of development is not supported by recent history. Neither does democracy alone end poverty, as is evident from India, the world's largest democracy.

There is no basis in the nature of the rights themselves for justifying the prioritization of either set of rights. It is an accident of history that they were ever separated, and self-interest that reinforced the fissure. Neither set of rights privileges particular models of economic policy. Provided minimum standards of health, education and social assistance are met, it is left to states to determine what combination of state and private action is best. But this is lost in the politics, ideology or blind loyalty to market economics.

Often, support for prioritization is simply pragmatic – grounded in the straightforward idea that you have to begin somewhere, or that "You can't do everything at once." People may accept that, while a full answer to poverty requires a holistic response, a state may just choose to tackle specific aspects first. Or they may see their specific contribution to solving one problem as intrinsically useful, and leave it to others to tackle other dimensions.

Such pragmatic prioritization may be understandable at an individual level, but it ought not to be the foundation for global anti-poverty policy. And yet the international community's largest and most significant, concerted effort to tackle poverty to date – the UN's MDGs – falls straight into the pragmatic sequencing trap.

The MDGs have been criticized for only going half-way – for example, to halve poverty and hunger by 2015. The real problem, however, is that, even in relation to half-goals, they only require half-measures. In doing so, they fail to address many of the factors that keep people poor.

Originally designed as a way to focus attention and highlight immediate and pressing priorities, the MDGs are increasingly being promoted as the solution to global poverty. The UNDP website says that the MDGs "respond to the world's main development challenges". The World Bank says the goals "guide the efforts of virtually all organizations working in development and have been commonly accepted as a framework for measuring development progress". UNICEF describes the targets as addressing "the most critical areas of human development".

The Millennium Declaration, from which the goals were drawn, in fact committed governments to the protection of all human rights. Indeed, in a dedicated section on human rights, UN member states committed themselves:

> *...To spare no effort to promote democracy and strengthen the rule of law...; to respect fully and uphold the Universal Declaration of Human Rights...; to implement the principles and practices of democracy and respect for human rights, including minority rights; to combat all forms of violence against women and to implement the Convention on the Elimination of All Forms of Discrimination against Women...; to work collectively for more inclusive political processes, allowing genuine participation by all citizens in all our countries; to ensure the freedom of the media to perform their essential role and the right of the public to have access to information.*[6]

Unlike the specific MDGs however, with their 20 targets and dozens of indicators to measure progress, there has been no further elaboration of these human rights provisions of the Millennium Declaration.

Here, starkly demonstrated, is the gap between acknowledgement and action with regard to human rights. The UN and all its member states are prepared to declare that progress in the fight to end poverty requires attention to a broader notion of human development, one that pays due regard to all human rights. But when concrete targets and indicators are agreed to measure that progress, there is no commitment to genuine participation, the rule of law, inclusive political processes, respect for minority rights, ending violence against women, and rights to information and free media. Yet, all of these are laid out in the Millennium Declaration.

Some might argue that goals such as the rule of law and minority rights cannot be translated into specific and measurable targets, with indicators to monitor progress. This is clearly nonsense. Such goals can be broken down into specific targets and indicators identified just as easily as those on environmental sustainability or the reduction of child mortality. The rule of law, for instance, might include targets to extend the provision of paralegal services, to enact laws guaranteeing the independence of the judiciary and to ensure that people are granted legal identity so that, for example, unlike Srey Mom's son, they can attend school. Protection of minority rights might translate into targets to improve access to education, to reduce the proportion of people in marginalized groups who live in poverty, and to abolish discriminatory laws.

Others might argue that because the human rights commitments governments make to freedom and non-discrimination are monitored separately, through the Geneva-based UN Human Rights Council, it would be unnecessary duplication to include these in the UN's anti-poverty programme. True, there are UN procedures and mechanisms in place to monitor the extent to which governments live up to the human rights commitments they make as members of the UN and through signing international treaties. But these procedures are often heavily politicized, and censure or approval is based on states' ability to win backing from their allies. Some procedures do operate independently from government influence, such as the treaty monitoring bodies and independent experts but, while they have often drawn attention to the failings of governments, their findings have little impact. Indeed, many states do not even meet their most basic treaty obligations to report periodically on their progress in implementing human rights treaties, or they submit reports years after the deadline for doing so.

We should welcome the global and shared commitment to end poverty that the MDGs represent. Setting goals implies making choices, and some desirable goals will be excluded, if only to ensure that the list is workable. But we should be clear about the politics underlying the choices. I have no doubt that the degree of unanimity achieved on the MDGs arises at least in part from what they exclude: guarantees against discrimination, rights to active participation of poor people, protection for minorities. Yet, these are essential for the fight against poverty; all are crucial for empowering communities to shape their own futures, and all are included in the Millennium Declaration. But none of them are subject to any concrete targets in the MDGs themselves. Future revisions to the MDGs should include specific goals that commit governments to protecting and fulfilling those rights that are essential to ending poverty.

The MDGs are a useful but partial response. They need fixing. Many will say, however, "These are worthwhile goals. Why make it all more complex?" There are two answers. The first is that, through their disjointed way of tackling the issues, the UN is sustaining the illusion that a piecemeal approach to human rights will address poverty. Human rights guarantees are fundamental to the fight against poverty. To exclude them from the major and high-level monitoring that accompanies the MDGs is to ensure that they continue to be marginalized and to perpetuate the idea that they can be postponed in the fight to end global poverty.

Secondly, and more fundamentally, reducing the MDGs to a largely technical process of counting drugs and mosquito nets, and assessing household surveys to determine income levels risks disempowering the poor – the very people who need to be most engaged if poverty is to be eradicated. Translating MDGs into the language of human rights, imbuing them with the spirit of human rights – and identifying targets and key indicators to concretize the achievement of those rights and make it possible to monitor them – would be an investment in empowerment and give an enormous boost to the profile and relevance of the MDGs in poor communities.

There is no linear solution to confront the vicious cycle of deprivation, insecurity, exclusion and voicelessness. They feed off each other. Srey Mom was evicted because she wields no power and has no voice; in turn, this is because she is poor. She is a "squatter" only because her poverty gives her no other choice and no possibility of "legal" residence. The MDGs will do little to address her plight if they do nothing to empower her.

ESCAPE FROM THE TRAP

The good news is that the traps which hold us back from pursuing human rights holistically can be overcome. I believe Amnesty International's journey, from defending a limited range of civil and political rights to working to protect all rights, is instructive.

Amnesty International was born in 1961, at the height of the Cold War. While supporting all the rights in the UDHR, it chose to concentrate on rights to free expression, fair trial and freedom from torture and other forms of ill-treatment, and the abolition of the death penalty. These rights were easily understood among the organization's membership, which was then located in Western Europe and North America. Provided Amnesty International defended these rights on both sides of the Iron Curtain, its members felt it could protect its independence from Cold War rivalries and not be accused of politicization. For some years, this approach worked: prisoners of conscience were released, the incidence of torture by state agents declined in many countries, formal and legal guarantees of due process and free speech were strengthened, and capital punishment was abolished in many states. At that time, many in Amnesty International felt that, for the sake of efficiency and effectiveness, they needed to focus on a limited range of rights. But in doing so, the organization inadvertently reinforced the ideological divide in human rights. According to some activists outside Amnesty International, particularly in the global South, the slanting of the organization's work in favour of civil and political rights fed the perception that economic and social rights were of lesser importance.

At the practical level, problems very soon started to become evident in terms of effectiveness and relevance. As tyrants fell from power and police states gave way to fragile democracies, Amnesty International found itself fighting to defend the same rights under new governments. Any drop in the practice of torture against political detainees seemed to be offset by widespread police brutality against poor people and marginalized communities. Instead of imprisonment, those suspected of disloyalty or opposition to the regime "disappeared" or were killed, and the perpetrators were difficult to identify. People living in poverty – Indigenous Peoples, landless peasants, religious and ethnic minorities, and those who sought to defend them, including trade unionists and community organizers – featured prominently in the lists of the missing and the dead. Massive human rights violations led to mass exodus, but the countries they fled to restricted the rights of refugees and asylum seekers. The issue was not only that it was wrong to return people to places where they risked torture or other ill-treatment, but that those people needed access to education, employment, housing and health-care in the countries where they sought asylum. Yet in all these cases, Amnesty International could only look at their suffering through a narrow prism of selected rights.

Above all else, when Amnesty International turned its attention to violence that was not perpetrated by the state, but which the state condoned or did too little to prevent, it was confronted with the truly horrifying reality of violence against women and the severe socio-economic discrimination as well as political disempowerment that these women faced. Working with partner and grassroots organizations, it learned that women living in poverty are at particular risk of violence, and that the state is least likely to intervene and offer them protection in this situation.

In country after country Amnesty International researchers found that they were isolating parts of the human rights problem. In Guatemala they campaigned for and gained the release of Indigenous leaders who protested against the dispossession of their land, but could not criticize the unlawful action of the state that had led to the protest in the first place. In Brazil they complained about police brutality against people living in slums, but were unable to condemn the conditions in those slums. In Saudi Arabia they condemned torture and ill-treatment of prisoners, but failed to highlight the exploitation of migrant workers.

Amnesty International was challenged, too, by the fact that, in too many cases, its traditional approach appeared to privilege elites within the countries where it was working. They would demand free speech on behalf of journalists and dissidents but not the right to education of poor children. They would observe high-profile political trials but fail to address impunity for violence against women. Amnesty International's approach meant that, even when it could make traditional appeals – for free expression, or against arbitrary arrest –

on behalf of poor and marginalized people, it did so knowing that it was ignoring other, equally important issues affecting the same people. It seemed increasingly problematic, for example, to protest against police violence when people who lived in slums were evicted, without asserting international standards that prohibit arbitrary evictions.

Throughout the 1990s Amnesty International debated the pros and cons of expanding its work, particularly as accelerating economic globalization forced attention to gross inequalities in standards of living worldwide. Ideological as well as practical aspects were thrashed out in heated debates within the organization. In addition to worries about politicization, some members felt that tackling economic and social rights would move the organization beyond its level of expertise and dilute the focus of its work, spreading limited resources over too wide a field. Others, including new members and partners from the global South, argued persuasively that if Amnesty International ignored the most pressing human rights problems of the day in the economic and social arena, it would lose impact and become irrelevant. Eventually, in August 2001, the membership voted to adopt a new mission, which included all the rights in the UDHR.

The organization's work with the Guarani-Kaiowá peoples in Brazil shows how we are now able to take a more holistic approach to human rights and so are better able to address the full dimension of poverty. The Guarani-Kaiowá peoples are struggling for recognition of their land rights, which are guaranteed under the Brazilian constitution. In 2003, Marcos Verón, the 72-year-old leader of the Guarani-Kaiowá peoples, led a small group to peacefully reoccupy a small area of claimed Indigenous territory in Mato Grosso do Sul. He was severely beaten by a group of men – thugs hired by local landowners – and died two days later.

Working with Survival International, an NGO that protects the rights of tribal and Indigenous Peoples, Amnesty International not only demanded that his killers be brought to justice, but also intervened to protest against the forced eviction of Verón's people from their lands. When state authorities suspended food aid to the group in an attempt to force them out, which led to child malnutrition, Amnesty International protested too, arguing that this was a blatant and unlawful attempt to use hunger as a political weapon, which violated their right to food. Local people believe our campaign worked: the food aid was resumed and evictions stopped. In one case, Amnesty International and its local partners forced the suspension of eviction orders affecting more than 1,000 people. These families are now permitted to live on the land where they had built homes, started schools, cultivated crops and reared animals.

THE FORGOTTEN PRISONER

If the rights of poor people are our starting point, then our lines of inquiry and advocacy ought to be driven by their needs and situation. The Guarani-Kaiowá peoples needed justice for their murdered leader; they also needed protection against unjust eviction, shelter, food and recognition of their land rights. All these rights are protected under international law. As in the case of Srey Mom, so too for the Guarani-Kaiowá peoples: deprivation, exclusion, insecurity and voicelessness require equal and simultaneous attention.

Dividing and diminishing rights according to which category they can be put in is a political game that serves no useful purpose in fighting poverty. Neither a piecemeal nor a sequencing approach to rights is likely to work. Nor can we rely on the market to promote human rights.

Today, eight years after that international meeting in Dakar, I am still challenged by the occasional journalist or Amnesty International member who feels our effectiveness is being diluted by working on all rights. My response is that the people for whom we campaign see no hierarchy in human rights, no separate categories of injustice. I tell them about Magdalena Duran, an Indigenous woman who is a street vendor in Mexico, and her husband who is a shoe-shiner. Magdalena was arrested in 2006 because she protested against laws that banned street trading. Amnesty International adopted her as a prisoner of conscience. I tried to visit her in prison in August 2007 but could not get permission. She became the focus of a worldwide campaign by the organization's members and was released in early 2008.

Amnesty International was founded in 1961 when a British lawyer, Peter Benenson, published an article in a London newspaper,

The Observer, entitled "The Forgotten Prisoners". He highlighted six cases of prisoners of conscience in western, socialist and less developed countries. They were all professional men – lawyers, academics, religious ministers, a doctor – and all but one were white. Forty-five years later, in 2007, Amnesty International was supporting a prisoner of conscience who was female, and an Indigenous Person and a street vendor. This, in microcosm, reflects the change that the human rights movement itself is undergoing to join the fight against poverty.

To insist on the rights of people living in poverty is to focus on those who have been excluded throughout history. They are the new forgotten prisoners.

SIX

NEEDLESS DEATHS – THE RIGHT TO SAFE MOTHERHOOD

AT THE AGE OF 16 I was sent to Ireland to continue my education. That same year one of my less affluent childhood playmates in Bangladesh, Asya, was married off by her parents to a man living in a remote village. A year later, I received a letter from my mother with the tragic news that my friend had died giving birth to her first child. Thirty-five years later, maternal mortality continues to be the leading cause of death for women of reproductive age in Bangladesh, as it is in most developing countries. Young mothers – aged 15-19 – are twice as likely to die as those in their 20s.

The magnitude of maternal mortality is horrifying. It has been described as "a global health emergency",[1] "a human rights calamity",[2] and "the biggest expression of brutality to women".[3] More than half a million women – to be accurate, many of them still girls – die every year due to complications related to pregnancy and childbirth; that's one woman dying somewhere in the world every minute. Millions more suffer from injuries, infections, diseases and disabilities that can cause lifelong suffering and debilitation. The effect on families and communities is devastating. Infants whose mothers die in the first six weeks of their life are between three and 10 times more likely to die themselves before reaching the age of two than children whose mothers survive.[4]

Women queuing outside a health centre in rural Huancavelica, Peru, September 2008. Maternal mortality rates in Peru are among the worst in South America. © Amnesty International

Maternal mortality figures are the strongest indicators of inequality between men and women and between rich and poor. Outside of war, there is no equivalent single cause of death or disability that affects only men on this scale. In every country of the world a poor woman faces a greater risk, on average, of dying in childbirth than a rich woman. More than 99 per cent of maternal deaths occur in developing countries.[5] Of the 10 countries with the highest ratios of maternal mortality, nine are in sub-Saharan Africa. The risk of maternal mortality over the course of a woman's lifetime in Sierra Leone is one in six. By comparison, in Sweden it is one in 17,400.

Maternal deaths are not inevitable. In most cases they could easily be prevented with the right medical care. Goal 5 of the UN MDGs seeks to improve maternal health by cutting maternal mortality by 75 per cent from 1990 levels by 2015. Very few countries are on track to reach that target. In fact, in almost two decades, the maternal mortality ratio has hardly budged.[6] In sub-Saharan Africa, where the problem is most acute, progress has been negligible.

There is so little sense of urgency to address this catastrophe that there are not even any truly reliable data on the extent of it. The statistics mentioned above are widely cited, but are also accepted by experts and policy-makers as no more than estimates. The problem is almost certainly worse than the data suggests. Some point to HIV/AIDS, insecurity, and the breakdown of health services in countries such as Zimbabwe as devastatingly exacerbating factors.

Why is there so little action in the face of such a wide-scale tragedy? Because maternal mortality is the ultimate illustration of the circle of human rights abuse – deprivation, exclusion, insecurity and powerlessness – which defines and perpetuates poverty. Poor women are deprived of their right to access basic health services. Funding maternal health services, particularly skilled birth attendants and emergency obstetric care, would go a long way to relieving the problem. But access to health-care is not the end of the story. Illegal botched abortions, sexual violence, child marriage, malnutrition, discrimination and isolation all significantly increase the risks of maternal mortality and disability.

Underlying the failure to tackle maternal mortality are deeper, more fundamental issues of the powerlessness of poor women. Who decides when a woman should marry? Who decides when she should conceive? Who decides whether she should use contraception, how many children she should have and how she should space their births? Who decides if and when she should seek medical assistance when she becomes pregnant? Assigned a low social and economic status, the woman who lives in poverty is rarely allowed to make these decisions herself. Enjoying no political power, it is also rare for her to have a say in decisions on how much the state should invest in maternal health-care services and how and where that care should be provided. Maternal mortality ratios are highest in countries and societies where women are denied the right to make those decisions.[7] In contrast, gender equality and empowerment lead women to demand – and obtain – family planning services, antenatal care and safe delivery.

The story of maternal mortality is a story of prejudice, discrimination, inertia and inaction, denying women their right to life, health and safe motherhood.

ROUTES BLOCKED TO BASIC CARE

Unsafe motherhood is a problem of deprivation: poor mothers are denied access to basic medical care that is their human right. Indeed, lack of access to medical care is a principal way in which women experience poverty, discrimination and exclusion in many societies. For pregnant women this can be fatal. They need trained birth attendants during delivery and, in the event of complications, access to well-equipped health centres and essential medicines. If caesarean sections need to be performed, for example, women need access to proper medical facilities where operations can be carried out. For serious complications at the birth, women need access to emergency obstetric care.

Weak and inadequate health systems are an important aspect of deprivation. But the cost of medical care is also a key factor in preventing women from getting the treatment they need. This is particularly so in societies where women are under-valued, since there is little inclination to spend large amounts on their medical care.

According to the WHO, 100 million people are pulled back into poverty each year through paying for health-care.[8] Fees for medical treatment ("user fees") and for transport to far-off clinics, to say nothing of loss of wages, can be prohibitive in many poor countries. In Nepal, the cost of a normal hospital delivery, including transport costs, is roughly one quarter of the country's average annual per capita income – far too much for many poor families to afford.[9] A complicated birth in Bangladesh that might require a caesarian section can cost anything from 90 to 140 per cent of the average annual income.[10] Time spent finding or borrowing the money to pay for health-care often delays the decision to seek medical help, with fatal consequences for many women.

Less developed countries face difficulties in providing this basic care, especially in inaccessible rural areas. The problem, however, is not only the availability of resources, but the political will to prioritize spending on maternal health and to provide it in a way that is accessible to the women who need it. Sri Lanka demonstrates that, where there is political will, such expenditure is not beyond the reach of developing countries. Over four decades Sri Lanka has cut its maternal mortality rates from 486 deaths per 100,000 live births to 24 deaths per 100,000 live births. Its lifetime risk of maternal death is significantly lower than those of Nepal, Bangladesh or Pakistan. Sri Lanka's success is attributed to a government commitment since the 1950s to provide health-care, including maternal health-care, through a widespread rural network that is open to all, targeted efforts to serve vulnerable groups, a commitment to providing information, and the professionalization and use of midwives, alongside broader social policies such as improving girls' education.[11] Its rates of contraceptive use are high, and its adolescent birth ratios low.

Greater investment in health-care is essential to achieving safe motherhood for all. Governments can and must provide better access to maternal health services for poor women and girls; doing so will certainly help to end many needless deaths in childbirth. But investment is unlikely to reach those who need it most without a conscious effort to target the most marginalized groups.

INVISIBLE AND EXCLUDED

The prevalence of maternal mortality is not evenly spread because access to medical services is skewed by a fatal intersection of inequalities: between rich and poor women, as I have already noted, but also between women living in cities and those in remote rural areas, and between women of different ethnicity, religion, caste, language, age and level of education.

One of the reasons that the MDG target to reduce maternal mortality will not be met is because the data fails to show who is being left out. It renders invisible those who require the most attention. There is only aggregate data – and no reporting to the UN on the extent to which the incidence of maternal mortality affects the poorest and most marginalized women. The global focus on improving health-care delivery to mothers in poor countries glosses over the obscene inequalities within countries and between groups of pregnant women.

Take the example of China. The Chinese government almost halved the number of maternal deaths between 1991 and 2004 (from 80 to 48.3 per 100,000 live births). Special maternal and infant health laws were passed, along with programmes to implement them. However, in a joint report with the UN in 2004, the government acknowledged that rates in remote rural areas were still between three and seven times higher than in urban areas, and that "marginalized and vulnerable population groups such as migrants and ethnic minorities" were not effectively covered by maternal and child health services.[12]

Statistics give a telling picture of the inequalities that persist within and between countries in the availability and access of maternal health-care to women. In a cross-regional study published by the WHO in 2006, the likelihood of a woman giving birth in the presence of a skilled professional – which is key to a safe and healthy delivery – was highly correlated with ethnicity, wealth, geography and maternal education. The study showed that in Kenya, for example, 71 per cent of births by Kikuyu women were supported by a skilled birth attendant, whereas only 27 per cent of pregnant women of the Mijikenda and Swahili ethnic groups received such care. In Ghana too, the dominant ethnic group is twice as likely to have had help from skilled birth attendants as the non-dominant groups. Turning from ethnic factors to income, we see the same discrepancies. In Nigeria, the country with the second highest number of maternal deaths per year in the world, 84 per cent of births among women of the top income quintile are likely to take place in the presence of a trained attendant. For the lowest quintile, the figure is 12 per cent. Wealthy women in India are four times more likely to have professionally attended births than their poor counterparts. In Bangladesh they are eight times more likely, and in Nepal, 11 times more likely. The urban-rural divide also affects maternal mortality in many countries where women in rural areas are isolated and ignored.[13] For instance, in Cambodia, Indigenous women in rural areas are at a disproportionately high risk of maternal death, and have reported discrimination from health-care staff when they have sought professional care.[14]

Well-off women are better able to access services in comparison with women living in poverty. In Nepal the lack of access to emergency obstetric care accounts for 75 per cent of all maternal deaths. A 2004 study measuring the use of emergency obstetric care – which makes the difference between life and death for many mothers – found that the principal users were high caste Brahmin/Chetri women. In one district, the rate of use was more than four times greater for high caste women than for all other women.[15] The Safe Motherhood project in Nepal has drafted a social inclusion strategy to lobby the government, and is working with marginalized women to raise awareness of their entitlements.[16]

Such disparities are not unique to developing countries but appear also in the developed world. African-American women in the USA are almost four times more likely to experience maternal mortality than white women.[17] Latina women have around a 65 per cent greater chance of dying in childbirth than white women.[18] In the middle income Latin American countries, maternal mortality is overall relatively low, but Indigenous women have a much higher maternal mortality ratio compared with the majority population.[19]

Discrimination in maternal mortality and provision of health-care can manifest itself in many different ways, and is not easily overcome without concrete and explicit measures. Bias can persist in the way health-care is provided or in how information is made available to pregnant women. Many women are shut out from health services simply because they are poor, illiterate, do not speak the language or are not given the information they need. Indigenous women in Peru have complained to Amnesty International that they are shunned by health workers for being poorly dressed or are accused of being dirty.[20] Cambodian Indigenous women who do not speak Khmer have reported that language barriers prevent them from obtaining maternal health-care.[21]

Tackling maternal mortality means tackling discrimination against women and their exclusion from decision-making. Equality and non-discrimination are fundamental principles of human rights. They demand action from those in power to prioritize those who are at the greatest risk. In Chapter 3, I mentioned the degree to which social attitudes feed discrimination against the poor. In the context of maternal health, the importance of taking a culturally sensitive approach to end exclusion cannot be over-emphasized.

To give an example, Peru has one of the highest rates of maternal and infant mortality in South America, especially among rural Indigenous women. In the village of San José de Secce and the communities of Oqopeqa, Punkumarqiri, Sañuq and Laupay, in the Ayacucho department of the Andes, an assessment carried out by a local NGO, Salud sin Límites Perú, found that women did not use the health facilities provided by the state. Their reluctance was partly because of the distance, cost and poor facilities, but also – and primarily – because the services did not match their cultural expectations. The population had no trust in the ability of the personnel or the services, and viewed attending the health facility as inconvenient and risky. The health services, on the other hand, were unresponsive to local cultural practices and sensitivities. In consultation with the communities, a culturally adapted project was put in place. Over a number of years communications were improved between health professionals and the community, with more user participation and a closer relationship between traditional midwives and health personnel. The environment of the delivery room, as well as care during delivery and the pre- and postnatal check ups were adapted to make them more sensitive to the local culture, such as women giving birth in upright positions or having their husbands hold them during delivery or returning the placenta to the family to bury. Health professionals were trained to be understanding of patients and to explain the procedures to users in their own language. An assessment of the project several years later showed a significant increase in deliveries at health centres, with a fall in mortality and morbidity rates.[22] This case study shows how exclusion can be overcome, and access to medical care improved when poor women are treated with respect and dignity.

INSECURITY AND VIOLENCE

A large tent made from blue plastic sheeting served as the main meeting place for the local NGO that provided support and counselling to rape survivors just outside Goma, in the eastern DRC. The facilities were very basic but every week hundreds of women turned up because that was the only place within reach where they could obtain medical help. The morning I visited the centre in 2003, there was a large crowd of women. Many of them had walked miles from remote rural areas. Some had babies in their arms or toddlers clutching their skirts; some of the mothers were themselves barely out of girlhood. They were survivors of a war in which rape and sexual mutilation has been widespread. They spoke to me of the unimaginable, but for them cruelly real, horrors of sexual violence, HIV and sexually transmitted disease. They spoke also of the complications of pregnancy and childbirth in a country that had virtually no health services at all. Over-stretched and over-worked NGOs, located in towns many miles away, were their only hope of medical help.[23]

Pregnancy is life-threatening for many poor women in times of peace; in times of war it can become a death sentence. Conflict significantly increases the rate of maternal mortality because of the collapse of health services on the one hand and the greater risk of sexual violence against women on the other. Even where health services exist, women may be unable to access them because of the prevailing insecurity. It is estimated that one third of all maternal deaths occur among the 14 per cent of the world's population who live in the most unstable and insecure countries.[24] There is a paradox though: where humanitarian relief operations in war are effective, maternal mortality rates may decline as emergency obstetric care is made available by NGOs, but they rise again when these programmes conclude.

It is not only in the midst of armed conflict that pregnant women confront life-threatening violence. All too often they are also at risk in the privacy of their homes. In one study in rural Gujarat, India, it was shown that intimate partner violence is the second highest cause of maternal mortality, accounting for 15.7 per cent of all maternal deaths. According to recent studies across the developing world, women who are the victims of family violence are systematically less likely to receive antenatal, delivery, and postnatal care. Women who are victims of intimate partner violence during pregnancies face grave physical and emotional consequences. One study in Uganda showed they are 37 per cent more likely to experience antenatal complications requiring hospitalization before delivery. They are also more likely to give birth to babies of low birth-weight, who have a higher risk of infant mortality.[25]

Gender-based violence contributes to unplanned pregnancies, abortions and the spread of sexually transmitted infections, including HIV and syphilis, which lead to a higher risk of neonatal and maternal deaths. Studies from Rwanda, Tanzania and South Africa indicate a threefold increase in the risk of HIV among women who have experienced violence compared with those who have not. In turn, in some populations, women living with HIV have been found to be around four times more likely to die in pregnancy or childbirth than a woman without HIV.[26] Reducing violence against women is not only important in itself, it would also help to reduce maternal mortality.

Female genital mutilation (FGM) is a specific form of violence against women and girls, and has potentially life-threatening health effects, including an increased risk of maternal mortality and injury in childbirth in certain cases. It is estimated that 135 million women and girls worldwide have had their genitals mutilated, although the practice is particularly concentrated in Africa.[27] Recent research shows that FGM increases the likelihood of haemorrhage and of obstructed labour requiring complicated emergency measures (such as caesarian section) that are less widely available than more routine procedures, particularly for poor communities.[28] A WHO study shows that

mortality rates among babies born to women who have undergone FGM are between 15 and 55 per cent higher than average.[29]

Violence against women is a stark reminder of the unequal power relations between men and women. In Chapter 4, I discussed how violence disproportionately affects poor women and keeps them poor. The impact of such violence on pregnant women is not just a specific example of this more general relationship. It is the most distressing illustration of inequality, which leaves the poorest women exposed to the most egregious forms of violence when they are most physically vulnerable.

Safe motherhood is about ensuring access to medical care. But it is also about ensuring that women are free from violence that forces them into pregnancy, endangers their health and physical integrity, or prevents them from accessing medical care when they are pregnant.

WOMEN'S VOICES AND CHOICES

Voices of poor women are rarely heard. When it comes to reproductive health, custom, culture and religion combine with poverty to silence women and deprive them of control over their bodies. Poor women are all too often denied control over their lives by their low status, even to the extent that they are the last in line for food in their own homes. How can they negotiate safe sex if they fear violence or are economically dependent on the man? How can they decide on the number and spacing of their children when they do not know what right they have to make that choice, or have no means to act on it? How can they speak up when law, culture, custom and religious practice subjugate them? If their voice is silenced at home, what chance do they have of making themselves heard in the public sphere? One study identified the lack of access to the political process on the part of those most directly affected by this issue – poor women with little education, who face significant gender discrimination in many poor countries – as a key factor in why the global initiative on maternal mortality has failed to achieve the kind of priority that other health initiatives such as HIV/AIDS have received.[30]

Previous pages: **Rehemi, 18, is waiting for an operation for the internal injuries she suffered when she was gang-raped by a group of seven rebels. North Kivu, Goma, Democratic Republic of the Congo.**
© Robin Hammond/Panos

Nowhere is poor women's powerlessness starker than in the area of reproductive and sexual health. Women have the right to information on sexual and reproductive health and the right to use contraception.[31] According to the UN Population Fund (UNFPA), access to reproductive health and family planning services for all could help avoid 35 per cent of maternal deaths, including from unsafe abortions. Yet, the UN agency says that 200 million women do not use effective contraception. According to the World Bank, across the world 137 million women have an unmet need for contraception. The UN admits that the MDG target of universal access to reproductive health remains "a distant dream".[32]

The battle for control over women's sexual choices is most devastatingly played out by state and society in the context of abortion. Unsafe abortion causes tens of thousands of deaths each year, and hundreds of thousands more women suffer serious health complications. It is often a direct result of women not knowing, or not being able to exercise, their right to reproductive health and family planning services. Many women who are driven to seek unsafe or unlawful abortions are married, poor and feel unable to provide for yet another child.[31] Most unsafe abortions occur in developing countries where the law prohibits it or, even if lawful, the facilities are not available or affordable for poor women, or social, cultural and religious taboos restrict women from accessing such services. Sixty-nine countries prohibit abortion in most cases, but Nicaragua, Chile and El Salvador forbid it under any circumstances, even after rape or when the mother's life is at risk. Such draconian laws – although mercifully rare, as 98 per cent of countries do allow for therapeutic abortion – mean poor women who resort to unsafe abortions at the hands of unqualified practitioners are refused medical help from state institutions if there are subsequent complications. Many die or suffer permanent damage to their fertility and other health as a result of lack of medical care. In Nicaragua the law goes further and prohibits medical service providers from treating a pregnant woman for an unrelated illness or injury if the treatment poses any risk of a miscarriage. Deliberately depriving women of medical treatment in this way amounts to torture – physical and psychological. The UN Committee against Torture concluded in

Malalai Kakar (left), head of Kabul's department for crimes against women, gathering evidence from victims of domestic abuse who would not have been able to report the crime to male officers. In September 2008, Malalai was assassinated by the Taliban. Kandahar Afghanistan.
© Ash Sweeting/Panos

May 2009 that the Nicaraguan State needed to reviseits laws on abortion if it didn't want to be in breach of its international legal obligations to protect human rights.[33]

Decriminalization and access to safe, legal abortion can reduce maternal mortality. In South Africa, for example, deaths from abortion complications decreased by 90 per cent between 1994 (when it was legalized) and 2000.[34] Another important way to reduce recourse to unsafe abortion is to expand and improve family planning services for all.

I began this chapter with the tragic story of Asya, who was forced into marriage at the age of 16. Under-age arranged marriages are yet another example of the way in which women are denied a voice in the fundamental decisions about their own lives. Births and marriages are not registered in many countries, so it is difficult to know exactly how many under-age marriages occur. But the practice is widespread in sub-

Saharan Africa and South Asia. In my own country, Bangladesh, more than half the girls between the ages of 15 and 19 are married, and the overwhelming majority of these marriages are arranged by their families. More than 57 per cent of them are mothers before they are 19 years old.[35] Child marriage exposes adolescent girls to many health risks. According to a recent report, "...the problem with children delivering children is that the young mothers are at a significantly higher risk than older women for debilitating illness and even death."[36] Yet, according to the UN, adolescent married women who ask for contraception are less likely to receive it than their older counterparts.[37]

Underage marriages are an abuse of a child's rights. It is no coincidence that underage marriages are most prevalent in the poorest countries – where maternal mortality ratios are highest. Culture and tradition, including religious and social taboos against premarital sex, along with poverty, lead many parents to marry off their young daughters, often to much older men. They may feel that it is their only option when they cannot feed their child or send her to school, or they may be tempted by a bride price that could rid them of other financial obligations. Many countries have enacted laws on the minimum age of marriage, but such laws are notoriously ignored. Social awareness and public education, alongside legislation, produce better results. But the real answer to breaking the practice of early marriage and teenage pregnancy is recognizing and providing for the equal rights of all girls to education and livelihood.[38] Teenage pregnancy is by no means limited to poor countries. But child marriage puts young girls at risk, and wherever it happens, experience shows that empowerment of women and girls is a key factor in reducing it.

Participation of poor people is well recognized as a critical factor in poverty-reduction programmes. Yet poor women of all ages are routinely excluded from information and decisions that affect their own health. In one study carried out in the Herat province of Afghanistan, which has one of the highest maternal mortality ratios in the world, 87 per cent of women reported having to get permission from their husbands or male relatives to access health-care.[39] In India, almost half of all women are not involved in decisions about their own health, including decisions relating to pregnancy and childbirth.[40] This often denies or delays treatment, increasing the risk of maternal death.

Breaking the barriers to increase participation of women may require dealing with cultural sensitivities, and understanding the social and cultural norms that hold women back. Here is an example of how culturally sensitive approaches have helped women in my country.

Visiting a maternal health class organized by the NGO BRAC in a village in Tangail in Bangladesh, I saw older women, clearly beyond childbearing age, alongside pregnant mothers. These older women were the mothers-in-law, and were part of the programme because they needed to be persuaded that their daughters-in-law required care during pregnancy – day-time rest, adequate food, lighter work – and also at childbirth. In Bangladesh much ill-treatment and discrimination against young married women happens in the home in extended family situations, often instigated by the husband's relations. The mother-in-law plays a critical role in the household and may assert her authority and subjugate the younger woman. In a society where women traditionally eat after everyone else, malnutrition is high among young pregnant women. In an effort to ameliorate this tradition, another Bangladeshi NGO, Gonoshasthaya Kendra, organizes *Bou-Shashuri* (daughter-in-law, mother-in-law) meetings, at which mothers-in-law are urged to ensure that pregnant women eat first with the children, rather than last, as is traditional for village women.

Access to information is key in breaking down the barriers of exclusion and overcoming discrimination. Very often women are deprived of or denied information, sometimes because of administrative oversight or lack of resources, but most often because of legal, social and cultural barriers that exclude women from decision-making, including those issues that most intimately affect their lives. If poor women are to use health services effectively, including contraception and family planning services, and understand their rights, then they must have information that is easily understood and freely disseminated, translated into minority languages or available in non-written formats – such as posters in community spaces, public service radio broadcasts and so on. Much, much more needs to be done to empower women – and information is a critical step in that process.

Poor and marginalized women should not be treated just as passive recipients of decisions made by others, but as empowered citizens. That will require a change in the mindset of policy-makers as well as health professionals, and greater co-operation across the disciplines of health and human rights. It will mean a greater effort to engage poor women, build their capacity to participate, and communicate with them in a language they understand. It will mean listening to their concerns and translating them into action. But above all, it will mean challenging the cultural and political norms and legal frameworks that discriminate against poor women, attack their physical integrity and limit their ability to make informed choices and decisions.

THE RIGHT TO SAFE MOTHERHOOD

There is a clear human rights case for safe motherhood. The right to health is well established in international law. Neglect, denial, discrimination and violence that take place before, during and after pregnancy are human rights abuses. An overwhelming majority of countries have ratified international treaties committing themselves to end such abuses. Maternal mortality is not a social problem that "just happens" – it is a terrible injustice that must be ended.

The travesty of millions of lives lost and scarred deserves much greater and more urgent attention. We need to name and shame all those who remain silent in the face of such a tragedy. Human rights activists have shifted the world agenda on torture and the death penalty – but neither of those take as many lives or create as much suffering for as many people as does maternal mortality. To quote the former UN High Commissioner for Human Rights, Mary Robinson: "Preventable maternal mortality and morbidity is a violation of women's rights to life, health, equality and non-discrimination. The time has come to treat this issue as a human rights violation, no less than torture, 'disappearances', arbitrary detention and prisoners of conscience."[41]

Unfortunately, we are still a long way from acknowledging that safe motherhood means the right of women to be mothers when they themselves choose, and to be able to do so without unnecessary risk. Access to appropriate medical care is essential to reducing the number of maternal deaths. But the lack of medical care is itself an outcome of discrimination and unequal treatment, of exclusion and marginalization as well as the lack of political power of poor women.

The medical solution to maternal mortality is crucial, and although well-understood, is often unavailable because of lack of investment of adequate resources. The socio-economic and political determinants of maternal mortality are also crucial, but are less well understood and often ignored. The solution to maternal mortality lies in tackling all facets of poverty – increasing voice, ending the exclusion of women and violence against them, and addressing deprivation by ensuring access to health services. The problems are interlinked, and so too are the solutions. The response will be inadequate if it is partial or sequenced.

In September 2008 I attended the UN High Level meeting on MDGs in New York. Governments, including many Heads of State and Foreign Ministers, were there to take stock and to recommit themselves to achieving the MDGs. In a session devoted to health, speaker after speaker drew attention to the need for increasing the capacity of health systems in poor countries, especially through foreign aid. Pressure was on governments – in poor countries to prioritize maternal health, and in rich countries to provide funding (a task made somewhat more difficult by the plunging share prices across town on Wall Street right at that moment.) Economist Jeffrey Sachs took the floor to argue for a massive increase in aid directed at health-care. He recalled how the world had eradicated smallpox through a vaccine and the scaling up of money, technology and management to deliver it. We could do the same, he argued, for malaria, tuberculosis and maternal mortality.

I do not disagree with him. Safe motherhood is a problem of capacity and resources – and there is a need for more international aid to boost both. But I do believe that safe motherhood is connected to the low political, social and economic status that women have in many countries, both at home and in the public sphere, so resources alone will not be enough – and indeed might not even be forthcoming for that very reason. The "vaccine" for safe motherhood requires more investment, not only in funding maternal health services but also in the empowerment of women. It demands an end to discrimination and an end to violence against women.

If the absence of medical care explains why women die in childbirth, their absence of power explains why there is so little urgency in taking action. It is the political marginalization of women that results in the marginalization of their health risks. Paul Hunt, the

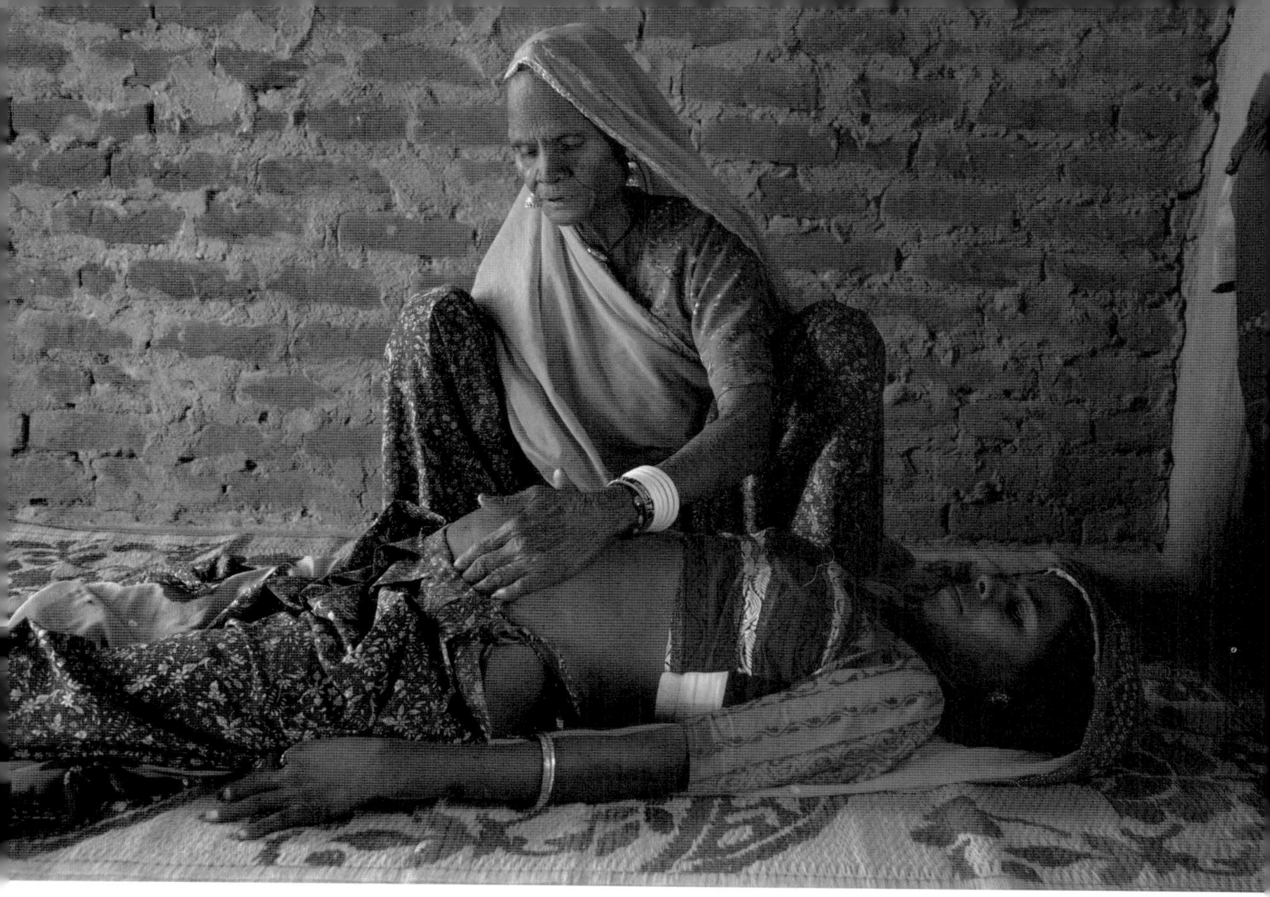

UN Special Rapporteur on the right to health, put it more provocatively: "I have a suspicion that if men had to give birth, mortality and morbidity arising from childbirth would be taken more seriously and attract more resources than they do today."[42]

A midwife checks a young woman who will give birth in a few days time. Rajasthan, India, 2007. © Robert Wallis/Panos

In a joint statement produced for the MDG Summit, UN agencies and the World Bank pledged to increase funding and attention to maternal health. They noted the need also to "tackle the root causes of maternal mortality and morbidity, including gender inequality, low access to education – especially for girls, child marriage and adolescent pregnancy".[43]

I would stress, therefore, that the political and social empowerment of women is crucial. We must especially champion and defend women's sexual and reproductive rights, including their right to contraception and to make decisions on the timing and spacing of their children, and on decisions to seek medical attention. Here, as elsewhere, the right to information is key, and much more must be done to provide women with the information they need to make these choices.

In addition to empowerment of women, concerted action is needed in three distinct areas.

1. MAKE THE PROBLEM VISIBLE

As a campaigner I know that the first step towards change is to throw light on the problem. If we are to advocate for more resources and better access for poor women to maternal health services, we need to make the injustices and issues more visible. Seven years on from the launch of MDG 5, there are still no accurate figures to measure maternal mortality. What we use are estimates or aggregates – which means not only that the real incidence of death and disability could be much higher but also that we do not know with precision how different groups of women are affected, and where the real problems lie. The absence of accurate data from countries with some of the worst maternal mortality ratios also means that it is not possible to assess what progress is being made nor to evaluate what are the most effective strategies to improve maternal health.

Maternal mortality ratios need to be supplemented with process indicators which can be disaggregated to show discrimination, and which are relevant then to programming and policy-making.

The data must be disaggregated along such lines as geography (urban/rural or isolated regions), race, ethnicity, age and caste. Some new indicators not always found in the health literature should also be included, such as information on sexual and reproductive health, participation and accountability.[44] Donors must be ready to provide international aid and technical assistance to help countries that have limited resources and skills develop reliable information systems.

Donor pressure, as well as civil society mobilization, can help overcome more than just technical know-how. It can push back the social and political constraints that shield the fundamental inequities underpinning this human rights catastrophe. It can demand that the discrimination be revealed, and lobby for societal change.

Better data leads to more meaningful monitoring and better assessment of national policies – giving credit where it is working and making a better case for change where that is needed – and so mobilizing national constituencies, people as well as governments, more effectively. The Safe Motherhood Initiative in Nepal, for example, by exposing the differential uptake of emergency obstetric care by low caste women in relation to upper caste women – because the services were less accessible to them – made a powerful argument as to why the government needed to spend more on reaching the poorest, most socially excluded women.[45]

2. MAKE SOLUTIONS EFFECTIVE AND ACCESSIBLE

Our aim must be universal provision of skilled birth attendants and access to emergency obstetric care. Maternal deaths are largely preventable if these services are provided. More resources are needed but the fact that some developing countries have made progress shows it is also about choices on how existing resources are spent.

The need to finance health-care must not create new barriers to access. A concrete way of improving access to health-care is to abolish "user fees", the charges paid by the patient to hospitals and clinics at the point of delivery of the service. People who live in poverty are instantly excluded from services if they have to pay for them. In 2005, at the World Health Assembly, 189 countries agreed that moving away from user fees for health was essential in order to reach MDGs 4 and 5. Many countries are choosing to abolish user charges. In Sri Lanka this has been highly successful: services are free at the point of access, and more than 95 per cent of women give birth with the support of a skilled midwife. Others have found the transition more difficult. This is a critical area for more international aid.

Transport costs, too, are very high, particularly for those women who live in the most isolated and inaccessible places and who, for that reason, are often the neediest. Building a more accessible health network is the obvious answer. There are creative, low-cost ways of doing so. Using paramedics, the NGO Gonoshasthaya Kendra in Bangladesh, for example, trained traditional birth assistants in remote villages, making it possible for skilled care to be available at almost 90 per cent of births in the villages it covered, compared with the national average of around 30 per cent. A combination of international aid, local resources and sensitivity to the problems of poor women can make a big difference.

Maternal health programmes must be designed to be inclusive. Poor women do not have the resources, skills or capacity to negotiate sophisticated health systems. It is important, therefore, to give particular attention to all those factors that discriminate against poor women and exclude them from accessing health-care, such as language barriers, cultural insensitivities and geographical isolation.

3. ENHANCE ACCOUNTABILITY

Human rights stipulate accountability. If safe motherhood is a right, then duty holders must be held to account for respecting, protecting and fulfilling it. Unless there are clear means of accountability to press for progress, that right will remain no more than an aspiration. By accountability, I do not mean just periodic UN Summits, important as they are as a means of visibility and peer pressure among governments and donors. I mean a range of different ways – political, local, legal and practical – to engage duty holders at different levels and enhance the participation of women themselves.

There are many ways in which accountability can be strengthened for fulfilling the right to safe motherhood. National human rights institutions should put the right to maternal health on their agenda. National and state parliaments should demand maternal death audits from governments, and hold annual reviews to assess policies, strategies and programmes. Because women's political power at national level is often marginal, it will be important to put pressure on these national institutions through international machinery, such as the Universal Periodic Review, which the UN Human Rights Council has instituted to assess the human rights record of all governments. Future UN meetings on MDGs should also insist on stronger national accountability because that is the level at which politicians have to be made to confront the truth. It is easy to spout rhetoric in New York or Geneva, but much harder to ignore facts at home.

It is closer to home that the real measures of accountability will have most effect. There are many good examples of how civil society is building accountability tools to assess the quality of services. They need to be supported, scaled up and shared across countries. For instance, a Dutch NGO, Aim for Human Rights, has developed a Health Rights of Women Assessment Instrument to analyze maternal health policies according to a country's human rights obligations. This tool has been used by a local NGO in Bangladesh to assess government policies on eclampsia, a major killer of pregnant women, and to make recommendations.[46] Another NGO in Bangladesh has made its own health workers in villages accountable to its local stakeholders through village health committees headed by women, and "death meetings", involving family members, teachers, priests, imams and others in the community to find out what went wrong and how it can be changed. By doing so, it claims to have brought down maternal mortality ratios to 40 per cent below the national average.[47]

Accountability can be difficult to implement but it can save lives by exposing poor policies and revealing good practices. Most importantly, it shifts the power balance between the women as rights holders and the state and health providers as duty holders.

The time has come to shame the world into greater action to address maternal mortality. All governments have limited budgets and, as I write, falling growth rates and shrinking economies will put greater pressure on spending. The question that has to be put bluntly, starkly and visibly is this: what value do we put on the lives of women?

The answer: no price, surely, is too high. But money alone will not solve this problem. At the UN MDG meeting in September 2008, Elaben Bhatt, founder of the Self-Employed Women's Association (SEWA) of India told world leaders: "Poverty is powerlessness. Poverty cannot be removed unless the poor have power to make decisions that affect their lives. So yes, poverty is a political issue." Nothing is more political than the persistence of maternal mortality.

SEVEN

THE GLOBAL SLUM – WINNING THE RIGHT TO THE CITY

MY MOTHER'S APARTMENT IN DHAKA is located in a well-to-do neighbourhood beside a small lake. From the balcony of the apartment you can see, on the other side of the water, the largest slum of the capital. It is a city of shacks, of corrugated roofs and bamboo walls. When the rains come in the monsoon season, the narrow lanes between the dwellings turn into streams of mud, and the sewers flood the flimsy homes. In the summer, as I watch the sun sparkle through the sprinklers and fountains in the garden below me, across the lake children cool off in the polluted water by the sewers. You can almost see the heat rising from the tin roofs, baking those who live there. In the morning I see streams of people leaving the slum and heading to work as rickshaw drivers, day labourers, factory workers or as maids or cleaners in apartment buildings like my mother's. At night, lights and air conditioning units whirr in the building where I stay, but the shacks on the other side are dark, with a few dim lights punctuating the gloom. Once in a while, the silence of the night is broken by screams and shouts, as police raid the slum. Maybe they have received a tip-off about illicit trade, prostitution or organized crime. More often they are collecting unpaid bribes or enforcing the law of the "slum lords".

Slums are vote banks for politicians in this city, and slum lords and local politicians work in tandem: the slum lord delivers the votes of the residents to the political party and, in exchange, he is left free to impose his power

Mumbai's biggest slum, Dharavi, is a thriving mix of poverty and enterprise that is home to over one million people. Mumbai, India, November 2008. © Mark Henley/Panos

over the people as he sees fit, from enforcing "rent" to running prostitution rings. Often, the only way to avoid eviction is to accept the oppression. Divided by the short stretch of water, the only experience that the slum dwellers and the residents of the wealthy neighbourhood share from time to time is the stench of the sewers when the wind blows in the wrong direction.

There are more than 200,000 communities in the world that can be defined as slums. They are currently home to more than 1 billion people, across all continents. The phenomenon is spreading at a terrifying speed. Some projections say that the number of people living in slums will double to 2 billion by 2030. If poverty is the world's worst human rights crisis, then slums are its "ground zero", where the magnitude of the calamity is plain for all to see.

Slums are caused by and deeply intertwined with a range of factors – such as rapid economic growth, natural disasters, war and human rights abuses. They dominate virtually all cities in the less developed world, and in a growing number of more developed countries as well. They stand as graphic testimonials to persistently failing economic and urban policies, and the unwillingness or inability – or both – of governments around the world to take the rights of all citizens equally seriously.

The growth of slum populations worldwide poses an enormous challenge. If this continues at the current rate, by mid-century our world will look ever more divided: the rich locked inside, the poor outside – a global slum at the margins of a global gated community. Here, perhaps, more than anywhere, we must mobilize for a comprehensive response and treat the problems of people who live in slums as a human rights crisis.

THE GLOBAL SLUM

They might be referred to as *bidonvilles*, the *ghetto* or the *hood*, *bustees* or *chawls*, *favelas*, *barrios populares*, or simply as "slums". These self-built, low-income neighbourhoods are each as unique and multifaceted as any other neighbourhood. They do, however, share common characteristics. These include inadequate housing, sanitation and drainage, poor water and electricity services, overcrowding, and exposure to toxic water, soil and air. Slums are characterized, too, by high levels of violence. Slums are generally built on land with the least economic value or development potential (but, ironically, that land often later becomes a prime location as cities grow and economies expand, creating pressure for them to be demolished to make way for development). They are usually classified as "illegal" or "unregularized". Above all, people who live in slums commonly have limited tenure rights or none at all. Treated as squatters, they face the risk of forcible or arbitrary eviction.

The proportion of populations in developing countries who live in slums is truly shocking – often well over 50 per cent. Some individual slums house millions of people. China tops the list, with some 193 million people living in slums; India comes a close second, with nearly 160 million. Brazil is a distant third: there 51.7 million people live in slums.[1]

These numbers are increasing everywhere. Each year, some 65 million new people are added to the population of the world's slums – that's an additional 130 people every minute. In contrast, there is very little upward mobility out of the slums. Once there, people are stuck.

This growth is driven by natural population increase and migration from the countryside to towns. Often people are lured to the city by the prospect of jobs and a better life. Booming economies have boosted this trend. Indeed, stimulating massive urbanization in particular areas may create economic efficiencies. Companies will cluster where the infrastructure and labour supply meet their needs. This is particularly marked where production is linked to overseas trade, and is therefore dependent on air- and seaports, or rail and road terminals. The prospect of work in the assembly plants was what brought the women I described in Chapter 1 to Ciudad Juárez from some of the poorest areas of Mexico.

The denial of human rights that goes along with the formation and expansion of slums is not well recognized. When people are pushed off their land or are driven out of their villages by persecution, war or famine, they flee to the city and end up in slums. Conflict-induced displacement and violence against women are two of the leading causes of people fleeing to slums to start a new life. When they get there, though, they discover that they are confronted with the same problems of deprivation, insecurity and exclusion that they left behind.

Women make up the bulk of the population of slums and often cite abuse and property disinheritance in their villages as the reason for their move to the city. Impoverishment for one reason or another is a key factor. In Cambodia, it is reported that 60 per cent of peasants who sell their land and move to urban slums do so to pay medical debts.[2] In Angola, the slums of Luanda house those who were displaced by decades of fighting in the rural areas during the civil war. In Kabul slums are burgeoning as people enter the city to escape insecurity and violence in the countryside.

How is it that no one noticed such overwhelming and rapid growth of slums, of the descent into them, and the inability of people to escape them? The truth is, they did. But those in power either did not listen or failed to put the right policies and mechanisms in place to halt the growth or improve the informal settlements. The growth of slums and informal housing arrangements are, in essence, the predictable outcome of decades of neglect of housing. One of the overriding factors is that the formal or legal housing, land and property sectors are simply inaccessible for poor people. We only have to look as far as the sub prime lending catastrophe in the USA to find a parallel for the disastrous results and inequities that flow from pumping money into housing in such a way that it outprices those with less means.

INSECURE, EXCLUDED, VOICELESS AND DEPRIVED

In my work as a refugee official and human rights activist, I have seen many slums – in Brazil, Bangladesh, India, Pakistan, Egypt, Mexico, Angola, South Africa and elsewhere. In every place I have been struck by the incredible ingenuity and perseverance of those who live in slums. With the state almost entirely absent in their communities, except as a predatory force, people have found creative ways to fend for themselves. But if there is a danger in painting too bleak a picture of slum life – one that obscures the fact that there is much joy as well as sorrow, success as well as hardship – there is, equally, the danger of romanticizing slums and the resilience of those who live in them. Movies like *Slumdog Millionaire* (2008) fail to fully capture the grim reality. The threats faced by people who live in slums and the deprivations they endure are multiple, and they compound each other into horrendous misery. The hardships are all the more striking in comparison with the way others live in the city.

To live in a slum is to live in insecurity, at risk of violence or natural disaster and in constant uncertainty, knowing that one's home and belongings, however meagre, might at any time be seized or destroyed without warning or legal recourse. The fear of being forcibly or arbitrarily evicted is compounded by other forms of insecurity. In Chapter 4, I described the plague of criminal violence in many slum communities. In the vacuum created by the absence of the state, criminal gangs often take over the running of the slum, controlling almost every aspect of life. The residents find themselves in double jeopardy, caught between criminal gangs and the police, oppressed by one and attacked by the other.

In a survey of women living in slums in six cities around the world, the Centre on Housing Rights and Evictions (COHRE) identified violence against women as "rampant" in slums and the "strongest cross-cutting theme" of their study.[3] Women experienced violence both within the home and in the slum community, on their way to or from work, or as they tried to use public sanitation facilities or open fields at night, or in the early hours of the morning. Women have also talked of the difficulties in reporting domestic or other forms of violence to the police because of negative perceptions of slum dwellers among the authorities, or simply because of the absence of police stations in slum areas.[4]

Less well known, perhaps, is the risk of natural disaster that destroys the lives and livelihoods of slum dwellers. Slums are often located in areas that are unfit for habitation, such as on garbage disposal sites or flood plains, near hazardous and toxic sites, or in polluted areas. At least three in every 10 non-permanent houses in cities in developing countries are located in dangerous areas that are prone to natural disasters. Because of the location of the homes, poor quality of construction, poor infrastructure and lack of information, people living in these areas, and in slums in general, are most at risk when natural or man-made disasters strike. Climate change is worsening the risks of natural disasters and it is predicted that these will continue to increase, with the greatest impact felt by populations already living in poverty.[5]

In 1984, around half a million people living in the city of Bhopal in India were exposed to toxic chemicals during a catastrophic gas leak from a pesticide plant run by the Union Carbide Corporation, later taken over by the Dow Chemical Company. The worst affected were people living in slums located around the factory. Amnesty International estimated that up to 10,000 people died in the immediate aftermath and at least 15,000 died in the eight-year period following the disaster. Hundreds of thousands more suffered, and continue to suffer, from debilitating illnesses.[6] Their suffering was compounded by the company withholding information about the nature of the substances that had leaked and their harmful effects.[7]

Such risks are symptomatic of a deeper problem: living in a slum on squatted land means, almost by definition, to live in illegality. The vast majority of people living in settlements or slums that governments consider irregular or "illegal", have limited or no security of tenure. This can be the case even when the inhabitants rent their homes or have purchased them. It is estimated that between 30 and 50 per cent of urban residents in the developing world lack any kind of legal document to show they have tenure security.[8] A lack of documentation or recognition of a formal address affects not just their rights to shelter but may limit their access to credit, public services, formal employment and the right to vote.

The absence of tenure security leads to forced evictions. This is the forcible removal of people from their homes without due process of law and without any arrangements made for alternative shelter. It is arbitrary and often carried out on a large scale. Recall the case of Srey Mom that I described at the beginning of Chapter 5, where entire communities were picked up and dumped in a remote location with scant regard for their homes, personal possessions, social networks, access to work including self-run informal enterprises, and access to services such as schools. Women suffer disproportionately from forced evictions; they are particularly vulnerable because of gender discrimination in relation to property rights that exists in many societies.[9]

The practice of forced eviction has been condemned as a gross violation of human rights under international law. A 2004 UN Commission on Human Rights resolution on the "Prohibition of forced evictions" unequivocally reaffirms "that the practice of forced eviction is contrary to laws that are in conformity with international human rights standards [and] constitutes a gross violation of a broad range of human rights, in particular the right to adequate housing".[10]

Despite repeated condemnation by the United Nations and many others of the practice of forced evictions, millions of inhabitants of slums are forcibly evicted annually, often with violence. In that process, other violations have been documented, including rape, arbitrary arrests and detention, torture and unlawful killings.[11] In the vast majority of slum eviction cases, there is no due process of law.

Mass forced evictions are on the increase as slums are demolished to make way for urban development or city "beautification" projects, or as part of the preparation for international mega-events. It is estimated that the Olympic Games alone have displaced more than 2 million people in the last 20 years.[12] Increasing land prices, land speculation and land-grabbing, as well as attempts to criminalize slums or to forcibly reverse rural-urban migration, also play a role in mass evictions. Six million people are displaced every year by urban development and transport programmes.[13] As UN-HABITAT notes, "it is always the poor who are evicted – wealthier population groups virtually never face forced eviction, and never mass eviction".[14]

In a selection of forced eviction cases in just seven countries – Bangladesh, China, India, Indonesia, Nigeria, South Africa and Zimbabwe – between 1995 and 2005, more than 10.2 million people faced forced eviction. This included the eviction in July 2000 of nearly 1 million people in Rainbow Town, Port Harcourt, Nigeria; more than 100,000 people in Jakarta in 2003-2004; 150,000 people in New Delhi and 77,000 in Kolkata (Calcutta), India, in 2004; and more than 300,000 people in Beijing, China as a result of preparations for the 2008 Olympic Games.[15] Other examples abound. At the end of 2008, at least 150,000 Cambodians were at risk of being evicted in the wake of development projects, land disputes and land-grabbing. This follows on the heels of 30,000 inhabitants of slums who were evicted between 1998 and 2003 in Phnom Penh alone.[16]

While all regions have witnessed large-scale forced evictions, Africa has perhaps fared worst. A recent study by Amnesty International and COHRE reveals that the practice of forced evictions has reached epidemic proportions in Africa, with more than 3 million people forcibly evicted from their homes since 2000.[17]

One of the worst cases of forced eviction in recent years was in Zimbabwe, when 700,000 people were evicted, losing their homes and much more. According to figures given by the government itself, 92,460 homes were destroyed between 18 May and 5 July 2005. The latest data from May 2006 show only 3,325 houses had been built by the government to replace those that were destroyed.[18]

The UN Special Envoy sent to investigate the incidents reported how locals referred to the government's May 2005 "Operation Murambatsvina" as "Operation Tsunami" because of its "speed and ferocity". The "operation" destroyed homes, business premises and vending sites, making an estimated 700,000 people homeless or jobless or both in cities across the country. A further 2.4 million people were affected in varying degrees. The hundreds of thousands of women, men and children who were made homeless had no access to food, water and sanitation, or health-care. Education for thousands of school-age children was disrupted. Many of the sick, including those with HIV and AIDS, no longer had access to care. The Special Envoy went on to say: "The vast majority of those directly and indirectly affected are the poor and disadvantaged segments of the population. They are, today, deeper in poverty, deprivation and destitution, and have been rendered more vulnerable."[19]

One of the simplest ways for authorities to convince themselves that they don't have to take the rights of more than a billion people seriously is by turning them into "'criminals'" – those they, and maybe their voters, perceive to deserve nothing. In Chapter 4, I mentioned Amnesty International's work in Brazil to expose the way in which negative perceptions of people living in slums have contributed to situations where the people are not given the protection of the police and are victims of both gang and police violence. In Brazil, Jamaica and Kenya, Amnesty International has documented the excessive use of force by the police while conducting operations in slums, including unlawful killings and, in some cases, extra-judicial killings.[20]

The term "slum" itself dates all the way back to 1812, when it was synonymous with "racket" or "criminal trade", and this perception of slums as criminal havens and zones of illegality unfortunately continues to pervade common connotations of lower-income neighbourhoods. This, in turn, assists in marginalizing slums even further from the political mainstream.[21] The reality is – and I can see it for myself whenever I look out from the balcony of my mother's apartment – that the vast majority of people who live in slums are hardworking, peaceful people who just want a better life for themselves and their children. They are forced into living "illegally" because there is no place for them in the "legal" housing sector.

Most slums are technically illegal. Land is often occupied by those without legal title to it; dwellings are often built in violation of local housing codes and regulations; electricity is often tapped without the knowledge of the company providing the service; drainage canals or public toilets are constructed in contravention of public health and safety rules and so on. But in the absence of affordable housing, poor people have no other choice. In the face of a legal order that in effect disenfranchises significant numbers (in some cases the majority) of a city's inhabitants, the excluded are demanding a "right to the city". Theirs is a claim for equal access to basic services and an equal right to participate in decision-making.

As it stands, the inhabitants of slums are excluded from access to many basic services. People living in slums at the peripheries of cities can spend up to 30 per cent of their income on transport or up to three to four hours walking to and from work or school.[22]

On average, people who live in slums are far more likely to suffer ill-health than city residents in general and have a shorter life expectancy.[23] Poor health is more influenced by housing and living conditions than almost any other factor, including income. According to one analyst, "Housing deprivation alone can lead to a 25 per cent greater risk of disability or severe ill health across the life course, with the risk increasing with exposure to poor housing in early childhood."[24] Another adds: "Overcrowding, poor water and sanitation, and insecure housing, and morbidity, are also related. In Sub-Saharan Africa, it is typical to witness a two- or even three-fold difference between the malnutrition levels of children living in slums, and those living in planned areas. While malnutrition is seen among 10 per cent in non-slum neighbourhoods, it is at endemic proportions within slums; 26 per cent in urban areas of Benin, Cameroon and Nigeria. Among the extremes, Ethiopia, Chad, Mali, Niger and Madagascar show malnutrition rates as high as 40 to 50 per cent among urban slum children, a situation worse than in rural parts of those countries."[25]

Access to water is a basic human right, necessary for life itself. But because many slums lack clean, piped water from municipal water supplies, inhabitants of slums throughout the world are often forced to

MUNICIPAL COUNCIL ELECTIONS
JULY 5TH 2008
Joseph Timothy Conteh
One Country
One People
LOCAL GOVERNMENT ELECTION 2008
CONSTITUENCY 107
VOTE
Class IV Social studie
Weather Climate and Season in Sierra leone:
1) WEATHER: refers to the condition or the days atmospheric condition of a Place.
eg the atmosphere may be dry
2) Climate is the average weather condition of a Place for a long Period of time:
3) Season Is the division of the Year according to the weather.
class III
Slow-moving

ClassII English 9/10/08
I get up at Six O'clock every day.
I wash my hands and Face. I Put on
My clocthes I clean my teeth. I eat my
breakFast I comb my
School at Seven
and English
One O'clack
Swamp

pay shockingly excessive rates for water from private vendors. In Faisalabad in Pakistan, for example, people living in slums are forced to pay an almost unimaginable 6,800 per cent more for water from water trucks than those who live in neighourhoods with access to piped water. In Manila, people in the slums pay 4,200 per cent more, in Mumbai 4,000 per cent more and in Phnom Penh 1,800 per cent more![26]

In Kenya, COHRE highlighted the fact that, although informal settlements housed approximately 55 per cent of the city's population, they were excluded from the city authority's planning and budgeting. While various water pipes cut through Kibera in Nairobi, residents were forced to buy water from entrepreneurs who charged between three and 30 times the normal council charge.[27] People who cannot afford to buy water have to use water from whatever sources they can find, even if they are polluted. As a result, residents of slums are extremely vulnerable to water-borne diseases. Most slums have few toilets or none at all, and, where they exist, they tend to be overused. Fees may also be charged to use the latrine, which many residents cannot afford.

People may be forced to use a "hanging latrine" (stalls made out of wood or rags, often precariously balanced over open water sources or mud pits, into which small children and women may and do fall) or "flying toilets" (because of lack of usable toilets, residents throw out their toilet waste in plastic bags on the roadside or on to crowded garbage heaps).[28]

People living in slums are frequently prevented from participating in the processes and decisions that affect their lives. Sometimes they are denied the right to vote because they have no address. Just as often, their vote – their voice – is stolen from them by manipulative slum lords and/or the corrupt politicians who pay them. If they are – rarely – consulted before an eviction, all too often their voices and suggestions are ignored. In slum upgrading processes, they are treated as passive recipients, not as stakeholders.

COHRE interviewed residents of informal settlements in Kenya and highlighted the fact that their strongest message was that they wished to be "treated as far as possible as partners in the development process, rather than as simply passive 'beneficiaries'". They also expressed frustration

Previous pages: **A class is taught in a narrow passage in Kroo Bay slum. Freetown, Sierra Leone, 2008. © Anna Kari/Documentography**

over the lack of information in relation to evictions, slum upgrading, land allocation and management, and access to essential services. Though initiatives to include slum upgrading in Kenya's national housing policy and launch pilot projects were considered positive, COHRE's mission found that residents of Soweto in Kibera "lacked a real voice in the project and feared that it would lead to their displacement and/or that they would be subjected to violence".[29]

The work of human rights defenders, often difficult and dangerous, is never more so than when giving voice to the issues facing people living in slums. Bienvenido Salinas, Director of the Saint Thomas Law Center, a unit of the Urban Poor Associates (UPA), in the Philippines, for example, received multiple death threats because of his work in support of housing rights for poor people in cities.[30] Zheng Enchong, a Chinese lawyer, was arrested, charged with disclosing state secrets, and sentenced to three years in prison in 2003 after he filed the case of 2,160 Shanghai evictees. People who repeatedly protested against a Shanghai redevelopment initiative were charged with "illegal assembly" and sentenced to "re-education through labour".[31]

I mentioned in Chapter 4 a lawyer and human rights defender who received numerous death threats for highlighting police brutality in the *favelas* in São Paolo, forcing her to leave the country temporarily to ensure her safety. She took me with her to visit a slum in São Paolo in 2003. Some of my colleagues on the Amnesty International delegation feared it might be too risky, but I wanted to see for myself the other side of her dangerous work – not just the threats from shadowy "officials" and their henchmen, but the insecurity presented by the communities themselves with whom she worked. We walked down narrow, dark lanes, flanked by teenage boys, smoking, staring at us, in some cases with open hostility, in others with edgy curiosity. She greeted them as friends. She understood their hostility, understood, too, how criminality – hooking up with the gangs and drug lords – was often the only way for them to survive. She took me to visit a family whose son had been shot in crossfire – the tragic consequence of living among, even when not participating in, such criminality. The relief on my colleagues' faces when I emerged unscathed was palpable. I had "survived" just under an hour. The residents, and the lawyer who guided me, have to make it through their whole lives.

Up until now I have focused on slums in the developing world. There are, however, remarkably similar issues of insecurity and deprivation in the poor neighbourhoods of cities in Europe and the USA, or in life on the reserves for Indigenous Peoples in Canada, the USA and Australia. For example, in Italy many Roma live in "camps for nomads", which are not legally recognized as housing, even though some of the camps have been authorized by the state. In 2008 the Italian government intensified forced evictions and the destruction of Roma camps because of a perception that the Roma represent a "security risk". Romani individuals and others who live in these camps are often denied local residence permits. As a result, they cannot register for the National Health Service or for a range of public services. They cannot even register car purchases or vote in public elections, despite the fact that they are Italian citizens.[32]

In Slovakia, Roma settlements are usually located several kilometres from the town or village where the rest of the population lives. The isolation of many of the settlements is increased by a total lack of public transport. They have no public facilities such as schools, medical centres, hospitals, libraries or public laundries. They have no electricity unless they obtain it through an illegal and often risky connection to the public supply.[33] When I worked for the UNHCR in the Balkan region, I saw first-hand how Roma settlements were pushed to the outskirts of cities such as Pristina in Kosovo and Skopje in Macedonia. The conditions there were not very different from those of slums in the cities of the global South.

A well-known report in the United States in 2002 documented "the systematic abuse of civil rights of homeless people", which, it said, were used "as a strategy to remove homeless people from sight by local governments and private business districts".[34] The study carried out surveys in 57 large American cities and found that none of them had sufficient accommodation for homeless people or programmes in place to tackle growing housing inaffordability, and, overall, that already scarce public resources were being diverted away from solutions to homelessness and towards criminalization of homeless people. In these and other urban centres in the world's most powerful nation, homeless people can be forcibly moved, fined or even imprisoned for sleeping in a park or a car or in the open. In San Francisco alone, some 43,000 people were cited for "quality of life" violations in a single year.

PROBLEM? WHAT PROBLEM?

The problems posed by slums, and the severity of the conditions facing the people who live in them, have not received anywhere near the attention they deserve. There is no concerted global effort to address the issue that begins to match the scale of the problem. In most countries it does not command sufficient political attention. The world's "Housing Agency", UN-HABITAT, while full of good intentions and with an excellent analysis of global housing conditions, remains one of the smallest, most under-funded and politically peripheral of all UN agencies – this is despite the fact it represents a worldwide constituency of more than one billion people.

The seventh MDG includes a target to "improve the lives of 100 million slum dwellers by 2020". This sounds a worthy objective. It recognizes people who live in slums as a distinct group with particular needs that must be addressed. But given that there are already significantly more than 1 billion slum dwellers, to speak of improving the lives of fewer than 10 per cent of them, and even then only by the year 2020 – five years later than the end point for the other MDG targets – is a pretty paltry response. By the time those 100 million lives are improved – if indeed they are – they will probably only make up 5 per cent of people living in slums worldwide.

It is as if we don't really know how to respond – a view confirmed by the fact that, for this MDG target, the only indicator to measure progress is to count the proportion of the urban population living in slums! In other words, no indicators that actually measure the "improvement" are sought. An indicator regarding the extension of security of tenure was dropped in 2008.

Perhaps the growth in slum populations is seen by political leaders and policy makers as a "stage" that all countries must go through as they develop – an inevitable consequence of rapid economic growth as people flock to the cities to find jobs. But the issue is not with the rise in urban population itself. Rather, it is that so much of this growth resides in the formation of slums. For the sake of better employment prospects, slum dwellers are denied a life that has dignity. This is a trade-off we should not tolerate. From a human rights perspective, it is unacceptable.

The right to an adequate standard of living, including the right to adequate housing, has been enshrined in the international human rights code for 60 years. Article 25 of the UDHR states explicitly:

> *Everyone has the right to a standard of living adequate for the health and well-being of himself and of his family, including food, clothing, housing and medical care and necessary social services, and the right to security in the event of unemployment, sickness, disability, widowhood, old age or other lack of livelihood in circumstances beyond his control.*[35]

Since 1948, the human right to adequate housing has been reaffirmed in numerous international conventions[36] and laws. The ICESCR, which entered into force on 3 January 1976, contains perhaps the most significant international legal source of the right to adequate housing.[37]

At the national level, nearly half of the world's constitutions contain explicit recognition of the right to adequate housing. A growing range of innovative national laws address various elements of this composite right in all regions of the world and representing every major legal system, culture, level of development, religion and economic system.[38]

Despite the existence of international standards and national laws, action to ensure housing has been sadly missing. At the national level, few governments have made a truly concerted effort to build or subsidize the building of adequate supplies of low-income housing and maintain it at a standard consistent with internationally recognized norms of adequacy. The right to housing has been largely left to the market to resolve. Yet, without strong state involvement, both in terms of supportive law and the provision of financial resources, it is clear that prevailing economic models will not result in the improvements required to transform the world's slums into the vibrant communities they could become with proper support and resources.

Improving slum conditions in a structured and sustainable manner is distressingly absent from the remit of most government housing bodies, despite the recognition of housing rights in national constitutions and laws. Public expenditure on housing remains extremely limited in virtually all countries, almost always lagging far behind health and education in national budgets. Efforts to provide housing at an affordable cost by the private sector have generally not achieved results (even when heavily subsidized or provided with tax incentives or other inducements to do so). Yet hand in hand with the forces of globalization, governments of all political hues are turning to the market as the source of hope for housing the hundreds of millions, if not billions, of people who today lack access to a safe, habitable and secure home. As a result, donor aid budgets, which have never been known for championing housing issues, have deprioritized it even further in recent years.

The market is a crucial link in any successful housing supply chain, but governments need to acknowledge that the market on its own has failed to provide affordable and accessible homes to all sectors of society, particularly those without the necessary financial resources or access to credit to enter into mortgage or other formal rental arrangements. Recent housing affordability and the sub prime mortgage crises in the rich world prove this point once again. Yet, if we analyze the dominant housing policy trends among national and international actors, it is clear that the market – even now – is seen by many as the "only real solution". Global housing policy debates tend to accept that only market-based solutions to the global housing crisis will prevail (despite such approaches arguably being the cause of the crisis in the first place!).

One approach favouring the market calls for people who live in slums to receive property titles – that is to give them properly recognized legal ownership of their dwellings. Doing so, it is argued, will ensure security of tenure, but will also give inhabitants of slums access to credit (as their homes can be used as collateral).[39] This is an option, and one that is increasingly gaining support.

Property ownership is not always possible nor always the best solution, and focusing on it must not exclude other options. One UN publication, for instance, points out that in many policy circles there is a structural bias against rental housing, although this form of housing provides shelter to perhaps one-third or more of humanity.[40] One housing expert argues that security of tenure can be achieved through several means other than the recognition of individual property rights. He talks of different "legal-political options", ranging from the transfer of

Irene Khan and Amnesty International delegates meet with members of the Guarda Civil outside a *favela* in São Paolo, Brazil, 2003.

individual ownership to various forms of leasehold and/or rent control to more innovative forms of collective ownership or occupation. He concludes: "Whatever the solution adopted, it will only work properly if it is the result of a democratic and transparent decision-making process which effectively incorporates the affected populations".[41]

It is clear that the crisis of the global slum will not be resolved overnight. It is equally clear that what has been attempted thus far has failed miserably. There must be a better way forward. New and different options need to be considered and developed and, if they are to be successful, then the people who live in slums themselves must be given a voice and a choice in that process.

WHERE DO WE GO FROM HERE?

The global slum crisis is a clear evidence of inequality entrenched so deeply that the world is physically divided into zones of affluence and zones of despair and deprivation. But how long can we sustain that degree of segregation without major social, political and economic problems? No country – even the wealthiest – will be immune from the consequences if we fail to act.

The challenge is enormous, but action on three fronts would make a significant impact. We need to: end the forced and arbitrary evictions of slum dwellers; secure tenure rights; and invest in slum upgrading. In each case, the active participation of the people who live in the slums is essential. Doing this will bolster their human rights, gradually reduce the deprivation that is commonplace within slums, enhance levels of security in the slum communities, and put a stop to their wholesale exclusion from the systems of power, rights and justice that their neighbours enjoy.

1. END FORCED EVICTIONS

Forced evictions are a gross violation of human rights, and governments should take all necessary measures, including the adoption of laws and policies that are in accordance with international human rights law, to prohibit and prevent them. As a first step, governments should impose a moratorium on mass forced evictions until such laws and policies are adopted and implemented. This is not an impossible or unthinkable measure, as there are many good examples of what can be achieved.

Considerable progress has been made in recent years in seeking to prevent the practice of forced evictions. Some of this has come about by exploring all feasible alternatives to eviction – in effect placing eviction at the bottom, rather than at the top of the list of policy options available to governments. The vast majority of planned forced evictions can be avoided, and it is possible to identify reasonable alternatives. There are numerous instances of planned evictions being cancelled, and drawing on such examples may encourage governments that wish to remove dwellers from their homes to reconsider.

In the case of Pom Mahakan in Bangkok, Thailand, a community of 300 residents located next to Mahakan Fort successfully resisted a planned forced eviction for several years after the Bangkok Metropolitan Administration (BMA) served the residents with a notice to vacate their homes in January 2003. In addition to holding protests, building barricades and organizing a night watch system, the residents put forward a highly innovative land-sharing plan as an alternative to eviction and relocation. Eventually, following continued resistance, interventions by international NGOs and a strong letter from the UN, the Bangkok Governor agreed to resolve the issue through negotiation. On 19 December 2005 the Governor confirmed that negotiations between the community, the BMA and the university had resulted in an agreement to preserve and develop the area as an "antique wooden house community", and the eviction was prevented.

In Brazil a different strategy is employed by the National Fight for Housing Movement, which aims to open negotiating space with the Brazilian government through the collective occupation of vacant land on 3 June each year in some important Brazilian cities such as Fortaleza, Belo Horizonte, Goiânia, Belém and São Paulo. This movement organizes an annual report on the number of forced evictions and families that have been victims of violations of the right to adequate housing. They send the report to the government authorities so that they, in turn, can take measures to resolve the reported conflicts.

2. SECURE TENURE RIGHTS

People living in slums must be guaranteed a minimum degree of security of tenure to protect them from forced evictions, harassment and other threats. Governments should review restrictive regulatory frameworks to develop fair, flexible and participatory models of tenure that are appropriate to the needs of people living in slums, and recognize the relationship between security of tenure and the realization of other human rights. Options to increase security of tenure can include the provision of individual titles, occupancy certificates, protection for tenants, communal land ownership and other solutions.

Indeed, many international bodies have recognized the centrality of security of tenure, and a range of initiatives is underway at the international level, including the UN's Global Campaign for Secure Tenure,[42] the Advisory Group on Forced Evictions (AGFE), the Cities Alliance and others. These can easily be expanded once greater attention is placed by the human rights community on the need to treat security of tenure as a distinct right, and as governments also wake up to these imperatives.

Treating security of tenure as an independent right, in effect is a recognition of the right of all people, in particular those who live in slums, to a right to security of place. The key challenge facing decision-makers in coming years will be how best to expand security of tenure protections, and at the same time not lose sight of the crucial fact that the provision of either tenure or title will not, by themselves, lead inevitably to the improvement of housing and living conditions, economic prospects and the overall enjoyment of human rights within slums. Preventing forced evictions and treating security of tenure as a distinct right are vital pieces of a considerably larger integrated policy framework that will be required for slum dwellers everywhere to enjoy all the rights to which they are entitled.

3. IMPROVE LIFE IN THE SLUMS

Governments must combat direct and indirect discrimination against people living in slums. Legislation and provisions that have a discriminatory affect (such as laws criminalizing homelessness or vagrancy, exclusion from residency, citizenship or other state benefits because of the lack of a "recognized" address, or discriminatory land and inheritance laws) must be reviewed and amended or repealed. Governments must also address the multiple forms of discrimination experienced by people because they live in slums. The issue of community policing is particularly critical.

Governments must ensure the availability of adequate housing, water, sanitation, health-care, and education to people living in slums. They must comply with their duty under international human rights law to prioritize the most vulnerable while allocating resources to ensure free and compulsory primary education, essential primary health-care, and other basic rights.

Slum upgrading, done correctly, can bring human rights to slums. Crucially, it presumes the recognition of the place of the slum within a given urban setting, and the right of that slum to exist as a community in which people as rights holders are allowed to dwell. Governments should adopt or include in their national housing policies a comprehensive plan for upgrading services and conditions in existing slums, and initiatives to provide affordable housing alternatives to people moving to cities. Those with experience argue that the essential ingredients include political will and leadership to drive the plan forward, clear targets, open and transparent land markets, the mobilization of both public and private resources, and realistic planning to prevent the growth of new slums.

The work of the Sindh Katchi Abadis Authority (SKAA) in Karachi, Pakistan has been widely hailed for its innovative approaches to slum regularization that are driven by the people who live in the slums themselves. Responsible for implementing the Katchi Abadi Improvement and Regularisation Programme (KAIRP), SKAA has succeeded in upgrading a large number of slums.[43]

The government of São Paulo has pursued particularly constructive policies on providing secure tenure to poor people in cities. Under a Legal Allotment Program, communities previously excluded from the benefits of legal development are improved and brought into the urban fold.[44] El Salvador's national housing policy promotes the legalization of land tenure and the participation of private sector developers in urban upgrading.

The Baan Mankong Program in Thailand enables poor communities to influence a national process of forging comprehensive solutions to problems of housing, land tenure and basic services in Thai cities. The programme channels government funds, in the form of infrastructure subsidies and soft housing loans, directly to poor communities, which plan and carry out improvements to their housing, environment and basic services, and they manage the budget themselves. All told, the Baan Mankong Program aims to reach 300,000 urban poor households in 2000 communities in 200 cities in five years.

4. MAKE PEOPLE PART OF THE SOLUTION

Underpinning all action is the need to recognize the rights of the people who live in slums and the contribution they make to a city. The participation of the communities themselves is crucial in addressing the discrimination and exclusion they experience in accessing their rights to adequate housing, water, sanitation, education, health, work and other services and resources. Lack of formal recognition means that residents are invisible in planning and budgeting processes. It heightens their insecurity in a discriminatory policing environment, and prevents them from seeking justice and remedy when their rights have been violated.

Governments must remove the barriers that prevent the active participation in public affairs, in slum upgrading programmes, and in other urban planning and budgeting processes of people living in slums. The inhabitants of slums must have access to relevant information on public processes and decisions, especially concerning housing, and urban planning and budgeting, as well as being included, consulted and listened to with regard to the decisions that impact on their lives directly or indirectly. Their rights to freedom of expression, peaceful assembly, to organize and to collective bargaining must be respected, and the government must create enabling conditions for human rights defenders to carry out their work.

Without the active participation of slum dwellers themselves, any well-intentioned policy is destined to fail. We need a vision that places housing and living conditions at the centre of the overall enjoyment of human rights. Policies, laws, projects and programmes need to be deeply influenced by the language of human rights and the sentiments and presumptions that rights bestow.

For too long, states have ignored slums and abdicated their responsibilities to those who live in them. Slum dwellers are all too often invisible to those who hold the reins of power and wealth. In some countries, urban maps leave slum areas entirely blank, as if they were empty wastelands! The problems of insecurity, inequality and deprivation that the people in those areas suffer are not set to disappear and are only likely to worsen, infecting all parts of the city. No scented gardens or grilled gates will keep away the stench of the sewers from the homes of the rich. The only answer is to recognize the right of slum dwellers to share the city with the same dignity and equality of opportunity as other residents, and to work with them to make that happen.

EIGHT
COMMODITIES BOOM, RIGHTS BUST

IN JANUARY 2009, AS STOCK markets around the world continued to tumble, I found myself at the World Economic Forum's annual meeting in Davos, Switzerland. I am one of several NGO representatives invited to these gatherings. I go because I see it as an opportunity to place human rights issues squarely in front of the world's economic and political elites. It is not always an easy task.

The 2009 meeting was a downbeat affair; everyone was gloomy in the face of what had emerged as a truly global recession. Beyond the gloom, what struck me most was the complete failure of the Davos attendees to accept any blame for this state of affairs. It was a "failure of government regulation", of "contagion that spread from the sub-prime mortgage market in the US" or of "debt-fuelled consumer spending".

Yet these same people at Davos were the principal cheerleaders for the model of economic growth that has led to the current crisis, a model built on freeing up global trade and investment, coupled with a light regulatory framework, and trust in multinational companies, including banks, to act in a "socially responsible" manner. Many of the big banks collapsing in debt are active participants in the World Economic Forum (though few showed up in Davos in 2009). Indeed, years from now, when historians seek to capture the spirit of free markets built on the globalizing economy that is the hallmark of the past 20 years, Davos will be iconic.

Oil refinery near Doba in Southern Chad, March 2007. The flow of oil has failed to improve lives of local people. © Teun Voeten/Panos

This is not to say there are no dissenting views. There is no shortage of good debate at Davos – critics are invited and there is an honest effort to include diverse perspectives. But the broad current flows powerfully in support of boosting global investment and trade, and indeed, at least prior to the current crisis, freeing up global finance.

With no apparent sense of irony, participants at the 2009 Davos meeting gathered under the banner, "Shaping the post-crisis world". The reasonable question from any one of the millions of people thrown out of work might have been: "Weren't you one of the architects of the crisis in the first place?" But this question wasn't asked, at least not in the many events I attended.

For me, those debates in Davos symbolize the power without accountability that is a feature of our world. In venues like Davos and elsewhere CEOs of the world's largest corporations, north and south, meet with trade, finance and foreign ministers, and sometimes with heads of government. Together they debate proposals on the global economy, environment and global social issues, including poverty, set the agenda and take decisions that impact on the lives of millions.

The rise of corporate power across borders has been a characteristic of economic globalization. Large companies headquartered in one country operate in multiple locations and impact on the lives and livelihoods of millions of people in dozens of other states. Yet, an understanding of their responsibility to respect human rights is only just beginning to emerge. Likewise, decisions of powerful governments and international financial institutions like the World Bank and the IMF are felt on lives and livelihoods across the world, way beyond the boundaries of any single nation state.

Few countries today can, on their own, truly master the problems of poverty within their borders. More often than not they may find themselves impoverished by actions taken elsewhere. Economic policy depends on trade and investment flows, the provision of foreign aid, and access to new technology. The economy of a poor country may be devastated by the subsidies provided by rich governments to producers in their own countries. When monies are misspent on arms, for personal enrichment, or on grandiose but misguided development projects in developing countries, foreign governments, companies and banks are often intimately connected, if not complicit, with the national government. At other times well-meaning national governments may find their ability to strengthen and defend human rights hamstrung by the power of foreign companies or the policies of donors driving development. Even where governments are well-intentioned, foreign governments and businesses may carry so much influence as to subvert or undermine local democratic processes.

Similarly, the threats to lives and livelihoods faced by poor people may originate abroad. The security of people's livelihoods can be put in jeopardy by world commodity markets, for instance when prices of basic foodstuffs increase dramatically, as they did in the period 2005-2008. International trade rules or practices may mean the crops on which poor farmers rely for a living are no longer competitive. Export-led job creation may deflate suddenly when demand abroad dries up and/or foreign companies abruptly withdraw their investments. Migrant workers may be sent home, remittances or revenues from exports may fall, and that, in turn, may mean less money for health, education and food programmes for very poor people.

In all these cases, therefore, it may be of little benefit to the individuals affected to rely on their own government to protect their rights and provide redress, because the power that needs to be checked or confronted resides outside the borders of their own country. What does the right to participate mean when the decisions that matter take place in foreign capitals or boardrooms? What does the right to security mean when one's own government lacks the means to guard against risks arising abroad?

If we are to act as if rights mattered, and accept that rights are a constraint on power, it should matter little where that power is exercised. Human rights are a truly revolutionary idea because they are based on the principle of universality and on the premise that *all* humans enjoy the same basic rights. One's own state is the primary duty holder in relation to these rights. It has been clear, however, from the adoption of the UDHR in 1948 that, in some cases, individuals will need to look beyond their own borders and to duty bearers other than their own state to respect and protect their rights.

This opens up a large arena of issues. Trade, investment, finance, aid; these and other areas of international action are all implicated. To explore the need for extending accountability across borders, and how this might be done, I will focus in this chapter on a small piece of that agenda – the impact of oil and mining companies in developing countries. The story of these countries – "cursed" by their resource wealth – is well known. But I believe it demonstrates in a clear and powerful way both the importance of human rights to the debate on poverty reduction, and the need for international accountability for state and corporate actors.

OIL, REPRESSION AND POVERTY

In the mid-1990s, massive oil reserves were discovered in one of Africa's smallest countries, Equatorial Guinea. Today, the economy of this tiny country of half a million people is almost entirely dependent on oil and gas revenues. The petroleum sector contributes around 80 per cent of GDP. The World Bank estimates that government oil revenue increased dramatically in value from US$3 million in 1993 to US$190 million in 2000 and US$3.3 billion in 2006. Equatorial Guinea is now the third largest producer of oil in Sub-Saharan Africa, after Angola and Nigeria.

The country's current ruler, President Teodoro Obiang Nguema Mbasogo, took power in a military coup d'état in 1979. He has held power through several fraudulent elections, including in 1996 when it was declared that he had won 99 per cent of the vote. The vast majority of the political opposition has been forced into exile, and there is currently only one opposition member in the 100-member legislature. Transparency International ranks the country in the top 10 of its list of corrupt states.

Unsurprisingly, therefore, the oil boom has not translated into benefits for the population. The country's average life expectancy of 50.4 years is one of the lowest in world. Only 44 per cent of the population has access to safe water and, between 1995 and 2002, almost 39 per cent of all children in the country under the age of five were malnourished.

Not only has the population not benefited, they have been impoverished further by new pressures resulting from the oil wealth flowing into the country. There is demand for land for commercial purposes, including for construction of luxury housing. In August 2006 the authorities engaged in a systematic practice of mass forced evictions, leaving hundreds of families homeless. In many cases, those who were uprooted possessed titles to the land. Amnesty International researchers concluded that residents were arbitrarily evicted, without consultation and with no opportunity to contest the eviction. Nor were they compensated for the loss of their homes.

Equatorial Guinea may be a particularly stark example of oil and mineral wealth making things worse for people living in poverty, but it is by no means exceptional. In Africa, other infamous examples include Angola, the DRC, Chad and Sudan, and in Asia, Myanmar. In all these countries, and others, we see a combination of massive oil and/or mineral wealth, repressive governments, widespread human rights abuses and the majority of the population living in absolute poverty.

Academics have warned for some time that the exploitation of a country's abundant natural resources may not result in benefits that are widely enjoyed by the population. This is especially so where the countries are characterized by high rates of poverty and profound inequality of income, figures that often worsen once mineral extraction begins. This anomaly is sometimes referred to as the "resource curse", or the "paradox of plenty" – where developing countries that are blessed with an abundance of oil, natural gas or minerals tend to have slower economic growth and higher rates of poverty than countries without such endowments.[1]

There is, in fact, a disturbing correlation between developing countries with generous natural resource endowments and the prevalence of authoritarian forms of government. Developing countries rich in oil, gas and mineral deposits have been found to be less democratic on average than those that do not enjoy such natural resources. They frequently lack an independent judiciary and respect for the rule of law. Resource rich countries in the developing world also suffer from higher rates of poverty and corruption, and are more prone to conflicts. Scholars who have examined this democratic deficit in oil producing countries have ruled out culture, colonial legacy, religion, and ethnic or linguistic tensions as the primary explanations for the failure of democracy to thrive.[2] Two principle explanations have emerged to explain the link, and both have important implications for human rights. The first explanation notes that oil producers are frequently "rentier states", which collect large profits from international sales of their oil exports, or from other external sources. The governments of these oil exporters combine the collection of these "rents" with low income taxes for their citizens and extensive patronage to relieve pressures from the public for greater accountability.[3]

A second explanation has been labelled the "repression effect" in which non-democratic regimes boost funding for internal security forces from oil and mineral revenues to ensure they maintain a grip on the reins of power and resist pressure from the public for an improvement in basic economic conditions.[4] Some observers suggest that control of oil revenues stifles modernization by providing the government with sufficient resources to suppress non-governmental and other actors who are independent of the government and who demand freedom and the rule of law.

Whatever the theory, the impact is clear – oil and mineral booms in many countries bring repression and continuing poverty. But who is to blame? The traditional response, at least of business, is to blame the local government, and hope for reform. The resources are needed, the argument goes, and businesses that extract them, or countries that import them, cannot be faulted if the places where they are found are poorly governed.

But this traditional position has come under pressure for change. In November 1995, Ken Saro-Wiwa, a Nigerian writer, was executed along with eight colleagues. Saro-Wiwa was an activist for the rights of the Ogoni people, whose lands and livelihoods in the Niger Delta had suffered enormous damage as a result of oil exploration and extraction. He had been campaigning loudly and visibly against the role played by foreign oil companies, including Shell and Chevron, in causing this devastation. Saro-Wiwa drew attention to the fact that the Ogoni had seen little benefit and much hardship from the exploitation of the Delta's resources. The military regime then in power arrested him on trumped-up charges and put him to death.

Saro-Wiwa's execution drew worldwide condemnation. In its wake, Shell and many other oil companies accepted that they couldn't ignore human rights issues. In 1998 Shell became the first major corporation, and the first oil company, to adopt an explicit human rights policy. This trend quickened. In a 1999 speech at Davos, then UN Secretary-General Kofi Annan challenged global companies to be champions of global values, including respect for human rights, the environment and core labour standards. The UN Global Compact was established to provide a means for companies to formally indicate commitments in these three areas, and to share information on implementation and good practice. Today, over 4,700 companies have signed up to the Global Compact, and more than 100 global companies have human rights policies that explicitly invoke the UDHR.

While some see it as a positive sign of growing commitment, others have criticized the UN Global Compact as an attempt at "blue wash" – no more than a public relations exercise under UN patronage. This may be too harsh. The Compact has increased awareness among companies about these issues. Still, in the absence of effective monitoring, or sanctions in the case of non-compliance, it is unlikely to bring about real and lasting change in corporate behaviour.

The UN expert on business and human rights has argued that assessing the human rights impacts of investment abroad ought to be part of the normal exercise of due diligence by any responsible company.[5] But neither such advice nor various voluntary codes of conduct – two of which I will examine later in this chapter – have led to significant change in the behaviour of companies or governments. The lure of profits and the competition to gain access to scarce resources mean that not all multinational oil and mineral companies are ready to commit themselves to respect human rights unless they are compelled to do so. Add to that pervasive corruption and the intransigence of some repressive governments, and it is clear that voluntary commitments are insufficient by themselves to address the problem. And as the cases that follow show, the commodity boom and rights bust dynamic continues to impoverish and keep people in poverty.

THE WORLD BANK AND CHAD

Chad is a poor country in the heart of Africa. In 2007, the UN HDI ranked it among the 10 poorest countries in the world, with 80 per cent of the population of 10 million living below the poverty line. Yet since 2003 the country has enjoyed substantial revenues from oil, brought to global markets by a high-profile oil pipeline project supported by the World Bank.

The Chad-Cameroon Oil and Pipeline project came about as a public-private partnership between the World Bank and a consortium led by Exxon. The World Bank participation helped in raising money on international capital markets. The project was funded despite the abysmal human rights record of Chadian President, Idriss Déby, who came to power in a military coup in 1990. His forces had been fighting a rebel movement since that time, and had carried out massacres and torture to subdue armed insurgents. In the 1990s, in the southern part of the country, where the majority of the state's oil reserves are found, Déby's military operations were particularly brutal – hundreds of people were summarily executed.

Many civil society actors were dismayed by the prospect that the project would go forward without tangible improvements in the country's human rights record and without adequate safeguards to ensure that revenues from the project would not be misused to prolong Déby's abusive rule.[6] In response to their criticism and pressure, a unique arrangement was set up whereby, in an agreement with the World Bank, the Chadian government committed itself to spend oil revenues on poverty alleviation. To this end, those revenues were to be set aside in a special account with independent oversight.

Problems arose almost immediately. With the first tranche of funds, Déby purchased military equipment. Three years into the project, with the oil flowing, it was evident Chad's population was not benefiting. Systematic and large scale embezzlement of state revenues triggered an unprecedented social crisis. The growing anger spurred opposition leaders and emboldened rebel groups. In April 2006, hundreds of rebels entered the capital, and battles in the streets killed an estimated 350 people. In the aftermath of that attack, Déby announced that even more of the country's oil revenues would go to buying weapons to fight the rebels.

In February 2008, armed groups mounted another offensive on the Chadian capital of N'Djamena. Hundreds of civilians were killed or injured, many homes damaged or destroyed. Some 50,000 refugees fled across the border into Cameroon. The government repelled the attack; it did so in part by relying on intelligence and ammunition from French military forces stationed in Chad. After government forces regained control, there were reports of enforced disappearances, arbitrary detention, extrajudicial executions and torture. The authorities also clamped down on independent journalists and human rights defenders, many of whom were forced to flee the country. Then, in March 2008, the government embarked on a campaign of forced evictions, demolishing houses and small businesses throughout the city. An Amnesty International research mission found that more than 60,000 people had been left homeless and without livelihoods, and thousands of children were unable to continue their schooling.[7]

The World Bank eventually pulled out, suspending US$124 million in loans and grants, and payment of an additional US$125 million in oil royalties. Chad's government had clearly reneged on its agreement that it would spend the vast majority of the oil wealth on poverty-reducing social expenditure. But this hasn't stopped the oil from flowing to foreign buyers. Although the demand for oil, and consequently the royalties, have decreased, the project is still enriching Déby's regime, and doing little for the people of Chad.

Déby was able to thumb his nose at the World Bank and ignore his pledges because other international actors – commercial and political – were not committed to enforcing them. What Chad shows is that repressive governments, flush with revenue from natural resources, can continue to impoverish their people as long as companies are willing to continue to put profit above the social or political costs of their activities, powerful governments are ready to support such alliances, and none of these actors incur any liability at home or abroad.

Some crimes are so heinous that their perpetrators can be brought to book in any country when they are immune from prosecution at home. Genocide, war crimes, crimes against humanity – those responsible may find themselves subject to "universal jurisdiction", and brought before courts abroad, as Chilean General Augusto Pinochet discovered on a shopping trip to London. This use of the courts in a country where the rule of law operates to enforce international law for crimes committed elsewhere, ought to be expanded. It may not be a crime to assist repressive regimes to develop their resources – but when this is done in the full knowledge that doing so will fund repression and enrich a corrupt political elite, questions of moral culpability arise.

THE SCRAMBLE FOR RESOURCES – EASTERN CONGO

Chad demonstrates the difficulty of influencing an intransigent government. A repressive state can act with impunity when markets exist for its oil and not all external actors with influence are ready to sign up to the same list of demands. This problem is, if anything, even worse where there is a weak state caught up in conflict. Many more actors – from warlords and guerrilla armies to regional and other governments – then play a role in mineral extraction and the raking off of profits. This is the situation in the DRC.

Natural resources lie at the heart of a brutal, devastating conflict in the DRC. The central African country has petroleum and vast mineral resources, including cobalt, copper, diamonds, gold, silver, tin and coltan, a metallic ore that is essential for producing the capacitors used in cell phones and other electronic devices. Yet, it is estimated that more than 80 per cent of the country's approximately 58 million people lived in absolute poverty in 2006.

After gaining independence, the country, then known as Zaire, was ruled by the brutal and corrupt dictator, Mobutu Sese Seko. In 1997, rebel leader Laurent Kabila assumed power with the support of forces from neighbouring Rwanda. During his tenure, Kabila signed numerous mining deals with multinational corporations to help finance his war against various rebel factions. In 2001, Kabila's son Joseph assumed the presidency after his father was assassinated. A tenuous peace deal was agreed in 2002, but fighting has continued.

Millions were killed in the war or as a result of the disease and malnutrition it caused, and other countries in the region became involved in the internal armed conflict. Government forces were supported by Angola, Namibia and Zimbabwe, while the rebels were supported by Uganda, Rwanda and Burundi. All sides were guilty of looting the country's resources. Thousands of tonnes of coltan were smuggled out of the country by Rwandan, Ugandan and Burundian rebels, according to a 2003 UN Security Council report.[8] An in-depth investigative report was produced by a panel of UN experts, but the governments of Uganda, Rwanda and Burundi protested, claiming it was inaccurate. The UN report described the brutal measures employed by the rebels to obtain the coltan, which included forced labour and murder. Most coltan mining in the DRC is done by informal artisanal miners rather than large-scale mining companies. The rebels used the civil population, including children, to extract the resources, frequently as forced labour.

As the conflict in the Congo raged from 1996 to 2003, both the rebels and government signed contracts with international mining companies. These contracts were of dubious legitimacy and were surrounded by persistent rumours that the unfavourable terms were due to the corrupt officials who signed them. In 2005, a Congolese parliamentary committee issued a report on its investigations into these contracts. The report found that dozens of contracts were either illegal or contained terms that were not in the interest of the Congolese people. It recommended cancellation or renegotiation of many of the agreements. The parliamentary committee also recommended investigation and prosecution of officials implicated in bribery schemes that resulted in the unfavourable terms.[9] No such prosecutions have been initiated, and, as of late 2008, renegotiation of contracts was continuing, though NGOs were criticizing the process for its lack of transparency.

Meanwhile, new investments in the country do not appear to be abating. In 2008, the state-owned China Metallurgical Group

Corporation, a resources development company, agreed to a joint venture set up by China to invest in a copper and cobalt mining project in the DRC. China agreed to provide almost US$6 billion to be spent on infrastructure and US$3 billion to be spent refurbishing the country's mining industry in return for mining rights stretching ahead 40 years. Infrastructure-related activities would include the building of more than 9,000km of roads and railways, as well as dams, schools, hospitals and housing. The deal sidelined large western mining groups that were also interested in developing the resources. It is indicative of the emergence of China on the global stage and the competition it represents to other more traditional players. We will have to see how the revenue will actually be spent. Though it seems a significant investment, critics argue that, in fact, the $9 billion is not much, given the 40-year lifespan of the contract.[10]

Those who are apprehensive about increasing extractive industry investment in the DRC are right to worry because the local courts appear unable to ensure that this activity does not increase insecurity, and therefore impoverishment. The case of Anvil Mining, an Australian-Canadian company, is instructive. It was accused of providing vehicles and other assistance to soldiers of the 62nd Brigade of the Congolese Armed Forces, which killed at least 73 civilians during an uprising in Kilwa in October 2004. Anvil Mining stated that its transport and equipment were requisitioned and that it had no choice in the matter.

The case created international concern and sparked a UN inquiry; eventually the Congolese authorities initiated criminal proceedings. In June 2007, however, a Congolese military court in Lubumbashi acquitted all those accused, including three employees of Anvil Mining who were on trial. Louise Arbour, then United Nations High Commissioner for Human Rights, issued a statement expressing her disquiet about the verdict. She stated: "I am concerned at the court's conclusions that the events in Kilwa were the accidental results of fighting, despite the presence at the trial of substantial eye-witness testimony and material evidence pointing to the commission of serious and deliberate human rights violations." She also condemned the use of a military

Previous pages: Young men dig for copper at a mine near Lubumbashi, Democratic Republic of the Congo. © Sven Torfinn/Panos

court to try civilians.[11] Efforts to initiate proceedings against Anvil in its Australian headquarters also failed.[12]

As in the case of Chad, so too in DRC, companies have been tempted by profit to ignore human rights, with devastating consequences. Even if some might have been inclined to do the right thing, there have been other less scrupulous competitors ready to move in. The government – supported by external allies and weakened by internal rivalries – has felt no commitment to respect human rights. A range of local political and military authorities control access to resources; and a range of external commercial interests are looking to buy them. This is an unregulated market, the consequences of which have proven deadly for the Congolese.

CORRUPTION – NIGERIA AND ANGOLA

Pervasive corruption is another factor that impoverishes people even as oil revenues fill state coffers. Consider Nigeria. Oil exploration in the Niger Delta goes back decades, and the diversion of revenues to enrich the political and military elite is notorious. Life expectancy in the country is only 47 years; 30 per cent of adults are illiterate; 52 per cent lack access to clean water; and 30 per cent of children are underweight. Since 1999, successive democratic governments have promised to end corruption and committed themselves to poverty reduction. The problems in the Delta are not easily solved, however. Civil unrest and outright banditry make the area one of the most violent in which oil companies do business. The violence finds its origin in the decades of neglect shown for the rights of the people living in the region, including by the oil companies involved. Many human rights groups, including Amnesty International, have reported on the widespread killings, hostage takings, attacks on civilians, environmental degradation and a climate of fear and impunity that characterize life in the Delta. Some of the oil companies have made efforts to invest locally, and to seek to minimize the violence. There is evidence, however, of continuing inadequate consultation with local people and poor responses to oil spills and other hazards that affect their health.[13]

Meanwhile, corruption continues. One recent investigation in Rivers State showed that many schools do not have even the most basic facilities, including sanitation facilities, safe drinking water and teaching materials. Some lack any physical structure to protect students from the weather or have classrooms that have been allowed to fall into a severe state of physical decay. Money transferred by the federal authorities to upgrade schools is just a part of the enormous sums lost to corruption or channelled into questionable and frivolous expenditures. Rivers State claims it publishes its budget each year, but state and local government budgets are treated as state secrets, and journalists are harassed for asking questions about the use of oil revenues.[14]

It is grotesque and immoral that the vast sums of money arising from these projects have been diverted away from schools and hospitals to enrich corrupt elites. It is also illegal. International human rights standards, to which Nigeria is a party, require that governments use all available resources to meet the basic rights of their people to health, education and shelter.

Or consider Angola. In 2004, Human Rights Watch reported that government funds that had disappeared between 1997 and 2002 were almost equal to the total social and humanitarian spending by the government and the UN combined, over that same period.[15] The IMF estimated that the government had mismanaged and misspent billions of dollars of oil revenues, and it conservatively estimated that, from 1997 to 2002, unaccounted funds amounted to US$4.22 billion. Those funds were not spent on health, education, or other social services, and their mismanagement came at the expense of Angolans enjoying basic rights.

Aware of the endemic corruption, and conscious of its negative impact on business, some companies tried to do the right thing. Under pressure from campaigners, BP sought to publish data on its revenue to the Angolan government. In 2001 BP told the UK campaigning organization, Global Witness, that it would publish financial data annually, specifically the total net production by each exploration or production block, and aggregate payments made to the Angolan state-owned oil company and to the Angolan government. BP also told Global Witness that the amount of the signature bonus payment it made for an offshore concession, Block Thirty-One, was recorded in the 1999 annual report for BP Exploration (Angola) Limited, available at Companies House in London, UK. In response, the Angolan state oil company, Sonangol, wrote to BP warning that its contracts would be in jeopardy if it continued to disclose "confidential" information.[16]

The letter had a chilling effect on the industry and on efforts to promote voluntary transparency. No other company has tried to undertake a similar effort in Angola, often citing the response by Sonangol as the reason they will not publish this data voluntarily.

Of course, the primary obligation for ensuring human rights must lie with the governments and courts in the country concerned. But foreign companies and international financial institutions also have a duty to respect the rights of the local population. They should also promote transparency so that local people can engage with their government to ensure that the money is devoted to poverty eradication. This is good for human rights and also good for business. However, the World Bank's efforts in Chad ran headlong into the intransigence of the largely unaccountable Chadian government. Similarly, some companies investing in the DRC made pledges to respect rights, but many others did not, and much of the mining is done under the auspices of local warlords sponsored by the government or neighbouring countries. Nigeria and Angola show that, where corruption reigns unchecked, for a company to be transparent may lead to loss of business. These realities have pushed big business and governments, with input from civil society, to work together to develop new models to promote change – with mixed results.

VOLUNTARISM AND BEYOND

Recognizing the problem but still wary of international regulation, companies, often prompted by and in co-operation with governments in states where they are headquartered, have attempted collective, though still voluntary efforts at standard-setting. Two such initiatives are worth looking at – the Voluntary Principles on Security and Human Rights, and the Extractive Industry Transparency Initiative.

The Voluntary Principles on Security and Human Rights were agreed in 2000, and now include 18 multinational oil and mining companies. They are sponsored by four governments (US, UK, Netherlands and Norway) and eight NGOs are also involved. Amnesty International is one of them. The principles commit companies to exercise due diligence in the hiring of security personnel, to ensure that any personnel act in accordance with international rules on the use of force, and that they are trained to this end. Though voluntary, the principles have been incorporated and adopted by other institutions, such as the International Finance Corporation (IFC) of the World Bank, which has adapted them and includes reference to them in contracts that are enforceable with respect to companies that receive project finance from the IFC.

The Voluntary Principles have met some success in setting a standard, but much less so in implementing it in practice. Until 2007, there were no rules or procedures that addressed transgressions. Those now in place are geared towards individual cases, and it is very hard to assess whether a company has implemented the principles consistently and throughout its operations. More importantly, there is little evidence that the Voluntary Principles have influenced governments, particularly those in resource-rich countries that have poor human rights records, to create an enabling environment in which the human rights addressed in the principles can be respected. Efforts are underway to strengthen the rules and compliance procedures for the Voluntary Principles, but progress has been slow and contentious, generating scepticism among some NGOs about their worthiness.

A second voluntary arrangement is the Extractive Industries Transparency Initiative (EITI), agreed in 2002. This initiative aims to encourage oil and mining companies to publicly disclose the revenue payments they make to governments. The idea is to encourage transparency, making it harder for corrupt and repressive governments to divert money away from useful social goals. Governments who sign up must disclose the revenues they receive and be subject to independent verification of those figures. This initiative was launched by former UK Prime Minister Tony Blair. More than 20 governments have become "candidate countries", committed to meet a number of criteria that promote transparency.

However, as yet only Azerbaijan is considered an "implementing country", compliant with the various information disclosure requirements regarding oil revenues.

EITI currently covers only government revenues – it does not cover government expenditures. Obviously, tracking the extent to which these go to poverty-reduction efforts and the progressive realization of economic and social rights is vital. EITI is a voluntary initiative; governments are not compelled to participate. The initiative requires that civil society organizations in the countries concerned participate in steps to publish the necessary data, including in drawing up the country's work plan and in the selection of auditors to verify the accuracy of financial information disclosed. However, some governments have prevented civil society from participating fully, as required by the initiative. For example, the governments of Gabon and the Republic of Congo both profess to be committed to the goals of the initiative, but they have repeatedly harassed activists who participate in EITI.[17] Some governments that are members, such as Equatorial Guinea, are so repressive that they do not allow independent civil society organizations to function in their countries.

The Voluntary Principles are just that – voluntary – and therefore only likely to be implemented by the willing. Furthermore, they only address the use of private or public security forces by the companies concerned. What of environmental impacts, arbitrary displacement, and the conflict-creating potential of these investments? All those consequences will keep people poor. Likewise, the EITI is optional; it has no means to enforce its provisions that require local participation, and even if it is followed, it only addresses the transparency of revenue, not expenditure. There is therefore no means of ensuring that states prioritize spending on basic rights to health, shelter, food and education in line with their human rights commitments.

I started this chapter by noting that the key problem we face is power without accountability. The record of the extractive industries in poor countries is, by and large, not a good one. Steps have been taken to improve that record, but more must be done. When we know that governments in these countries will not or cannot curb corporate malpractice – on the contrary they seek to benefit from it – trying to protect human rights by relying solely on voluntary compliance by all parties or the good intentions of outside investors to prod them to do so seems inadequate.

The cases above illustrate what is happening in repressive countries, and/or countries riven by conflict. Some might argue that in other countries, where governments are more open and more committed to poverty reduction, significant advantages for the poor have come from investment in oil and mineral extraction. True, developing countries with oil and mineral resources like Malaysia, Brazil and Mexico have made progress in tackling poverty. But even countries like these are often unwilling to adopt the reforms that would allow them to manage and account to the public for the revenue flows from their new investment. They have too rarely put into place procedures and systems to assess and to effectively regulate and monitor the environmental and human rights impact of investments. There are countervailing pressures – to attract investment, to bring the resources quickly to market, and to reduce costs – that weigh heavily against effective regulation in these areas.

The case for change is strong. We see new trends and support for more regulation emerging in the financial sector on a range of issues. Take taxation. For years, global banks and investors were able to opt out of national regulations on transparency and tax by placing their investments in tax havens abroad. In the wake of the financial crisis, the world powers, in the form of the G20, decided to close this loophole. Jurisdictions that do not abide by minimal rules on financial transparency and disclosure will be named and shamed, and forced to comply.

We need a similar approach on human rights in the extractive sector. In rich, developed countries, oil and mining companies are required to follow laws on consultation with affected communities, on security, on environmental assessments, and on transparency. Although these are not always adequate or enforced, there is at least a clear legal framework. Why shouldn't there be similar rules when such companies invest abroad? "There will be no more tax havens," the G20 declared at their London meeting in April 2009. Using the same logic, the G20 (who make up 80 per cent of the world economy) could decide to insist that the rule of law and transparency should guide investment in and exploitation of natural resources.

International human rights and environmental standards – to which all governments pay lip service – provide a ready-made code against which to judge compliance.

Standards are only effective to the extent that they are enforced. Much oil and mineral extraction occurs in poor countries and conflict-prone regions, where the state machinery for oversight and enforcement is weak or the political will to enforce them is lacking or both. That is why we also need systems that cut across borders to uphold standards – such systems are needed not only to bring the rich to heel on tax evasion, as the G20 announced, but also to bring governments and companies to account for impoverishing people and abusing their rights.

NEXT TIME – A BOOM FOR HUMAN RIGHTS

The governments of Angola, Chad, Equatorial Guinea, Nigeria, the DRC and others have pledged to respect and protect human rights, and pledged also to progressively meet the basic needs of their citizens for food, shelter, health and education. But when they can't or won't honour these pledges, outside investors and governments should not be complicit in ongoing abuse. The traditional approach is to recognize the sovereign right of a government (regardless of how it came to power or how it rules) to exploit its mineral resources. How can outsiders tell an independent country what to do with its oil, gold or copper?

Human rights are universal. Upholding them should be everybody's business. The obligation to act should trump concerns about sovereignty when a country's record is utterly dismal. The problem is to find an effective response that changes state and corporate behaviour without hurting the people even more. The UN could ban outside investment in the country, or ban the purchase by foreign buyers of its resources until it reformed. But such sanctions are a blunt weapon, and more likely to hurt poor people than those in power. The solution must be to ensure that clear rules – on security, respect for rights and consultation with local communities, and transparency – are in place to regulate the behaviour of foreign investors, and that they can be enforced when compliance is lacking. The rules need to cover three major issues.

1. NO MORE LOOPHOLES

It is good news that foreign governments and multinational companies have seen the need to adopt measures like the Voluntary Principles and EITI. It means they recognize the problem – that investment in oil and mineral extraction in poorer countries may lead to insecurity, further corruption and deny to the poor the investments in health, education and shelter that they need. But experience has shown that these measures have not been good enough in practice and more needs to be done.

One way to promote transparency is to empower local communities, and I discuss that below. But these local actors will always have less power than large multinational companies, so what hope do they have in influencing the states where such corporations are headquartered? This problem of power means we must look to laws that operate across borders to provide clear duties to respect the rights of local people.

The UN expert on business and human rights has shied away from recommending the creation of new standards for companies. He has, instead, clarified the duty of companies to respect human rights and called on them to strengthen their policies and procedures so that they are better able to do so. But in my view, there is a role for new international rules to make clear that the principles of respect for rights and transparency found in the Voluntary Principles and EITI are not optional. We can't wait for governments and companies to act individually. International rules in most areas are meant to lead, not follow, and it is leadership we need. These rules, too, should uphold the participation rights of local communities. It is crucial that companies from China and other large, emerging economies are included. The G20 might, therefore, be a good venue for this process.

These rules should additionally make clear that individuals alleging human rights abuses can seek redress in the countries where large oil and mining companies are headquartered, when redress at home isn't feasible. The UN expert has stressed the duties on headquarter states to enact and enforce national laws to ensure that their companies respect human rights abroad. Few do so adequately. Setting a clear international standard that gives standing to individuals to complain from abroad would be a stimulus to countries where these companies are incorporated to put such laws in place.

2. LISTEN TO LOCAL COMMUNITIES

People have the right to participate in development decisions that impact on their lives, including decisions on the use of the benefits from these projects. This right to participate includes respect for the rights to assembly, expression and political participation, and to seek, receive and impart information. It also includes the right to open governance processes that are inclusive of people living in poverty, providing meaningful consultation and transparency in development efforts.

This participation must be "active, free and meaningful," according to the UN Declaration on the Right to Development. To ensure that participation is not ceremonial or *pro forma* and is, instead, truly meaningful, access to information is key. Individuals cannot meaningfully participate without comprehensive and timely access to information on development processes, government policies and budgets, and on procedures for redress or access to complaints mechanisms.

One indication of the acceptance of meaningful participation, access to information and access to review by an independent court or other body, is their inclusion in a growing number of international instruments, including in the 1992 Rio Declaration on the Environment and Development. The Rio Declaration laid the foundation for a more detailed treatment of the right to participation and access to information. This was the Convention on Access to Information, Public Participation in Decision-making and Access to Justice in Environmental Matters, also known as the Aarhus Convention, which came into force in 2001.

The convention has been signed by about 40 parties, including the European Union and governments of Europe and

Central Asia, and is only binding on those states. It is only intended to provide for participatory, informational and procedural rights in environmental policy-making matters. It would not apply to a broader range of development issues, for example those relating to the right to education or right to health. However, it is illustrative of the growing attempts to identify basic minimum requirements for meaningful public participation in development decision-making.

The convention covers public participation in three kinds of government actions: on specific activities or investment projects; on policy-making, including planning and programming; and on executive regulation and rule-making. For example, the convention provides for five measures that governments must provide for participation to be meaningful on specific activities or investment projects:

- The first measure is related to timing – it requires participation prior to a government decision being made. It stresses "*early* public participation, when *all* options are open and effective public participation can take place." (My emphasis.)
- It requires that governments must inform the public about specific proposed decisions related to activities under consideration, and about the procedures and possibilities of participating.
- The public should be allowed to submit comments or express views at hearings or inquiries.
- The authorities must take due account of the views expressed. This requirement to take due account does not amount to a veto, but the authorities cannot discard the public's comments or opinions without considering them seriously, and must state the reasons and bases upon which its decision was made.
- Finally, the convention provides that meaningful participation must include the right to have a government action or decision legally reviewed by a court or another independent and impartial body established by law.

Indigenous Peoples have been particularly severely affected by oil and mineral extraction. Their lands are intimately linked to their livelihood and culture, and there has been some effort to ensure their participation rights. The ILO's Convention (No. 169), concerning

Indigenous and Tribal Peoples in Independent Countries, provides for their rights to participate in efforts to improve their quality of life and work, and their levels of health and education. The convention further requires governments to fulfil the right by providing information in circumstances of particular public interest, for example when it would be in the interest of protecting the public's health. In September 2007 the UN adopted the Declaration on the Rights of Indigenous Peoples. The Declaration urges governments to incorporate in their national legislation the principle of "free, prior and informed *consent*" (my emphasis) of Indigenous Peoples regarding potential development projects or other activities carried out on their lands. This includes access to information and meaningful participation for Indigenous Peoples.

Both the Aarhus Convention and the UN Declaration on the Rights of Indigenous Peoples provide useful examples of what can be achieved in the form of international standard-setting. The Indigenous Peoples' declaration is more controversial, as its inclusion of a "consent" requirement in effect gives these communities a veto over development projects. But why not, when their very survival as a people is at stake? Governments claim that extracting oil and minerals will advance development and end poverty. Company advertisements in glossy news magazines make the same claim. So why shouldn't those who are expected to benefit from the development be given a voice in the decision on whether to proceed or not?

3. FOLLOW THE MONEY

I have spoken several times of the importance of information in making participation rights meaningful. Information on government budgets, on how money is allocated and how it is actually spent, can be a powerful tool in holding governments to their obligations to fulfil basic rights to health, education, shelter and food. In many countries, however, such information is not readily available or easily accessible. Indeed, in some countries budget information and the budget-making process are treated as a state secret. There is, therefore, no way to debate what resources are available or what is being spent. Any trade-offs are unknown. In Chapter 2, I spoke of the

An Atacameño Indigenous leader points out to Irene Khan the damage done to land and livelihoods of the local Indigenous community by water shortages and pollution resulting from copper mining in the region. Chiu-Chiu, Chile 2008.

work of the MKSS in India, which has championed the right to information. The right to information became central to the group's work due to the refusal of government authorities to pay the wages due to poor labourers for their work on public projects.

The MKSS showed what could be done at the village level, when local authorities had to open their books. The same transparency must be in place as regards the central government's budget. The ability of the public, the media and civil society to access timely and accurate budget information is essential for public participation. It enhances the accountability of government, improves decision-making, provides better information to legislators, enhances government credibility with its citizens, and assists in fighting against corruption. Budget transparency should include disclosure to the public of a complete and comprehensive picture of government finances and financial activities. These include the revenues received from extractive and other sources, government expenditures, the debt it plans to incur, government assets and any commitments or activities that might have future budget implications. Moreover, the public should have access to regular updates on all these issues. This information is critical for ensuring accountability to citizens, and would increase the likelihood that extractive revenues will be used to combat poverty.

In countries that are reliant on extractive industries, fluctuating commodity prices frequently result in revenue windfalls, and regularly updated public information is important for accounting for them. Such countries are also renowned for boom and bust cycles in which governments embark on spending and debt sprees when commodity prices are high, followed by default on debt when prices and revenues plummet. In some cases, such painful cycles have been followed by the adoption of important government financial management and freedom of information reforms.

Mexico is one such example. A traumatizing financial crisis in the mid-1990s caused the government to adopt widespread austerity measures in 1995. This was followed in the late 1990s by the publication of a series of reports of the existence of secret presidential slush funds. This caused a public outcry as it contrasted sharply with the austerity measures the public was asked to bear. This galvanized civil society to push for increased access to official information, including on the budget. In 2002, a right to information law was adopted, and a commission appointed to oversee the law's implementation.

Civil society groups, such as Mexico's Fundar Center for Research and Analysis, have subsequently used previously unavailable information to advocate for increased spending on reducing poverty. For example, Fundar, in co-operation with a coalition of civil society partners, successfully advocated for a US$50 million increase in emergency health-care, arguing that the spending was essential to increase access to women's obstetric care in poor, Indigenous communities and to meet the government's obligation to address high maternal mortality rates.

AN URGENT NEED FOR ACTION

It is hard to predict the impact of the current downturn. The commodity boom is over for now. But although the demand for oil and other minerals has slowed, new investments continue and will almost certainly pick up in the years ahead. In April 2009 a consortium of European companies, led by E.ON, the top German power and gas supplier, announced that they had entered into a contract to exploit Equatorial Guinea's large natural gas reserves. The human rights situation in that country remains grim. At the same time, the Chinese deal in the DRC is just one of many the country's extractive sector is pursuing in Africa and elsewhere.[18] There are no grounds for complacency, and much urgency to press on with action to ensure the voice and security of poor people and to end their impoverishment, deprivation and exclusion.

I felt the urgency palpably as I sat in the airport lounge at Calama in northern Chile waiting for the evening flight back to Santiago last year. I had just been to Chiu Chiu and seen for myself the slow death of an Indigenous community as their underground water sources are diverted, diminished and polluted by the activities of the nearby copper mines. With no prospects, and growing environmental hazards, the young are abandoning the villages and drifting to the cities. The community is gradually losing its way of life and its identity. The elders spoke to me of their fears that their very existence as a people is threatened.

The airport, on the other hand, was clearly thriving. The departure lounge was filled with men in dark suits and sturdy boots, carrying briefcases marked with the names of leading US business schools or multinational companies. Chile's economy depends on the copper mines, and economic growth has brought prosperity to the country. Chile is a democratic country and a far cry from the egregious cases that I have highlighted in this chapter. But the issue is the same: in a globalized economy, big business and foreign governments are as much players in determining the human rights impact on people as the national government. They should not be allowed to shirk or shrug away their responsibilities. This is the new frontier of human rights – and it needs new systems to ensure respect and accountability for human rights if people living in poverty are to have their voices heard and their interests protected.

NINE
CLAIMING RIGHTS – LEGAL EMPOWERMENT TO END POVERTY

THE GEOGRAPHY OF BANGLADESH, AT the delta of three major rivers, means that land is continuously being lost or gained by riverbank erosion. As a result, every year, thousands of families are displaced, and they move either to freshly created land (known as *char*) and start a new life, even if it is with the constant uncertainty of being dispossessed by nature again, or are left landless and destitute. Thousands of hectares of land are destroyed but also rebuilt every year. The state policy is to distribute the *char* to poor, landless farmers, but a badly organized and corrupt land registration system means that the claims are rarely recorded and, historically, the poor people have been left unprotected and at the mercy of the rural elite. In recent years the poor people on the *chars* have discovered yet another threat to their land and livelihood with the emergence of industrial farming of shrimps for export in these coastal areas. Local entrepreneurs are increasingly occupying their land illegally, often using violent means, in order to set up shrimp farms.

The case of Char Jabbar in Noakhali district of southern Bangladesh shows not just how the law is failing the people, but also how people are organizing themselves to defend their rights. The families in Char Jabbar had moved to this newly formed area and begun to cultivate after losing their previous land to river erosion some years ago. They joined Nijera Kori (NK), a Bangladeshi NGO committed to the empowerment

Women at BRAC's legal literacy class in Tangail, Bangladesh, January 2008. © Amin/Amnesty International

of poor people through collective mobilization, and started the process of applying for land title of the *char*. Two years later, the registration still had not occurred. Instead, a group of businessmen from a neighbouring town had, with the connivance of the local land registration officials, obtained a lease for this land with the intention of using it for export-oriented industrial shrimp farming. When the organizer of NK moved into the area to offer protection to the families, he was arrested on a false charge lodged by one of the entrepreneurs. When the local NK groups learnt that the businessmen were trying to hire some local people to destroy the harvest and seize the land, they took the initiative to contact those who were being hired and persuaded them not to fight against fellow landless people. NK then took legal action, as a result of which the High Court issued an injunction forbidding the business people from entering the *char* area and prohibiting the local authorities from issuing leases for shrimp farming. Nevertheless, the leasing continued illegally.[1]

The Char Jabbar case shows not just the deprivation, insecurity, and exclusion of the people living in poverty but also their struggle to claim their rights through their own action. In previous chapters I have tried to show the importance of the active participation of those living in poverty in finding solutions to their problems. In this chapter I will argue that the law, and in particular knowledge of rights protected by law and backed by social mobilization, can be a powerful tool to this end.

Human rights are guaranteed by international law, and it is through laws that a state assigns and apportions the duties that must be met to give effect to human rights. Laws are an essential step in enforcing rights. But law on its own rarely provides the whole solution for people living in poverty. As we saw in Chapter 3, entrenched racism and bigotry can persist and deny opportunity to poor people, even in the face of good laws. Or where governments lack resources or capacity, legislation on its own will not change much unless it is followed by effective implementation, as happened to the *char* dwellers in Bangladesh. But law is always a crucial piece of the puzzle.

I am a lawyer by training. I took up the study of law because I saw it as a tool for social change. Good laws, fairly administered, can transform societies. But how is one to judge good laws? And how do we ensure they are enforced? More fundamentally, how to do both in ways that make the law work for people living in poverty who, in every country, face particular difficulties in seeking the protection of law?

I believe that the best way to do that is to empower people to claim their rights and to engage with the institutions that set and administer the laws. This approach is called *legal empowerment*. It is a bottom-up effort to arm those living in poverty with knowledge of their rights so that they can effectively engage official institutions.

POVERTY, POWER AND LAW

Poverty is about lack of power. A farmer is poor to the extent that he or she lacks money to feed their family. But farmers are also impoverished if their control over the land that they till is subject to the whims of a feudal landowner or corrupt government official. People living in slums may rise above an income-based poverty level if they can scrape together $2 per day; but they remain poor – and in fact can be plunged back below the $2 benchmark – if their homes are demolished at a moment's notice. Street vendors may make a minimal living plying newspapers on a busy city street, but police who extract bribes or beat them exacerbate their poverty and deny them a way out of it.

Law can be a tremendous force for protecting the rights of those living in poverty to challenge and gain power. International human rights law is designed to give people the means to protect and demand their rights, as claims on those exercising power. There is undoubtedly an important ethical component to the idea of human rights, a plea that every human being – in the words of the UDHR – "act towards one another in a spirit of brotherhood". But few would rely simply on the goodwill of others to protect their rights. Law is essential both as a shield against the kinds of harm that cause or perpetuate poverty, and as a weapon for helping people increase their freedom. Legal empowerment is about using that shield and wielding that weapon.

The irony is that, for most people living in poverty, the law is often not a liberating force but a means of oppression that perpetuates their deprivation, exclusion, insecurity and voicelessness. Many poor people regard the law as something to be avoided.

The law may exclude poor people from its protection directly, for example, when they are denied citizenship or identity cards; this, in turn, may deny them rights, benefits and access to government services such as health and education. The UN Commission on Legal Empowerment of the Poor (CLEP) (which I will look at in more detail later in the chapter) claims that tens of millions of people across the globe lack a formally documented legal identity.[2] Citing a UNICEF statistic, the Commission suggests that more than 70 per cent of children in the least developed countries do not have birth certificates or similar registration documents.[3]

Exclusion may be *de facto* as well as *de jure*. That is, even if the law ostensibly serves those living in poverty, it may force people to negotiate nearly impassable bureaucratic barriers (often paying bribes in the process) in order to work, go to school or be treated in hospital, legally. The upshot is that poor people may be better off living outside the ambit of the law, even if doing so keeps them poor.

The law may be used to control poor people rather than to promote their freedom. It may – contrary to international standards – bar demonstrations, limit people's ability to organize, constrain their speech or prevent the press from airing their grievances. Or the law may facilitate the exploitation of poor people. For instance, the law may permit compensation so low and employment conditions so onerous that the workers remain poor. It may skew land rights in favour of landowners and against tenant farmers. Or it may mandate that such rights only involve individual property ownership, contrary to the communal use and mores of many cultural minorities. This in turn may enable the government or private interests to seize property legally from under the noses of those minorities.

Some laws go beyond exploiting or controlling people living in poverty, to create a situation in which being poor itself invokes criminal sanctions. Poor people living in cities may face anti-squatting ordinances that deny them housing. Rural residents may encounter regulations that prevent them from seeking legal employment in the cities. Street vendors may encounter rules that block them from making a living. This is not to say that societies must simply let everyone live anywhere or do anything they want but that, by penalizing poor urban citizens, street vendors and other impoverished groups simply for the situation they find themselves in, the law frequently frustrates both their hopes and their prospects for economic progress.

The law may instil fear in poor people. It might equally breed contempt or indifference, for instance when laws are not enforced in practice. A country may have rules in place to protect people against abusive landlords, officials, spouses and the police but such legal protection means nothing if those who would like to ignore it are free to do so, or if corruption, repression, bias or incapacity tilt the courts, the police, land registration bodies, labour tribunals or other government institutions. In all too many countries it is common to hear the refrain: "We have plenty of good laws but they just aren't enforced."

All this leaves poor people victimized, rather than protected, by the law. In fact, in many countries the wealthy and well-connected make the law and can evade the law at their choosing, while poor and powerless people frequently find that the law is ignored to their detriment, or when enforced, it is only ever used against them. In the World Bank's *Voices of the Poor*,[4] many people spoke of the state as a source of oppression and fear rather than protection. Many poor people feel that they are often better off steering clear of the law and legal institutions.

WOMEN, LAW AND POWER

In several chapters in this book I have described the experiences of poor women – killed in Ciudad Juárez, raped in Darfur, evicted forcibly in Cambodia, compelled into under-age marriage in Bangladesh, or forced into prison in Afghanistan for running away from domestic violence. They were denied the protection of the law because they were poor but also because they were women.

Gender discrimination impoverishes women and traps them in poverty. Often the discrimination is social and cultural, but much of it is also legal. Despite progress over the past few decades, laws and legal systems in many societies continue to discriminate against women and perpetuate their poverty in a host of ways. They deny or limit women's land rights or inheritance rights. They grant a husband control over his spouse's assets. They constrain women's rights to work, allow them to be paid less, restrict their right to run a business, obtain credit, vote or participate in politics – or place such decisions under the control of their husbands, fathers or brothers. They fail to protect women against domestic violence or female genital mutilation. They define rape and relevant standards of proof so tightly that prosecutions become nearly impossible – and police and prosecutors become disinclined to pursue such cases.

In a growing array of countries, a plethora of relatively progressive laws have been adopted to end discrimination against women but have not been enforced. And even where laws are fair, the legal system has been unable to overcome longstanding social practices that have oppressed women. In Bangladesh, for example, the practice of dowry has been outlawed, however it regularly continues to be paid, impoverishing the woman and her family, and is the source of much domestic violence. A host of laudable micro-credit programmes empower women economically in Bangladesh but because they are discriminated against in other spheres of life, such as inheritance, marriage, divorce or child custody issues, their gains are fragile. Women who are widowed, divorced or abandoned are at a significantly increased risk of being poor.[5]

JUSTICE – SUPPLY AND DEMAND

We face a conundrum. To be effective, rights must be incorporated in laws and enforced on the ground. But for good reasons poor people, and especially poor women, distrust the law and its institutions. They distrust the law because they often lack the power to make it work for them. Knowledge and action to claim rights can alter both the power imbalance and the disillusionment. Claiming rights through law places both constraints and duties on those who wield power, and makes poor people themselves the main protagonists in the struggle for legal reform.

To put it another way, the "supply" of law and justice, fairly administered, is crucially dependent on the "demand" for it. Enacting

Local community rules for use of the only well and source of clean drinking water in Kroo Bay Slum. Freetown, Sierra Leone, 2007.
© Aubrey Wade/Panos

good laws and reforming institutions is important, but so, too, is stimulating the demand that the law delivers in a way that benefits people living in poverty.

Many governments and experts recognize the importance of law to sustainable development. But their overwhelming focus is on the supply side – in other words on the legal and judicial systems. These are largely top-down efforts to reform legal institutions, train judges and police, and improve the capacity of justice institutions. For the World Bank, which probably spends more on law-specific programmes than any donor agency, it would be fair to estimate that 90 per cent or more – possibly much more – of its money goes to supply-side activities. It does have a promising Justice for the Poor (J4P) programme in a handful of countries, but its budget is dwarfed by the Bank's other legal initiatives. The spending imbalance is even more skewed for the other major multilateral financial institutions.

Let me be clear. The goals of these supply-side initiatives are important: to establish independent judiciaries is essential, as is the need to improve security through better policing. We all want the courts and the police to operate more fairly and effectively. Indeed, this is an area on which many of Amnesty International's recommendations to national governments and the international community are focused. Where there is a real lack of capacity, it makes sense to find resources, including through foreign aid, to boost that capacity.

But for people living in poverty, the law so often fails, not due to incapacity but because of pervasive corruption, repression and deep-seated prejudices. A top-down approach places tremendous faith in government officials who, in many cases are hostile to the rule of law and to poor people.

Take Cambodia. The country has seen wave after wave of efforts, spurred by foreign aid, to train and otherwise aid the country's judges and other legal officials to do their jobs better. It has received foreign funding for new courthouses, better case management systems and associated efforts to improve the delivery of justice. Countless foreign consultants have drafted laws for Cambodia, including, in recent years, civil and criminal codes based on Japanese and French models respectively. But there is little to show for it. The law, the police and the courts are all implicated in the continuing forcible eviction of thousands of people from the slums (discussed in Chapter 5), in defiance of Cambodia's international human rights obligations. The country's bar association tried to stymie the work of a hybrid international-Cambodian tribunal, hearing the cases of Khmer Rouge officials who oversaw the mass murder of fellow Cambodians in the late 1970s.

Numerous other examples could be given. Of course, reforming the law and the institutions that deliver it are long-term undertakings and they should not be abandoned quickly. The truth is, however, that evidence for the success of such approaches is weak. A recent World Bank report on its support for the related field of public sector reform suggests a problematic track record for supply-side programmes.[6]

This is why we need to examine what else has to happen to make legal reform effective for people living in poverty. I would say stimulate the demand side. The bottom-up demand for justice by those who need it most has the potential to force action from sclerotic state structures. The goal should be to assist those living in poverty to understand and act on their legal rights – often in combination with non-governmental and governmental allies – in ways that engage the state or those exercising power. Strategies will be as diverse as local circumstances dictate and allow. The following examples show the richness of approaches and the amazing and impressive outcomes they produce when people themselves generate a demand for justice – from litigation to paralegal aid, reform of traditional systems of justice and social mobilization and solidarity actions.

USING THE COURTS

A classic use of the law involves litigation through the courts. Urban waste recyclers, waste-pickers or scavengers are an extremely marginalized group, who struggle to survive by collecting garbage, using what they need and then separating and classifying what can be sold to industrial recyclers. You will find them – mostly women and children – toiling around the trash heaps of any poor city. The example of the Recyclers Association of Bogotá (ARB) shows how litigation strategies can help protect a marginalized group's access to their means of economic survival.

In 1994, Bogotá's official cleaning and waste management services went on strike for six months. The city issued an urgent appeal to the recyclers of the informal economy to manage the growing piles of garbage. They moved more than 50,000 tonnes of garbage, preventing a public health emergency, and winning a city prize for public service. But at the same time, Bogotá city law prevented recyclers from bidding for city waste contracts. It also deemed all garbage left outside residences as the private property of the corporation that had the contract. So waste-picking was potentially illegal.

The ARB organized and grew quickly after the crisis, and began providing waste services for towns surrounding Bogotá, where the regulations allowed them to operate legally. At the same time, they took the City of Bogotá to court. First they challenged the law that excluded NGOs and co-operatives from the public service market, and, in 2003, key aspects of it were declared unconstitutional. Then they successfully challenged a 2002 National Decree which privatized the ownership of garbage.

The City of Bogotá then set such narrow demands on contractors bidding for waste management that ARB was blocked from even bidding. This time, the organization filed a Writ of Human Rights Protection regarding the lack of substantial competitive opportunities for organized poor people in the bidding process. The Constitutional Court not only validated ARB's claims, but recognized the need for affirmative action to encourage the entrance of waste recycler co-operatives into the industry. ARB's legal strategy paved the way for the recognition of waste recycler co-operatives, helping to guarantee their right to a livelihood.[7]

Litigation strategies stand a much better chance of success where formal guarantees of rights exist. Crucial to ARB's success was the ability to launch a human rights petition to the Constitutional Court. Constitutional protection of human rights is key because this makes clear, at least formally, that the state is committed to human rights. International human rights standards have played a crucial role in this regard. Dozens of constitutions have drawn directly on the language in the UDHR or international human rights treaties to provide this formal commitment to human rights.

Another interesting point about the ARB case is that it litigated an economic right. In Chapter 5, I discussed the regrettable Cold War division of human rights into two categories: civil and political rights, and economic, social and cultural rights. One effect of that division has been that many countries do not offer the same level of protection to economic and social rights. On the other hand, dozens of national constitutions do protect economic and social rights, and these rights have been adjudicated in many courts.[8] Recently, the United Nations made a significant step forward by adopting a protocol that will allow individuals to petition UN bodies when they believe their economic, social and cultural rights have been violated. Up till now, this has only been possible for civil and political rights. This should stimulate efforts to protect key economic and social rights through law.

BEYOND THE COURTS

My understanding of legal empowerment and the use of rights extends far beyond litigation and the courts, however. Courts are remote, often biased, and litigation may be expensive or not allowed. Moreover, the aim should be to strengthen poor people's ability to engage with those who actually administer the law. Land registration bureaux, local government agencies, those administering rural relief schemes – this is the sharp end at which people living in poverty must engage. Legal empowerment strategies can spur legal reform – improving laws, regulations, ordinances and institutions which take crucial justice decisions that have an impact on poverty. Again, the relevant institutions are not simply courts, but those that set and implement rights involving land, gender, the environment, labour and a host of other concerns.

A movement of Alternative Law Groups (ALG) in the Philippines shows what's possible. Filipino NGO attorneys have used legal and organizing tools to advance the rights of disadvantaged groups, including women, farmers, Indigenous Peoples, union workers and the urban people living in poverty. They have often, though not exclusively, used strategies that make those populations more legally self-sufficient and less dependent on lawyers. The ALGs are noteworthy in that they operate in manifold ways, which include legislative lobbying, grassroots aid and ensuring that reforms which are good in theory, are enforced on the ground in practice. Most of the laws that address the needs of poor people, along with many related regulations adopted in the Philippines over the past two decades, have had substantial input from these NGOs. They themselves would correctly emphasize, however, that they generally play supportive roles – helping broad civil society coalitions on the policy and legal reform level, as well as assisting at the community level.

Over the years, various studies have documented the impact of ALGs to various degrees. A seven-country Asian Development Bank review of legal empowerment, published in 2001, discusses various types of work carried out by ALGs and their impact. It also includes a combination of survey research, observation of focus group discussions and interviews with government officials that confirms the contribution of one ALG, Kaisahan, to land reform in sample districts in the country.[9]

Knowledge of the law and the rights it protects – or ought to protect – is key, but so too are skills in advocacy, negotiation and mediation. One strategy has been to train paralegals (non-lawyers with legal knowledge and skills) so that poor people themselves and other non-lawyers shoulder the load of advancing their rights. A recent example of this is in Liberia, which is one of the poorest countries in the world. The country suffered years of devastating civil war and horrifying human rights abuses from 1989 to 2003. As the country slowly began rebuilding in the wake of the trauma, the Open Society Justice Initiative worked with local groups to launch a legal services project that became an NGO called Timap for Justice. Given the paucity of lawyers in the country, and the fact that they were almost exclusively concentrated in the capital, Monrovia, Timap made the best of a bad situation by training paralegals to mediate some disputes and advocate for disadvantaged people in others. Through an evolving mixture of paralegal and mediation activities, Timap has had initial success in addressing land and petty corruption issues in which power, poverty and human rights intersect.[10] Its progress was considered impressive enough for the World Bank's J4P programme to step in with considerably expanded funds, and for neighbouring countries to start exploring ways of replicating the Timap experience. Timap demonstrates that a more decentralized, bottom-up approach can yield concrete, promising benefits for advancing the rights and power of poor people.

Most disputes involving rural poor people in developing countries are processed by traditional justice systems. Operating with or without the recognition or endorsement of the state, they often have an important "legal" impact on poor people's daily lives. Take the case of *shalish*, or informal village councils that settle disputes in Bangladesh on family, property and other civil issues. People turn to *shalish* because it is more geographically accessible, comprehensible and affordable (being free) than the formal court system, which is slow, cumbersome and beset by corruption. But the *shalish* is plagued by gender and class biases, and often operates in ways that perpetuate the influence of elites and the powerlessness of those living in poverty.

A variety of legal aid, community development and women's NGOs in Bangladesh are working to reform

Previous pages: **Movimento Sem Terra (MST) – landless agricultural workers' movement. Brazil, August 2003. © Paul Smith/Panos**

shalish. Their approaches include: co-opting the informal panels that conduct the mediations; organizing independent panels themselves; providing training on the more progressive aspects of national law; and encouraging the participation of women in these processes that historically have been exclusively reserved for men.

As the work of leading scholars like Naila Kabeer has shown, the empowerment of people living in poverty, including poor women, clearly goes beyond the realm of law and lawyers. It is often builds on, or otherwise involves, a range of actions in other fields that are not specific to law.[11] It can include community organization, the formation of groups and use of media, for example. And addressing legal and human rights is integrated with reproductive health, natural resources management, urban housing and other issues. The focus is on providing those living in poverty with the tools to claim their rights.

For many groups, empowerment efforts are embedded in broader strategies and activities that help poor people assert their rights and influence underlying – and often anti-poor – community dynamics. Some NGOs integrate empowerment in broader socio-economic development efforts, such as those focusing on livelihood, literacy and health. Others, among them NK, one of whose cases I described at the beginning of this chapter, have focused on social mobilization, solidarity and the collective power of poor people to fight exploitation and oppression through a variety of non-legal as well as legal means.

Senegal provides an example of how knowledge of human rights can be integrated into projects aimed at improving health and ending harmful traditional practices. In 2001, the African NGO Tostan (Breakthrough) launched a two-year project geared toward reducing female genital mutilation (FGM) and otherwise bettering the lives of village women in one small part of the country. The project featured education for both women and men concerning general hygiene, problem solving, women's health and human rights. The initiative was evaluated by the Population Council, an international research and development NGO. It surveyed women and men in 20 of the 90 villages where the Tostan project took place, and in 20 similar "control villages" where it did not.[11] The research found significant decreases in the reported frequency of FGM in the project communities. It further found that, in comparison with the control populations, both women and men in the target villages came away with greater awareness of the issues around FGM, reproductive health, violence against women and human rights.

MAKING INTERNATIONAL LINKS

I argued in Chapter 8 that power must be checked abroad as well as at home. Examples abound of local groups combining with international NGOs to claim their rights more effectively. In 1999, the Wassa Association of Communities Affected by Mining (WACAM) in western Ghana, together with the Berlin-based Food First Information and Action Network (FIAN), carried out a study on the impact of the Iduapriem gold mine, documenting forced resettlement, lack of compensation, loss of land, water pollution, serious health impacts, and harassment by security forces. All of these problems were evident around numerous mines in Ghana, and FIAN and WACAM chose this case for a focused campaign.

Over the next few years, WACAM and FIAN combined local awareness-raising with an innovative international approach to influence the mine owners through their investors and lenders. FIAN organized public events in Germany on cyanide-based mining and its effects, and invited the German Investment and Development Company (DEG). They also had private meetings with DEG, and presented a list of recommendations for action. DEG, with its reputation at stake, found it was in its own interests to respond. The campaigners then began also to approach the mine's larger lender, the IFC.

The lenders and the mining company defended themselves against all of FIAN's claims, but with WACAM as a local partner constantly monitoring, every defensive claim made by the company could be quickly investigated and answered. The Ghanaian Commission for Human Rights carried out its own investigation, calling attention to gross violations of human rights around the mine. FIAN lobbied the German Parliament to adopt a resolution criticizing cyanide-based mining. After various modes of pressure, the lenders agreed to join a field visit with FIAN and WACAM. They visited some of the worst hit villages, and emerged with a joint action plan to address concerns about water, land and compensation, health, education, employment and ongoing community consultation. After this victory FIAN and WACAM continued to work together on monitoring the implementation of the action points.[12]

The crucial agents for change in all these examples are poor communities and their allies, and the crucial venue the local communities, even if in some cases litigation results in rulings by national courts, or in alliances abroad to bring added pressure on the government or multinational companies. This is not to say, however, that international actors are marginal. On the contrary, by supporting local initiatives, they can help them grow and gain influence. There are encouraging signs that major donor agencies are open to new approaches. Both the World Bank and the UNDP have shown increasing interest in legal empowerment initiatives. Launched in 2002, the Bank's J4P programme has been its first, and largest, effort to look at the demand-side of the justice equation. J4P-related initiatives have started in Cambodia, Sierra Leone (including support for the NGO Timap for Justice) and Kenya, with plans for expansion into additional countries. It features a combination of support for NGO legal services for people living in poverty, other paralegal and mediation activities and related research.[13]

The UNDP's Legal Empowerment and Assistance for the Disadvantaged project (LEAD) is essentially a grant-making project that was launched in partnership with the government of Indonesia in 2007. It is initially operating in three provinces, though it also has the potential to support worthwhile initiatives elsewhere, including on a national scale. LEAD is potentially significant in at least two regards. Firstly, as with J4P for the World Bank, LEAD represents UNDP's first large-scale foray into legal empowerment. In addition, its funding mechanism is something of a departure from how the agency often operates. UNDP opted to make grants to Indonesian NGOs rather than implementing the project itself, because experience across the globe suggests that, as a matter of both principle and practice, this way of disbursing funds is the most flexible and effective way of supporting legal empowerment.[14]

These are small steps. The overwhelming majority of governments' efforts and donor money still go to more top-down approaches. Additionally, the bulk of the World Bank's spending on legal reform is targeted at improving the capacity of justice systems to set and administer rules on contracts and other regulations needed in a market economy. But this could change. It would happen faster if all actors were ready to acknowledge the importance of the full dimension of human rights to ending poverty.

THE WAY FORWARD

The importance of law to development was given high-level attention by the Commission for Legal Empowerment of the Poor (CLEP). This UNDP-assisted body was launched in 2006 and reported in 2008. The Commission's high-profile membership included Madeleine Albright, Larry Summers, Hernando de Soto, Fazel Abed (the head of BRAC) and Mary Robinson. The Commission made a major contribution by stressing the importance of law to advancing the rights of people living in poverty. It placed emphasis on law as a means to protect livelihoods and economic assets. Three of the four pillars of legal empowerment identified by the Commission "are derived from the livelihoods of the poor: property rights, labour rights, and business rights."[15] The fourth pillar is access to justice and the rule of law, which comprises the "enabling framework" for the realization of these rights.

Nevertheless, many of the recommendations emerging from the Commission advocate a top-down approach – despite being about bottom-up development. They emphasize the centrality of political leadership rather than poor people themselves. The CLEP report argues that a "comprehensive [legal empowerment] agenda will be best run ... by presidents and prime ministers in cooperation with ministers of finance, justice, and labour," while "citizens and grass-roots organizations" play a supportive role in "educating the public and rallying around the themes of legal empowerment."[16] Political leadership is, of course, highly desirable, to the extent that it is really dedicated to policies which address the needs and interests of poor people, to human rights, to battling corruption and to sustaining more than its own power. But the legal empowerment examples I provide above challenge the assumption that it is the crucial element. Those examples illuminate the efforts of poor people themselves, and what they and their civil society allies can accomplish, even in the absence of political leadership.

We need to be bolder, and step up our efforts to empower poor people through law and rights. There are no easy answers. Pushing through laws that benefit and support those living in poverty is usually a struggle. And as we've seen, reforming laws is not like turning on a light switch – even when new laws are enacted, they are not self-executing. They often encounter ingrained interests and attitudes that frustrate their enforcement. But much can be done to assist those who are struggling locally to make the law work for poor people.

1. MAKE LEGAL EMPOWERMENT A MILLENNIUM DEVELOPMENT GOAL

The MDGs currently do not acknowledge access to justice as a crucial element in the struggle against poverty. A legal empowerment goal would set this straight. Targets might include the extension of legal and paralegal services to people living in poverty, and expansion of training in law and rights – legal literacy. They might also include ways to measure the opening of democratic space to allow greater civil society mobilization in this area.

Some people may be concerned that this would overburden the judiciary; that the so-called demand would vastly exceed the supposed supply. But as I've already emphasized, legal empowerment is not just about taking cases to court; it requires a far broader view of what the law is all about. In fact, it is more concerned with governance. Through legal empowerment, those living in poverty can exercise their rights to access land, or to ameliorate the gender and other biases that permeate many traditional justice systems, or to ensure that their government delivers the health, education and other services to which they are entitled and for which resources are available, or to participate in community and government decision-making that vitally affects their lives and livelihoods.

2. INCREASE INTERNATIONAL SUPPORT FOR LEGAL EMPOWERMENT

This clearly goes hand in hand with making legal empowerment a MDG. Financial and political support should be available for both stand-alone legal empowerment projects as well as complementing government-centred justice projects with legal empowerment initiatives, to ensure people can make use of improved government institutions. But legal empowerment support should go beyond the strictly legal field, and should also support the integration of justice components into social mobilization of poor communities and into community-based socio-economic development efforts, such as public health, reproductive health and natural resources management. So many development efforts hinge on people actually receiving the services to which they're entitled, and legal empowerment can help ensure that those living in poverty really do benefit from such efforts, rather than being bystanders as resources are siphoned off or otherwise wasted.

Support should also be provided for a pipeline of development-oriented lawyers and other professionals who can help make legal empowerment a reality. Law school is the crucially formative time in providing attorneys with skills and perspectives that shape their future careers. Yet, with some notable exceptions, legal education across the globe is not overly concerned with how to work with those living in poverty, listen to them, learn from them or train them.

3. CHAMPION AND DEFEND POOR PEOPLE'S RIGHT TO ORGANIZE

As I've stressed throughout this book, it is crucial that people living in poverty are active participants in programmes designed to improve their situation. They must be able to come together and organize for this purpose. Collective efforts to claim rights through law will usually stand a far greater chance of success than individual efforts. The examples above are just a small sample of what can be achieved.

Those living in poverty are better able to organize themselves in countries where there are vibrant civil societies. In almost 50 countries, there are restrictions on the right of people to organize independently to advance their interests. The CLEP rightly pointed to the potential benefit to poor people if the law were to work for them rather than against them. As I hope I've shown in this chapter, poor people themselves will be the main protagonists in this effort. The minimum first step, therefore, is to be much more vigorous in demanding the space for them to do so.

In Chapter 5, I spoke of Amnesty International's work to defend the rights of the Guarani-Kaiowá peoples of Brazil who were organizing to protect their land. In Cambodia we have condemned the harassment and wrongful arrest and imprisonment of those struggling to end forced evictions. In Ethiopia we recently spoke out against a draft bill that criminalizes human rights activities and gives the government wide-ranging power to control civil society groups. It isn't always easy to get international attention for these and many, many other situations where poor people are denied a voice.

Sometimes the international community speaks out to defend the rights of people to organize, but not always nor consistently. Countries which resort to repression can too often count on the support, or at least indifference, of powerful trading and security partners. If we were serious about ending poverty, defending the right of poor people to organize to demand their rights wouldn't be an option, but an obligation on all states enforced.

TEN

FROM ACKNOWLEDGEMENT TO ACTION – A CAMPAIGN FOR THE RIGHTS OF POOR PEOPLE

PEOPLE LIVING IN POVERTY ARE trapped – lacking those things that are essential to a life in dignity and kept poor because they are excluded, ignored, and threatened with violence and insecurity. Rights are a way out of that trap. Why?

Put simply, respect for human rights demands inclusion, demands that people have a say, and demands that those in power provide protection against the types of threats faced by those in poverty. It requires also that we recognize that everyone is entitled to those things that are essential to a dignified life – food, water, basic health-care, education and shelter. These rights and protections – with their basis in universal standards – give to people living in poverty a tool to change the power imbalance that keeps them poor.

Those living in poverty need more assets; economic growth can help them by providing better jobs, new and more secure markets, and greater opportunities. But they need more power, too, not least to protect those assets. A focus on the rights of poor people highlights the full spectrum of forces that are at work to keep them poor, even as it equips them with claims for recognition in the political, social and economic domains.

I have written this book in the hope that it will fulfil two aims. Firstly, I hope it will convince you that attention to human rights must be at the centre of our efforts to end poverty. Secondly, I want it to show that there can be

Faced with physical and fuel insecurity, girls carry bricks of mud and donkey dung back to Kalma camp for internally displaced persons. Nyala, Darfur March 2007.
© Sven Torfinn/Panos

no sequenced or partial approach to human rights if we want to tackle poverty. Demanding participation rights is as important as directing resources to meet basic needs for food, health and shelter; protecting people against violence is as crucial as ending discrimination.

We can dramatically reduce the incidence of maternal mortality by improving the capacity of health-care systems in poor countries to deliver emergency obstetric care, by ending the human rights abuses that increase risks in pregnancy, including gender violence, and by empowering women to claim their rights, including their sexual and reproductive rights.

We can improve the lives of people who live in slums by ending forced evictions, by working to provide secure tenure and by working with the residents themselves to provide better health, education, policing and sanitation services in their communities. And we can ensure that the next commodity boom is not again a human rights bust, if we insist on the full participation rights of affected communities, if we apply the same rules of transparency in poor countries as we expect in rich countries, and if we demand that revenues go to finance the fulfilment of basic rights.

Each of these cases shows how we can create a virtuous cycle of rights to end the vicious circle of abuse. The struggle on these and many other issues will play out in an infinite variety of ways in communities worldwide.

Action at the global level must support those struggles. How? First, through global acknowledgement that rights matter. Despite the rhetorical support given by many governments to human rights, when it comes to poverty, powerful governments have yet to accept the relevance of the full gamut of rights across all four dimensions of the problem. I mentioned earlier that China had not yet accepted basic freedoms and participation rights. Its continued reluctance to ratify the UN Convention on Civil and Political Rights (ICCPR) is yet one more piece of evidence of that failure. All the other G20 nations, apart from the absolute monarchy in Saudia Arabia, have done so. At the same time, the United States has failed to ratify the UN Convention on Economic, Social and Cultural Rights (ICESCR). Successive US administrations have not supported UN initiatives in regard to these rights and, at times, have actively opposed them.

The USA and China – the G2 – are global economic leaders. The USA exercises enormous influence in the UN and international financial institutions, and China's influence is growing. How they perceive human rights matters, their competing world views – each pushing a hierarchy of rights with a different set on top – are an obstacle to action on poverty.

But this can change. In its Human Rights Action Plan, published in 2008, the Chinese Government has not ruled out ratifying the ICCPR – in due course. Change is in the air in Washington, DC, too. Prompted by stark market failures and an emerging consensus that the USA must find a way to guarantee universal health-care, talking about human rights in the social and economic spheres is no longer taboo. The joint ratification by these two countries of the two Covenants would send a powerful message, and could signal a new willingness in their respective countries and in their policies abroad to bring human rights fully to bear on the problem of poverty. Their G20 partners and other governments should encourage them to take that step.

Treaties, like laws, must be implemented to be meaningful. Once we acknowledge the importance of rights, we need to move to action to make that acknowledgement real. The current international plan to eradicate poverty is centred on the MDGs. They represent an important global commitment to end poverty. The goals, however, do little to address the exclusion, insecurity and voicelessness that drive and deepen poverty. The MDGs largely de-link rights from development; at best they narrow a broad conception of human rights into an arbitrary and diminished set of indicators. The MDG endpoint is 2015. Many of the targets – indeed most – are unlikely to be met by then.

We must work to make the MDGs more effective by insisting that countries provide disaggregated data to expose the problems of exclusion that are hidden in the aggregate figures provided now. What is visible is harder to ignore.

But we must look to the future and be bolder in 2015. Setting aside piecemeal efforts, governments must launch a global human rights action plan to end poverty. In the past, the international community has captured its commitment on major issues in ambitious and elaborate action plans – in Rio in 1992 on the environment, in Cairo in 1994 on population, in Beijing in 1995 on women, and the same year in Copenhagen on development. Such plans helped to galvanize world attention, but in many respects failed miserably to deliver outcomes because they lacked resources but also clear targets of the kind the MDGs contain. The MDGs, on the other hand, have provided precision, and the deadlines they include create an impetus to action – but only by ignoring action in key areas of vital concern to those living in poverty. A global human rights plan should draw on both experiences and avoid their worst mistakes. It must match ambition with effectiveness.

Recasting the global effort to eradicate poverty in terms of human rights would bring several distinct advantages. Firstly, it would sharpen our focus on the question of accountability. Governments have made commitments to meet MDG targets but continue to fail to do so. If "targets" are explicitly identified as fulfilling rights, and not merely as pledges regarding the shape of government policy, then there is a clear duty to take certain steps. This duty falls first and foremost on governments in respect of the poor in their own countries. But duties fall, too, on other actors: governments abroad, international organizations and private companies, indeed all who exercise power and influence over decisions that impact on the lives of the poor. Human rights obligations, true to the universal nature of the claims they buttress, know no borders.

Secondly, a human rights plan to end poverty must necessarily look at deprivation and exclusion, insecurity and voicelessness. It would acknowledge more accurately the lived experience of poor people. It would broaden the existing approach of the MDGs, although priorities would still need to be set and choices made. This will not be easy, not least for human rights advocates who have traditionally set high demands for immediate progress on many issues. But a plan conceived in rights terms would at least address those human rights abuses that keep people poor, and not, as with the MDGs, largely ignore the problem of discrimination or the issues of empowerment.

Thirdly, a human rights plan should set targets that speak directly to the issues of power. For example, by insisting on the right to information or eradication of violence against women or giving slum communities a right to a hearing on issues affecting them, it would create a potent force for mobilizing people. It would encourage civil society to engage more effectively with the pledges their governments make, and see if they are being met. The success of the plan should not be measured in debates in the UN General Assembly, but in its impact on the ground.

An additional aspect of the human rights plan should be to engage a new constituency – the human rights system itself – in the fight against poverty. Poverty is the world's worst human rights crisis. Yet the UN's inter-governmental and expert machinery set up to advance human rights have given it far too little attention. The UN has prioritized action to end poverty, but its Human Rights Council has not risen to the challenge. The issue is often relegated to bodies with narrow mandates on specific economic and social rights. To break free from Cold War categorizations, the UN Human Rights Council should ask all the UN's human rights experts and human rights monitoring bodies to report on the manner in which poor people are affected by the rights abuses in their respective areas of competence. For some time now, development agencies have adopted a "rights based approach" so that poverty-reduction efforts take account of rights. But we might also attack the problem from the other side, so to speak, by asking those who work to protect rights to also take full account of poverty. This would finally put to rest the notion that certain categories of rights are more or less important in the struggle to end poverty. It would also encourage the human rights system to respond effectively to emerging challenges that are likely to impact adversely on poor people, such as climate change.

The UN's human rights system is not the only culprit to ignore or compartmentalize poverty. As I mentioned in Chapter 5, Amnesty International was among those who ignored issues of economic and social rights for many years. If the global human rights movement is to offer real solutions to the world's worst human rights crisis – poverty – it must rediscover the unity of purpose expressed in the UDHR 60 years ago. As this book goes to press, I am proud that Amnesty International has begun a campaign for the rights of those living in poverty – a campaign for human dignity.

The worldwide human rights movement today is a powerful force. When Amnesty International began its work in the early 1960s, in many countries it was the only organization speaking out in defence of human rights. When it speaks now, it raises its voice alongside many others, even in the most repressive countries – proof of the bravery of the defenders of human rights who live in those countries. Coalitions are now regularly built among national and international, small and big human rights groups around specific human rights demands. The results have been impressive, from controlling the banning of landmines to the setting up of the International Criminal Court or the abolition of the death penalty. The commitment to combatting poverty must also become a call of the global human rights movement.

Looking to the future, the task is to translate universal rights into universal justice. The need to look beyond borders to identify duties to respect and fulfil rights is apparent. It is at the heart of the problem of the global scramble for resources; it arises too, and will do so ever more prominently, in debates on climate change. This is the new human rights agenda. How to give those living in poverty a say in decisions made in distant capitals and boardrooms? How to protect them from foreign threats to lives and livelihoods? And how to challenge global discrimination that appears to replicate, at least in its results, the most egregious inequality within countries? The rights framework tells us that global inequalities in access to rights must narrow, not widen. If not, insecurities will grow, including in the rich world, for the consequences of continuing to deny dignity to billions of people will be conflict and instability.

But why should you listen to me? I've argued that to end poverty we need to focus on respect for human rights. The Commission on Growth and Development, which reported in March 2008, placed the emphasis – understandably – on strategies to achieve economic growth. The CLEP urges us to focus on the law as a means to protect the assets and rights of the poor. The UN is urging renewed attention to successfully completing the MDG agenda. Al Gore and many others point to the urgency of tackling climate change, which is bound to have the greatest impact on the poor. Jeffrey Sachs places the emphasis on more foreign aid, better spent. Others decry the value of aid, and its corrupting influence, and place the emphasis on markets, innovation and entrepreneurship. You may have heard too of the "Tobin" tax – to raise money for development by taxing foreign currency transactions. Muhammad Yunus, the founder of Grameen Bank, urges us to prioritize micro-credit.

There are, indeed, many solutions on offer. But what else would you expect? Amartya Sen is right: to end poverty is to win freedom. There are many paths to freedom, and no single road to happiness. There is, therefore, no single solution to ending poverty. There is merit in many of the ideas being proposed. Future global commissions will be formed, and they will generate new proposals. Out of the current economic crisis we may see, at last, a real restructuring of the international economic system that might provide more stable and equitable outcomes.

I want you to listen to me, however, because I believe that, whatever else may change, and whatever other economic, political or legal solutions are proffered, full respect for the rights of the poor is a constant. Respect for these rights must be at the core of any particular strategy, above all, because only in this way will the people who stand to gain or lose the most by the success or failure of the strategy get their say. Respect for human rights is not another strategy – it is rather *an essential piece of any strategy*.

Looking back, I see several key moments in the history of human emancipation. The abolition of slavery, the achievement of universal suffrage and the emancipation of women, the end of colonialism, the victory over fascism, the end of apartheid, the fall of the Berlin Wall. Each struggle has its own history and dynamics. But at the very core of each of these great struggles was the claim that individuals had rights that could not be denied, rights that transcended race, religion, gender, class or citizenship, and rights that took precedence over any particular economic or political policy. These struggles have, in turn, inspired and been inspired by the language of Article 1 of the UDHR: "All human beings are born free and equal, in dignity and in rights."

The struggle to end poverty is no less momentous. It is this generation's great struggle. We will win it if we put freedom, justice and equality at its core.

Overleaf: Women of Zimbabwe Arise, rural meeting Sibasa Insiza. The meeting was part of a wider consultation on WOZA's People's Charter, Zimbabwe. © WOZA

ENDNOTES

CHAPTER ONE

1 J. Sachs, *The End of Poverty: How we can make it happen in our lifetime*, Penguin, 2005.

2 Center for Economic and Social Rights, Fact Sheet No. 8, *Bangladesh*, http://www.cesr.org/downloads/bangladesh%20WEB.pdf

3 Commission on Legal Empowerment of the Poor, Final Report of the Commission, *Making the Law Work for Everyone*, 2008.

4 M. Yunus, "The problem of poverty in Bangladesh", 25 February 2008, http://muhammadyunus.org/content/view/114/127/lang,en/

5 D. Narayan (Ed), R. Patel, K. Schafft, A. Rademacher and S. Koch-Schulte, *Voices of the Poor: Crying out for change*, Oxford University Press, World Bank Publication Series, 2000, p2.

6 World Bank, *Voices of the Poor*, p236.

7 The argument for an effective state as essential to poverty reduction is made most recently in D. Green and M. Fried (Ed), *From Poverty to Power*, Oxfam International, 2008.

CHAPTER TWO

1 "Building collaborative partnerships to develop a Local Housing Board", New Tactics in Human Rights, www.newtactics.org/es/tactics/building-collaborative-partnerships-develop-local-housing-board

2 Joint World Bank/IMF 2005 PRS Review, World Bank, 2005, fn 107, p42. http://web.worldbank.org/WBSITE/EXTERNAL/TOPICS/EXTPOVERTY/EXTPRS/0,,contentMDK:20343412~pagePK:210058~piPK:210062~theSitePK:384201,00.html

3 UN *Human Development Report 2005*, p59.

4 M. Matsumara, "Democracy as Economic Strategy", *Policy Innovations* 2007.

5 See X. Li in M. Nussbaum and J. Glover (Eds), *Women, Culture and Development: A study of human capabilities*, Oxford University Press, 1995.

6 "The ghost of illiteracy returns to haunt country", *China Daily*, 2 April 2007.

7 See www.chinareform.org

8 Amnesty International, *People's Republic of China. Internal migrants: Discrimination and abuse. The human cost of an economic 'miracle'* (Index: ASA 17/008/2007).

9 Amnesty International, *People's Republic of China. Internal migrants: Discrimination and abuse. The human cost of an economic 'miracle'* (Index: ASA 17/008/2007).

10 C. Coonan, "China 'suppressed report on pollution deaths'", *The Independent*, 4 July 2007 and World Bank, *Cost of Pollution in China: Economic Estimates of Physical Damages*, http://web.worldbank.org/WBSITE/EXTERNAL/COUNTRIES/EASTASIAPACIFICEXT/EXTEAPREGTOPENVIRONMENT/0,,contentMDK:21252897~pagePK:34004173~piPK:34003707~theSitePK:502886,00.html

11 A. Sen, *Poverty and Famines: An Essay on Entitlement and Deprivation*, Clarendon Press, Oxford, 1981.

12 A. Sen correctly points out that the evidence we have in terms of fairly comprehensive inter-country comparisons "have not provided any confirmation of this thesis" and that such claims regarding the benefits of denying rights in pursuit of development have been based on "very selective and limited information, rather than on any general statistical testing over the wide-ranging data that are available." A. Sen, *Development as Freedom*, Oxford University Press, 1999, p15 and 149.

13 D. Kaufman, "Human Rights and Governance: The Empirical Challenge", 2005. Revised draft of paper presented at 2004 Conference on Human Rights and development – towards mutual reinforcement.

14 K. Deininger and P. Mpuga, "Economic and Welfare Impact of the Abolition of Health User Fees:

Evidence from Uganda", *Journal of African Economies*, Oxford University Press, Vol 14(1), pp55-91, March 2005.

15 Right to Know, Right to Live: Building a campaign for the right to information and accountability. New Tactics project. http://www.newwtactics.org/sites/newtactics.org/files/Sowmya_notebook.pdf p6.

16 R. Reinikka and J. Svensson, "The power of information: Evidence from a newspaper campaign to reduce capture", World Bank working paper 2003.

17 P. Collier, *The Bottom Billion: Why the poorest countries are failing and what can be done about it*, Oxford University Press, 2007.

18 J. Isham, D. Kaufmann and L. Pritchett, "Civil Liberties, Democracy, and the Performance of Government Projects", *World Bank Economic Review*, May 1997. (Isham, Kaufmann and Pritchett, May 1997).

19 Harvard Project on American Indian Economic Development, *The State of the Native Nations: Conditions under US policies of self-determination*, Oxford University Press, 2007.

20 Health Canada, "The Evaluation of the First Nations and Inuit Health Transfer Policy: Final Report", 2005.

CHAPTER THREE

1 See www.dalitfoundation.org/whoaredalits011

2 L. Bandeira Beato, "Inequality and Human Rights of African Descendants in Brazil", *Journal of Black studies*, Vol 34, No 6, pp766-786.

3 J. Vandemoortele, *Are the MDGs feasible?*, UNDP, New York, 2002.

4 UN Millennium Project, "Halving hunger: It can be done", 2005, p5.

5 *The Persistence and Mutation of Racism*, International Council on Human Rights Policy, 2000.

6 *Indicators for Monitoring the MDGs – Definitions, concept and sources*, UN, New York.

7 *Claiming the Millennium Development Goals: A human rights approach*, UN, 2008, www.ohchr.org/Documents/Publications/Claiming_MDGs_en.pdf

8 *En-gendering the Millennium Development Goals (MDGs) on Health*, Department of Gender and Women's Health, World Health Organization, 2003.

9 G. Hall and H. Patrinos, *Indigenous Peoples, Poverty and Human Development in Latin America: 1994-2004*, Palgrave Macmillan, 2005.

10 *Indigenous Peoples and the Millennium Development Goals*, UN Permanent Forum on Indigenous Issues, www.un.org/esa/socdev/unpfii/en/mdgs.html

11 Indigenous Peoples figure prominently in statistics on poverty in rich countries, but the MDGs only cover low- and middle-income countries.

12 http://209.85.215.104/search?q=cache:vfd10-t3kz0J:www.odi.org.uk/edc/papers/EUPovertyFocusinMICFinal%252BAnnexes.pdf+POVERTY+IN+MIDDLE+INCOME+COUNTRIES+41&hl=en&ct=clnk&cd=7&gl=us

13 *Achieving the Millennium Development Goals: The Middle-Income Countries*, www.unicef.org/lac/spbarbados/Planning/donors/MIC_DFID_2004.pdf

14 S. Burd-Sharps, K. Lewis, E. Borges Martins, *The Measure of America*, American Human Development Report, 2008-2009, Social Science Research Council and Columbia University Press, 2008.

15 European Roma Rights Centre, *Ambulance Not on the Way: The disgrace of health care for Roma in Europe*, 2006.

16 Cited in *Ambulance Not on the Way: The discrace of health care for Roma in Europe.* European Roma Rights Centre, p.9.

17 *Racial and Economic Exclusion: Policy Implications*, International Council on Human Rights Policy (ICHRP), 2001, www.ichrp.org/en/projects/113s

18 T. Homer-Dixon, *The Upside of Down: Catastrophe, creativity and the renewal of civilisation,* Souvenir Press, 2007, p190.

CHAPTER FOUR

1 "Obesity and overweight", World Health Organization, 2003, www.who.int/dietphysicalactivity/media/en/gsfs_obesity.pdf

2 F. Stewart and V. Fitzgerald, *War and Underdevelopment, Volume 1: The Economic and Social Consequences of Conflict*, Oxford University Press, 2000, p1.

3 R. Draman, "Poverty and conflict in Africa: Explaining a complex relationship", document prepared for Experts Group Meeting on Africa-Canada Parliamentary Strengthening Program, Addis Ababa, 19-23 May 2003.

4 Blomberg et al, "On the Conflict Poverty-Nexus", *Economics & Politics*, 18, November 2006, p3. This paper finds some evidence to suggest that such self-reinforcing cyclical dynamics exist in the relationship between poverty and both internal and external conflicts, particularly in those places where capital formation starts from lower levels.

5 Luckham et al, "Conflict and poverty in Sub-Saharan Africa: An assessment of the issues and evidence," *Institute of Development Studies Working Paper 128*, p1.

6 P. Collier, "On the economic consequences of civil war", *Oxford Economic Papers*, January 1999.

7 P. Justino, "On the links between violent conflict and chronic poverty: How much do we really know?", *Chronic Poverty Research Centre Working Paper 61*, July 2006, p12.

8 This overview comes largely from World Health Organization, *World Report on Violence and Health*, 2002, pp222-224. (WHO, *World Report on Violence and Health*, 2002.)

9 For discussion of particular plight of refugees, see WHO, *World Report on Violence and Health*, 2002, p225.

10 WHO, *World Report on Violence and Health*, 2002, p223.

11 WHO, *World Report on Violence and Health*, 2002, p879.

12 L. Bailey, "The Impact of Conflict on Poverty", World Bank, 2006, pp12-14. (L. Bailey, 2006.) See also P. Collier, *The Bottom Billion*, Oxford University Press 2007, cf p27-32.

13 P. Justino and P. Verwimp, "Poverty Dynamics, Violent Conflict and Convergence in Rwanda", *MICROCON Research Working Paper No. 4*, March 2008.

14 P. Collier, *The Bottom Billion*, Oxford University Press, 2007, pp124-134.

15 *Proactive Presence*, Centre for Humanitarian Dialogue, February 2008.

16 Amnesty International, *Democratic Republic of the Congo: North Kivu – No end to war on women and children* (Index: AFR 62/005/2008).

17 Amnesty International, *Brazil: "They come in shooting": Policing socially excluded communities* (Index: AMR 19/025/2005), p18.

18 Amnesty International, *Kenya: Police operations against Mungiki must comply with Kenya's obligations under international human rights law* (Index: AFR 32/008/2007).

19 *Crime, Public Order and Human Rights*, International Council on Human Rights Policy (ICHRP), December 2003. (*Crime, Public Order and Human Rights*, ICHRP).

20 *Crime, Public Order and Human Rights*, ICHRP.

21 D. Narayan et al, *Voices of the Poor: Crying out for change*, Oxford University Press, World Bank Publication Series, 2000, p163.

22 M. Ruteere and M.E. Pommerolle, "Democratizing security or decentralizing repression? The ambiguities of community policing in Kenya", in *African Affairs* 102, 2003, pp587-604.

23 A.N. Roy, former Mumbai police commissioner, cited in *Chicago Tribune*, 16 March 2007.

24 L. Heise and C. Garcia-Moreno in E. G. Krug, L. L. Dahlberg, J. A. Mercy, A. B. Zwi and R. Lozano (Eds), World Health Organization, *World Report on Violence and Health*, 2002.

25 *Ending Violence Against Women: From words to action*, Study of the Secretary-General, 9 October 2006, p38, www.un.org/womenwatch/daw/vaw/launch/english/v.a.w-exeE-use.pdf

26 *Women, Slums and Urbanisation: Examining the causes and consequences*, Centre on Housing Rights and Evictions (COHRE), 2008. (COHRE 2008).

27 World Health Organization, *Addressing Violence Against Women and Achieving the Millennium Development Goals*, 2005, pp9-10.

28 R. Jewkes, "Intimate partner violence: Causes and prevention", *The Lancet*, Vol 359, Issue 9315, 20 April 2002, p1424-1429.

29 Amnesty International, *Safe Schools – Every girl's right* (Index: ACT 77/001/2008).

30 Amnesty International, *Jamaica: Sexual violence against women and girls in Jamaica: "Just a little sex"* (Index: AMR 38/002/2006). (AI, Safe schools.)

31 S. Tropp and M. Ellsberg, "Addressing violence against women within the education sector", World Bank, 2005, p2.

32 Human Rights Watch, *Failing Our Children: Barriers to the right to education*, September 2005.

33 WHO, *Multi-country Study on Women's Health and Domestic Violence Against Women*, World Health Organization, 2005, Chapters 4 and 6.

34 L. Smith and L. Haddad, *Overcoming Child Malnutrition in Developing Countries: Past performance, future possibilities*, Draft 2020 Vision for Food, Agriculture, and the Environment Discussion Paper, International Food Policy Research Institute, 1999.

35 L. Heise, M. Ellsberg and M. Gottemoeller, "Ending Violence Against Women", *Population Reports*, Series L No. 11, Population Information Program, Johns Hopkins University School of Public Health, 1999. (Heise, Ellsberg and Gottemoeller, 1999).

36 Human Rights Watch, *Just Die Quietly: Domestic violence and women's vulnerability to HIV in Uganda*, 2003, www.hrw.org/reports/2003/uganda0803/ (HRW, *Just Die Quietly*).

37 Human Rights Watch, *Hidden in the Mealie Meal: Gender-based abuses and women's HIV treatment in Zambia*, 2007. (HRW, *Hidden in the Mealie Meal*).

38 International Clinical Epidemiologists Network (INCLEN), *A Summary Report for a Multi-Site Household Survey: Domestic violence in India*, 2000. (*Multi-Site Household Survey: Domestic violence in India*).

39 A.R. Morrison and M.B. Orlando, "Social and economic costs of domestic violence", in Morrison and Biehl (Eds), *Too Close to Home: Domestic Violence in the Americas*, 1999, p54.

CHAPTER FIVE

1 "Righting Wrongs", *The Economist*, 16 August 2001.

2 A. Neier, "Social and economic rights: A critique", *Human Rights Brief*, Vol 13, Issue 2, Winter 2006. A. Neier is President of the Open Society Institute and former Executive Director of Human Rights Watch.

3 Article 2 of the ICESCR provides for progressive realization of economic, social and cultural rights: "Each State Party to the present Covenant undertakes to take steps, individually and through international assistance and co-operation, especially economic and technical, to the maximum of its available resources, with a view to achieving progressively the full realization of the rights recognized in the present Covenant by all appropriate means, including particularly the adoption of legislative measures."

4 S. M. Lipset "Some social requisites of Democracy – Economic development and political legitimacy", *American Political Science Review* 53, pp69-105

5 A. Przeworski, M. E. Alvarez, J. A. Cheibub and F. Limongi, *Democracy Development: Political Institutions and well-being in the world 1950-1990*, New York, Cambridge University Press 2000.

6 United Nations Millenium Declaration; General Assembly resolution 55/2; 8 September 2000.

CHAPTER SIX

1 UK House of Commons International Development Committee. *Maternal Health*, 5th Report of Session 2007-08, 2 March 2008. Available at, http://www.publications.parliament.uk/pa/cm200708/cmselect/cmintdev/cmintdev/66/66ipdf

2 P. Hunt, UN Special Rapporteur on the Right to Health.

3 Jens Stoltenberg, Prime Minister of Norway at the UN high-level meeting on Millennium Development Goals, September 2008.

4 DFID, *Maternal Health Strategy, Reducing Maternal Deaths: Evidence and action*, June 2008. (DFID, 2008).

5 UNICEF, *Progress for Children: A report card on maternal mortality*, No. 7, 2008.

6 UN Millennium Development Report, 2008, p25.

7 In countries with the same level of economic development, maternal mortality is inversely proportional to the status of women, according to the United Nations Population Fund (UNFPA).

8 WHO, *World Health Report 2005 – Make Every Mother and Child Count.*

9 DFID, 2008, p28.

10 Richard Horton, "Healthy motherhood: an urgent call to action", *The Lancet*, Vol 368, Issue 9542, 30 September 2006, p1129.

11 The maternal mortality ratio in Sri Lanka is 1 in 850, compared with 1 in 34 in Nepal, 1 in 51 in Bangladesh and 1 in 74 in Pakistan. See Center for Global Development, www.cgdev.org/section/initiatives/_active/millionssaved/studies/case_6

12 *Joint Review of Maternal and Child Survival Strategies in China*, UNFPA, UNICEF, WHO and the Chinese Ministry of Health, December 2006.

13 M.E. Wirth et al, "Setting the stage for equity-sensitive monitoring of the maternal and child health Millennium Development Goals, *Bulletin of the World Health Organization*, 84, 2006, pp519-527.

14 Health Unlimited, "Indigenous women working towards improved maternal health: Ratanakiri Province, Cambodia", Action Research to Advocacy Initiative, May 2006. (*Health Unlimited*, 2006).

15 DFID, "How to reduce maternal deaths: Rights and responsibilities", February 2005. (*DFID*, 2005).

16 C. E. Barker, C. E. Bird, A. Pradhan, G. Shakyad, "Safe Motherhood Programme: Support to Safe Motherhood Programme in Nepal: An integrated approach", *Reproductive Health Matters*, 1 November 2007.

17 Miniño et al, "Deaths: Final data for 2004", *National Vital Statistics Report*, Vol. 55, No. 19.

18 M. B. Flanders-Stepans, "Alarming racial differences in maternal mortality", *The Journal of Perinatal Education*, Vol 9(2), Spring 2000, pp50–51. Available at, www.pubmedcentral.nih.gov/articlerender.fcgi?artid=1595019

19 S. Stereker, "Reproductive health in Latin America – maternal death and adolescent pregnancy" 9 April 2008. Available at, http://www.no-fortress-europe.en/upload/GVE_NGL_stereke.pdf

20 Amnesty International, *Peru: Poor and excluded women – denial of the right to maternal and child health* (Index: AMR 46/004/2006).

21 Health Unlimited, 2006.

22 Amnesty International, *Peru: Poor and excluded women – denial of the right to maternal and child health* (Index: AMR 46/004/2006).

23 Amnesty International, *Democratic Republic of Congo: "Our brothers who help kill us": Economic exploitation and human rights abuses in the east* (Index: AFR 62/010/2003).

24 DFID, "Why we need to work more effectively in fragile states", January 2005.

25 J. Cook, "Acknowledging a persistent truth: domestic violence in pregnancy", *Journal of the Royal Society of Medicine*, Vol 101, No. 7, 2008, pp358-363.

26 UK House of Commons, International Development Committee.

27 Amnesty International USA, *Female Genital Mutilation: A fact sheet*, www.amnestyusa.org/violence-against-women/female-genital-mutilation—fgm/page.do?id=1108439&n1=3&n2=39

28 *Eliminating Female Genital Mutilation: An Interagency Statement*, OHCRH, UNAIDS, UNDP, UNECA, UNESCO, UNFPA, UNHCR, UNICEF, UNIFEM and WHO, 2008, p11. (WHO 2008.) A WHO report also suggests a link between FGM and higher maternal mortality rates: "Female genital mutilation and obstetric outcome: WHO collaborative prospective study in six African countries", *The Lancet*, 2006, 367, pp1835-41.

29 WHO 2008, p11.

30 J. Shiffman and S. Smith, "Generation of political priority for global health initiatives: A framework and case study of maternal mortality", *The Lancet*, Vol 370, Issue 9595, 13 October 2007, pp1370-79.

31 Article 12, of the Convention on the Elimination of All Forms of Discrimination Against Women (CEDAW), says: "States Parties shall take all appropriate measures to eliminate discrimination against women in the field of health care in order to

ensure, on a basis of equality of men and women, access to health care services, including those related to family planning."

32 Committing to action: achieving the MDGs, July 2008. Available at, http://www.un.org/milleniumgoals/2008highlevel/pdf/committing/pdf.

33 Amnesty International *Nicaragua: The impact of the complete ban of Abortion*: Briefing to the UN Committee Against Torture (Index: AMR 43/005/2009).

34 UK House of Commons International Development Committee.

35 UN Bangladesh Common Country Assessment 2005. Available at http://www.un-bd.org/bgd/index.html

36 N. M. Nour, "Health consequences of child marriage in Africa", *Emerging Infectious Diseases Journal,* Vol 12, No. 11, November 2006, www.cdc.gov/ncidod/EID/vol12no11/06-0510.htm

37 UN, *The Millennium Development Goals Report,* 2008, cf p27.

38 *Ending Child Marriage: A guide for global policy action*, IPPF, 2007.

39 Physicians for Human Rights, "Maternal mortality in Herat Province, Afghanistan: The need to protect women's rights", in S. Gruskin, M. A. Grodin, G. J. Annas, *Perspectives on Health and Human Rights*, Routledge, 2005.

40 S. Roy, "Negligence kills 1.3 lakh mothers a year in India", *Merinews*, 22 April 2008, www.merinews.com/catFull.jsp?articleID=132896

41 Mary Robinson speaking at the Women Deliver conference, 2007.

42 Report of the Special Rapporteur on the right to health to the UN General Assembly, 2006.

43 UNICEF, *The State of the World's Children 2009: Maternal and Newborn Health.* Panel: UN agencies strengthen their collaboration in support of maternal and newborn health, pp.102-3.

44 P. Hunt and J. Bueno de Mesquita, *Reducing Maternal Mortality: The contribution of the right to the highest attainable standard of health*, UNPFA. (Hunt and Bueno de Mesquita).

45 DFID, 2005.

46 Hunt and Bueno de Mesquita.

47 "Time to act", *Development and Co-operation Journal*, Issue 9, 2008.

CHAPTER SEVEN

1 M. Davis, *Planet of Slums*, Verso, London & New York 2006.

2 S. de Dianous, "Les damnés de la terre du cambodge", *Le Monde diplomatique*, September 2004, p20.

3 Centre on Housing Rights and Evictions, *Women, Slums and Urbanisation: Examining the causes and consequences*, COHRE, 2008, p14. (Women, Slums and Urbanisation).

4 See Amnesty International, *Picking Up the Pieces: Women's experience of urban violence in Brazil* (Index: AMR 19/001/2008), pp49-50. See also *Women, Slums and Urbanisation*, pp79, 103 and 109.

5 *State of World Population 2007*, United Nations Population Fund (UNFPA), 2007, pp58-61.

6 Amnesty International, *Clouds of Injustice: Bhopal disaster 20 years on* (Index: ASA 20/015/2004), pp1-18.

7 Amnesty International, *Clouds of Injustice*, pp8-10, 12, 18-19.

8 UN-HABITAT, *State of the World's Cities 2006/7*, p92.

9 See *Report of the Special Rapporteur on adequate housing as a component of the right to an adequate standard of living*, Human Rights Council, 4 Session (UN Doc. A/HRC/4/18, 5 February 2007). See also, *Violence: The impact of forced evictions on women in Palestine, India and Nigeria and Women, Slums and Urbanisation*, COHRE, 2008. (COHRE, *Violence: The impact of forced evictions.*)

10 Commission on Human Rights Resolution 2004/28 (10 April 2004).

11 See for instance, World Organisation Against Torture (OMCT), *Compilation of Urgent Appeals and Letters, Programme on Economic, Social and Cultural Rights, January-December 2003*, available at: www.omct.org/pdf/ESCR/OMCT%20Appeals%202003_ESCR.pdf See also COHRE, *Violence: The impact of forced evictions.*

12 COHRE and RUIG/GIAN Joint Media Statement, "The Olympic Games have displaced more than two million people in the last 20 years", 5 June 2007, available at www.cohre.org/store/attachments/Olympics%20Media%20Release.doc

13 UN-HABITAT, *Global Report on Human Settlements 2007: Enhancing urban security and safety*, p129 (UN-HABITAT, *Global Report on Human Settlements 2007*).

14 UN-HABITAT, *Global Report on Human Settlements 2007*, p124.

15 COHRE, Global Survey on Forced Evictions, Vol. 7, 1998, Vol. 8, 2002, Vol. 9, 2003, Vol. 10, 2006. See also, Human Rights Watch, *Demolished: Forced evictions and the tenants' rights movement in China*, 2004.

16 Amnesty International, *Rights Razed: Forced evictions in Cambodia* (Index: ASA 23/002/2008). (Amnesty International, *Rights Razed*).

17 Amnesty International and COHRE press release, "Forced evictions reach crisis levels in Africa: More than 3 million evicted since 2000, 4 October 2006, available at, www.cohre.org/view_page.php?page_id=257#i530 See also: Amnesty International, *Mass forced evictions in Luanda – a call for a human rights-based housing policy* (Index: AFR 12/008/2003).

18 Amnesty International, *Zimbabwe: No justice for victims of forced evictions* (Index: AFR 46/005/2006), p11.

19 UN-HABITAT, *Fact-Finding Mission to Zimbabwe to Assess the Scope and Impact of Operation Murambatsvina*, Report by the UN Special Envoy on Human Settlements Issues in Zimbabwe Mrs Anna Kajumulo Tibaijuka, 18 July 2005, p7.

20 Amnesty International, *"Let them kill each other": Public security in Jamaica's inner cities* (Index: AMR 38/001/2008), Amnesty International, *Brazil: "They come in shooting" – Policing socially excluded communities* (Index: AMR 19/033/2005) and Amnesty International, *Kenya: Police operations against Mungiki must comply with Kenya's obligations under international human rights law* (Index: AFR 32/008/2007).

21 The first published definition is thought to occur in the 1812 book by convict writer J. H. Vaux, *A New and Comprehensive Vocabulary of the Flash Language*, Dodo Press, 2008, cited in *Dublin Slums, 1800-1925* by J. Prunty, Irish Academic Press, 1995. See also: J.A. Yelling, *Slums and Slum Clearance in Victorian London*, London 1986, London Research Series in Geography, No. 10, Unwin Hyman, 1986.

22 R. Holden, 'Urban Sanitation Technologies: The Challenges of Reaching the Urban Poor', IRC Symposium: Sanitation for the Urban Poor, 19-21 November 2008, p.3.

23 *The State of the World's Cities Report 2006/2007*, p29.

24 N. You, "Cities, climate change and global health" in *Habitat Debate*, December 2007, p4.

25 Bazoglu and Mboup, "Do cities give the poor better chances of survival?" in *Habitat Debate*, December 2007, p10. See also: S. Merkel et al, *Meeting the Health Needs of the Urban Poor in African Informal Settlements*, USAID, 2007.

26 M. Davis, *Planet of Slums*, Verso, London & New York, 2006, p145.

27 COHRE, *Listening to the Poor? Housing rights in Nairobi*, Kenya, COHRE Mission Report, June 2006, p42. (COHRE, *Listening to the Poor?*)

28 COHRE, *Listening to the Poor?*, p3.

29 COHRE, *Listening to the Poor?*, p13 & pp26-27.

30 Frontline, *Philippines: Death threats against human rights defender*, 26 February 2005, available at www.frontlinedefenders.org/node/58

31 HIC-HLRN and COHRE, Joint Parallel Report on China submitted to the UN Committee on Economic, Social and Cultural Rights, 2005.

32 See Joint submission by the European Roma Rights Centre (ERRC), the Centre on Housing Rights and Evictions (COHRE), OsservAzione and Sucar Drom to the UN Committee on the Elimination of Racial Discrimination, 72nd session, January 2008, available at: www.errc.org/db/02/9B/m0000029B.pdf (Joint submission by ERRC et al.) and Amnesty International, *Italy: The witch-hunt against Roma people must end* (Index: EUR 30/006/2008).

33 Amnesty International, *Slovakia: Still separate, still unequal* (Index: EUR 72/001/2007), pp8-9, 13.

34 National Coalition for the Homeless and the National Law Center on Homelessness and Poverty, *Illegal to be Homeless: The criminalization of homelessness in the United States*, Washington, DC, 2002.

35 Universal Declaration of Human Rights, Article 25(I).

36 The International Covenant on Economic, Social and Cultural Rights (Article 11(1)), the International Convention on the Elimination of All Forms of Racial Discrimination (Article 5(e)(iii)), the Convention on the Rights of the Child (Article 27(3)); the Convention on the Elimination of All Forms of Discrimination Against Women (Article 14(2)h), the International Convention on the Protection of the Rights of All Migrant Workers and Members of Their Families (Article 43(1)(d)), ILO Recommendation No. 115 on Workers' Housing, and numerous others.

37 "The States Parties to the present Covenant recognize the right of everyone to an adequate standard of living for himself and his family, including adequate food, clothing and housing, and to the continuous improvement of living conditions. The States Parties will take appropriate steps to ensure the realization of this right, recognizing to this effect the essential importance of international co-operation based on free consent."

38 See for example: Article 26(1), South Africa; Article 13(9), Philippines; Article 47, Spain; Article 23(3), Belgium; Article 178, Honduras; Article 4, Mexico; Article 64, Nicaragua; Article 65(1), Portugal. See also: UN-HABITAT and UN-OHCHR, *Housing Rights Legislation*, Nairobi, 2002.

39 See, for instance, H. de Soto and F. Cheneval, *Realizing Property Rights* (Swiss Human Rights Book, Vol 1), Rüffer & Rub, 2006.

40 UN-HABITAT, *Rental Housing: An essential option for the urban poor in developing countries*, Nairobi, 2003, pp103-130.

41 UN-HABITAT, E. Fernandes, "The illegal city" in *Habitat Debate*, Vol 5, No. 3, 1999, p12.

42 See the description of the campaign in Chris Williams, "The global campaign for secure tenure" in *Seminar on Securing Land for the Urban Poor*, UN-HABITAT and ESCAP, 2001, pp25-34.

43 Aquila Ismail (Ed), *The Story of SKAA – Sindh Katchi Abadis Authority*, City Press, Karachi, 2004, p.9 (*The Story of SKAA*).

44 Prefecture of São Paulo, *The Regularization of Allotments in the Municipal District of São Paulo*, 2003, p8.

CHAPTER EIGHT

1 R. M. Auty, "Natural resource endowment, the state, and development strategy," in *The Journal of International Development*, Vol 9, No. 4, 1997 pp651-663. Also see T. L. Karl, *The Paradox of Plenty: Oil booms and petro-states*, University of California Press, 1997; and J. D. Sachs and A. M. Warner, "Natural resource abundance and economic growth," in G. M. Meirer and J. E. Rauch (Eds), *Leading Issues In Economic Development*, Oxford University Press, 2000. More recent work has included E.H. Bulte, R. Damania, and R. T. Deacon, "Resource intensity, institutions and development", *World Development* 33(7), July 2005, pp1029-1044; and P. Collier and B. Goderis, "Commodity prices, growth and the natural resource curse: Reconciling a conundrum", Centre for the Study of African Economies Working Paper Series, University of Oxford, 2007.

2 For example, see M.L. Ross, "Does oil hinder democracy?", *World Politics* 53, April 2001, pp325-61, and K.K. Tsui, "More oil, less democracy: Theory and evidence from crude oil discoveries", University of Chicago, Job Market Paper, November 2005.

3 For example, see H. Mahdavy, "The patterns and problems of economic development in rentier states: The case of Iran", in M.A. Cook (Ed), *Studies in Economic History of the Middle East*, Oxford University Press, 1970; and H. Beblawi, *The Rentier State*, Croom Helm, 1987.

4 Some examples include J. Clark, "Petro-politics in Congo", *Journal of Democracy*, July 1997; and T. Skocpol, "Rentier state and Shi'a Islam in the Iranian Revolution", *Theory and Society*, April 1982.

5 "Protect, respect and remedy – A framework for business and human rights", report of J. Ruggie, Special Representative of the Secretary-General on the issue of human rights and transnational corporations and other business enterprise, 2008 (A/HRC/8/5).

6 "Chad's Oil: Miracle or mirage?", Bank Information Center and Catholic Relief Services, 17 February, 2005, www.bicusa.org/en/Project.26.aspx

7 Amnesty International, *Double Misfortune: Deepening human rights crisis in Chad* (Index: AFR 20/007/2008).

8 *Final Report of the Panel of Experts on the Illegal Exploitation of Natural Resources and Other Forms*

of Wealth in the Democratic Republic of the Congo*, United Nations Security Council, 2003 (S/2003/1027).

9 The Special Parliamentary Commission in the Democratic Republic of the Congo, led by Member of Parliament Christophe Lutundula, issued its findings in June 2005. The commission report, known as the Lutundula Report, is entitled,"Assemblée nationale commission spéciale chargée de l'éxamen de la validité des conventions à caractère économique et financier: conclues pendant les guerres de 1996-1997 et de 1998".

10 T. Whewell, "China to seal $9bn DR Congo deal", *BBC Newsnight Online*, 14 April 2008, http://news.bbc.co.uk/1/hi/programmes/newsnight/7343060.stm

11 UN press release, "High Commissioner for Human Rights concerned at Kilwa military trial in the Democratic Republic of the Congo", 4 July 2007.

12 Full details of the case can be found in "The Kilwa Appeal – A travesty of justice" 5 May 2008, Rights and Accountability in Development and Global Witness, http://raid-uk.org/docs/kilwa_trial/kilwa_update_may_2008.doc

13 Amnesty International, *Nigeria: Petroleum, Pollution and Poverty in the Niger Delta* (Index: AFR 44/017/2009). See also Human Rights Watch, "The Warri Crisis: Fueling violence", 17 December 2003, and Human Rights Watch, "Politics as war: The human rights impact and causes of post-election violence in Rivers State, Nigeria", 26 March 2008.

14 Human Rights Watch, "Chop fine: The human rights impact of local government corruption and mismanagement in Rivers State, Nigeria", 31 January 2007, www.hrw.org/en/reports/2007/01/30/chop-fine

15 Human Rights Watch, "Some transparency, no accountability: The use of oil revenues in Angola and its impact on human rights", 12 January 2004, www.hrw.org/en/reports/2004/01/12/some-transparency-no-accountability-0

16 Global Witness press release, "Campaign success: BP makes move for transparency in Angola,"; Global Witness report, "All the President's Men: The devastating story of oil and banking in Angola's privatized war," 1 March, 2002, www.globalwitness.org/media_library_get.php/141/All_the_Presidents_Men.pdf

17 Publish What You Pay International press release, "PWYP expresses concern over harassment and intimidation of anti-corruption campaigners in Gabon", 31 July 2008, www.publishwhatyoupay.org/en/resources/pwyp-expresses-concern-over-harassment-and-intimidation-anti-corruption-campaigners-gabon. PWYP statement to the African Union: For an open and inclusive debate on revenue transparency, 5 February 2009.

18 A. Zafar, "The growing relationship between China and Sub-Saharan Africa: Macroeconomic, trade, investment and aid links", *The World Bank Research Observer*, Vol 22, No. 1, Spring 2007, p113.

CHAPTER NINE

1 N. Kabeer, "Making rights work for the poor: Nijera Kori and the construction of 'collective capabilities' in rural Bangladesh", *IDS Working Paper* 200, September 2003.

2 Commission on Legal Empowerment of the Poor, *Making the Law Work for Everyone: Volume One, Report of the Commission on Legal Empowerment of the Poor*, Toppan Printing Company America Inc, 2008, p32. (Commission on Legal Empowerment of the Poor, Volume One.)

3 Commission on Legal Empowerment of the Poor, Volume One, p32, footnote 26, citing UNICEF, *The "Rights" Start to Life: A statistical analysis of birth registration 2005*, available at www.unicef.org/sowc06/pdfs/BirthReg10a_rev.pdf

4 D. Narayan-Parker (Ed), R. Patel, K. Schafft, A. Rademacher and S. Koch-Schulte, *Voices of the Poor: Crying out for change*, Oxford University Press, World Bank Publication Series, 2000. (World Bank, *Voices of the Poor*).

5 *Human Rights in Bangladesh*, reports published annually by A. O. Shalish Kendra (ASK), available at www.askbd.org/web/?page_id=430

6 World Bank Independent Evaluation Group, *Public Sector Reform: What works and why? An IEG evaluation of World Bank support*, 2008.

7 A. Ruiz-Restrepo, *Access to Justice: Bridging the gap between principle and practice – Innovation 2*, ImprovingAccess.org at www.improvingaccess.org/materials/access-to-justice-bridging-the-gap-between-principle-and-practice—-innovation-2

8 See, for example, International Court of Justice, *Courts and the Legal Enforcement of Economic, Social and Cultural Rights*, 2008, which cites cases from national courts in over 25 countries.

9 S. Golub and K. McQuay, "Legal empowerment: Advancing good governance and poverty reduction", in *Law and Policy Reform at the Asian Development Bank*, 2001 Edition, Office of the General Counsel, Asian Development Bank. (Golub and McQuay.) The Kaisahan research is detailed in "Appendix 1: The impact of legal empowerment activities on agrarian reform implementation in the Philippines", in Golub and McQuay, pp135-149.

10 For descriptions of Timap's work, *see* V. Maru, *Between Law and Society: Paralegals and the provision of primary justice services in Sierra Leone*, Open Society Institute, 2006; and V. Maru, "Between law and society: Paralegals and the provision of justice services in Sierra Leone and worldwide," *The Yale Journal of International Law*, 2006, pp427-428.

11 N. J. Diop et al, The Tostan Program: *Evaluation of a community-based education program in Senegal*, Population Council, 2004.

12 This action is described in detail in *Leveraging the Money: Enforcing human rights by influencing financial institutions*, New Tactics Project 2004, http://www.newtactics.org

13 Further information on Justice for the Poor can be found at: www.worldbank.org/justiceforthepoor

14 Further information on LEAD can be found at: www.lead-project.org/

15 Commission on Legal Empowerment of the Poor, Volume 1, p31.

16 Commission on Legal Empowerment of the Poor, *Volume 1*, p9.

INDEX

D

I

J

K

L

M

N

O

P

R

S

T

U

V

W

Y

Z

www.demanddignity.amnesty.org